THE LIFE AND TEACHINGS OF SRI RAMANUJACHARYA

THE
LIFE AND TEACHINGS
OF
SRI RAMANUJACHARYA

BY

C. R. SRINIVASA AIYENGAR

GYAN

Published by

Gyan Publishing House
5, Ansari Road
Daryaganj, New Delhi-110002
Phone: 011-47034999, 9811692060
E-mail: books@gyanbooks.com

Distribution Network
gyanbooks.com
India, USA, Canada, UK, Australia

ISBN: 978-93-6208-164-3 (PB)
First Published, 1908

2nd Impression 2024

Printed at: Gyan Press, Delhi.

THE LIFE AND TEACHINGS OF SRI RAMANUJACHARYA
Author: C. R. SRINIVASA AIYENGAR

ॐ

THE
LIFE AND TEACHINGS
OF
SRI RAMANUJACHARYA

BY

C. R. SRINIVASA AIYENGAR, B. A.

1908.

Published by:

R. VENKATESHWAR & CO.,

Madras.

[Price Rs. 2.

A MODERN PREFACE.

IT was night, and silence still reigned over the place—silence in the author's study, save for the tickings of the clock on the mantel piece, the ominous heart-beats of Father Time: silence without, save for the sighing breeze, wafting through the open window the distant hum of the busy city, as, like a wilful child, it sobbed itself to sleep.

In his den the author sat, his legs on the table before him, and his chair tilted back, in Yankee fashion, at an angle that was dangerously close to the line of equilibrium. He was in a fix, the author; before him, on the table, lay the last letter from his patient, long-suffering publisher, calling, in no gentle tones, for the promised preface that never came. And yet, for the life of him, he could not manage to extract one from his poor over-worked brain. With closed eyes and fingers tightly clasped around his head he sat, as if he would force the unwilling one from out of its dark abode. And upon him thus wrestling with his stubborn Muse, the silent hours stole on. The table lamp flared up, as if in angry protest at being kept awake so late to no purpose; and close upon it the clock struck the hour of midnight.

The last stroke was still upon the air, when there came a knock at the study door, and roused the author from his deep reverie, back to the world and its sorrows. "One more hour," cried he, "another messenger of Time, posting from the dark realms of the Future, on to the regions of the Dead Past. The world has grown older by an hour and I no wiser." With that, there strode into the room, all unbidden, the impatient visitor.

The author half turned himself in his chair to see who his midnight guest might be, and was greeted by "Hullo! old boy, not yet abed? How does my little busy bee? Improving each shining hour and gathering wisdom all day long?"

With a heavy sigh, he resigned himself to the inevitable and made himself ready for a pretty long spell of boredom; for, the man before him was no other than Nârada Ṣâstri, whom the naughty world was not ashamed to call meddling, inquisitive, and what not. Busy men steered clear of him, and our author, naturally of no sweet temper, was now in no mood to stand the bustling gaiety of the irrepressible Nârada. But, he was in a tight corner and no mistake; so, forcing up a rebellious smile, he hastened to welcome the old gentleman.

Author.—"Very glad to see you. It is an age since you have shown your bright and cheery face here in this gloomy den of mine. To what do I owe this welcome visit, all unexpected?"

Nârada.—"Oh, don't speak of it; and now that I come to notice it, what have you been doing to yourself? You look clean washed out."

Author.—(*aside*) What kindness! Curse it, he speaks as if his blessed visit was the best invigorator possible. (*aloud*) Nothing remarkable. Only a preface to my *Life of Râmânuja* that I cannot, for the life of me, manage.

Nârada.—What! Life of Râmânuja!! You have written one and *I* do not know it! Poor boy! You must have been hard pressed indeed to write it without my help. You little know what you have lost. Such valuable sources of information! Such rare books! Such eye-openers for the Orientalists! What madness possessed you to do it? Of course you had to write your precious life out of that apology for one—The Viṣishtâdwaita Catechism?

Author.—I don't know. (*With a regretful look*) Oh! that you were here! But yet, let me console myself with at least knowing what priceless treasures I have been denied to possess.

Nârada.—Would you? Well, it would be a lesson to you not to make such a fool of yourself another time. (*He straightens himself and puts out his chest—then with a triumphant air*) Now look here, your 'Life,' is it not a bald catch-penny affair, like the accounts in *Who's Who* or Beeton's Biography—a dry matter-of-fact record of dates, names, places and events? Come, don't deny it.

Author.—No. What on earth made you think that *I*, of all men would go in for such trash? You have heard of Edwin Arnold's *Light of Asia*; you have read it, eh! good. Arnold wrote the life of Lord Buddha as a devout Buddhist would have done it, who loved the Master for his love of men. Well, my work is a similar attempt, however humble, in that direction; and I opine that a 'Life' written on any other lines is not worth the rag on which it is scribbled. I love Râmânuja for his love of us. I write not for the Orientalists, or their pale imitators in India; but I aim to bring home to the hearts of all good men and true, the priceless Doctrine of Devotion enshrined in his teachings; the grand Personality that was the living exponent thereof; the broad love that embraced all Humanity and knew no distinction of caste or creed, race or color, rank or sex; and the spirit of perfect self-sacrifice that made him dare his Teacher's curse and the horrors of eternal damnation, that mankind may drink of the Waters of Life.

Nârada.—Stop, stop. What! No scientific treatment! No historical criticism! How did you fix the date of Râmânuja and his works?

Author.—(*with rising anger*) Enough ! What care I about your coins and inscriptions, your pillars and mounds, the dry bones of History. To me it is of far more importance how a man lived and worked among his fellows, than when and where he was born and died ; where he was at a particular date ; when he wrote such and such a book ; whether he was tall or short, dark or fair, single or married, a flesh-eater or a vegetarian, a teetotaller or no ; what particular dress he affected, and so on. And yet, more important still it is to me what a man thought and wrote, than how he lived and died. Your Orientalists ! Heaven save me from the brood. Mischief enough they have done, those human ghouls that haunt the charnel-houses of Antiquity, where rot the bones of men and events of the Dead Past. They have played sad havoc with the fair traditions of our forefathers, that placed ideas before facts and theories, and the development of a nation's heart before 'historical finds' or 'valuable discoveries.' Many a young man of promise they have turned away to paths uncongenial, where his bray betrays the animal within the skin. You will find no such antiquarian twaddle in my book. But yet, when I come to think of it, I too have thrown a sop to the Orientalist Cerberus ; I too have burnt incense to strange gods and lit a candle at the altar of the Prince of Darkness—I mean my notes and the comparative references therein.

Nârada.—(*taken aback*) But the sources of information—

Author.—(*impatiently*) Come now ; have done with your blessed sources. Trot them out, I say.

Nârada.—(*brightening up*) Of course the Visishtâdwaita Catechism is your sheet-anchor.

Author.—Hold there! Who said so? In fact, I have made very little use of it.

Nârada.—Well. Have you ever heard of the Guru Parampara? The Tengalai, fuller and more circumstantial, and the Vaḏagalai, differing from it upon many an important point.

Author.—(*with a pitying smile*) Unfortunately *that* is my sheet-anchor, the Tengalai Parampara; and my 'Life' is based upon it. And as for the other, I refer you to my notes to see if I have omitted any material point where they differ from or supplement one another.

Nârada.—Ah! Is it so? What about the Pal̄a Naḏai Vil̲akkam? (*Aside*) I am sure he has never heard of it.

Author.—Very much indebted am I to that valuable compilation for the clear light it throws on many a dark point.

Nârada.—(*aside*) Curse my luck! (*Aloud*) May be you have had access to another rare book, Peria Tirumuḏi Aḏaivu?

Author.—Look here. Have done with your pin-pricks. I cannot offord to be fooling with you thus, at this unearthly hour of the night. Here is the list of the books I have used in my work. See if you can add anything to it. But mind, this excludes priceless oral information derived from traditional teachings that will never be soiled by printer's ink.

Nârada.—(*with a look of blank despair*) reads:—

1. The Guru Parampara, Tengalai (1880)
2. Do. Vaḏagalai.
3. Pal̄a Naḏai Vil̲akkam.
4. Peria Tirumuḏi Aḏaivu.
5. Râmânujâchârya Divya Charitai.
6. Vârttâ Mâlai.

7. Âlvâr Charitram.

8. Hari Samaya Dîpam.

9. The Divya Prabandha.

(*To himself*). The sly rogue! He has exhausted every Tamil work known upon the subject; why, I am sure some of them I have never heard of. (*Reads aloud*)

10. Divya Sûri Charitram.

11. Srî Bhâshyam.

12. Prapannâmritam.

(*To himself.*) The devil! He has used it! And I have been moving Heaven and Earth to have a sight of that *rara avis*! These are Samskrita. What next? (*Reads aloud.*)

13. The Visishtâdvaita Catechism.

14. Life of Râmânuja by Govindâchârlu.

Author.—Unfortunately that book was sent to me when more than three-fourths of my work was in print; and I could make very little use of it.

Nârada.—(*with an air of ill-concealed spite*) And how pray, did you get access to all these varied sources and rare?

Author.—Oh! No secret about it. My respected friend Sathakopa Râmânujâchârya—I dare say you know him—the Tamil Pandit of the College here, what do I not owe him? Ever affable and obliging to a degree, he placed his valuable library at my disposal and his profound erudition; he allowed me to draw upon his remarkable memory, the inexhaustible store-house of many a traditional teaching, many a priceless mystery connected with Doctrine and Worship. I cannot enough thank the noble gentleman.

Nârada.—(*to himself*) A blessed exhibition have I been making of myself during the last hour—and all for the edification of this irreverent rascal, who took me in with his airs of idiotic vacuity and blank ignorance. I have caught a Tartar and no mistake. 'Discretion is the bettter part of valor' and in that better part of it I shall beat a prudent retreat ere I am floored. (*Musing*). What! to think that I, Nârada Şâstri, the highest authority living, nay, for the matter of that, or dead, on everything connected with History, Antiquities and Religion, the member of all the learned Societies in Europe and America, to be cornered by a slip of a boy!! I fear my anger will get the better of me if I stay here any longer and I shall be tempted to do him some mischief. (*Aloud, with a wan smile*). Very glad to hear of your success. You know I am ever at your service. But now, are we not robbing ourselves of the sweet sleep that our over-worked brains stand so much in need of? *Au revoir*. (*Exit*).

Author.—(*Yawning awfully*). A good riddance. Hope I have laboured hard to earn his lasting hatred; but it is a nice set off against his tiresome visits and peacock airs of patronage. Heigho! Here remains this precious preface to be written. (*Stops suddenly and cries*). My gods! Where have my wits gone to? Why, this eternal bore and the hard dressing I gave him; this is as good as any orthodox preface. And, by the shades of the Orientalists, it *shall* be one.—(*Exit*).

A FRIEND OF THE AUTHOR.

List of References—Abbreviations.

1.	Tengalai Guruparamparai (Edition of 1880) ..	.. T. G. (1880)
2.	Prapannâmṛitam ..	.. Prap.
3.	Divyasûri Charitram	.. D. C.
4.	Vadagalai Guruparamparai	.. V. G.
5.	Palanadai Viḷakkam	.. Pal.
6.	Peria Tirumuḏi Aḏaivu	.. Per.
7.	Ramanujacharya Divya Charitai ..	.. R. C.
8.	Vârttâ Mâlai ..	.. Var.
9.	Life of the Alvars	.. L. A.
10.	Viṣishtâdvaita Catechism	.. V. C.
11.	Vinôdarasa Manjari	.. V. M.

Table of Transliteration.

आ = â	घ = gh	ड = ḏẖ	ध = dh
ई = î	छ = chh	ढ = ḏẖ	फ = ph
ऊ = û	झ = jh	ण = ṉ	भ = bh
ऋ = ṛi	ञ = ñ	त = t	श = ṣ
ए = ê	ट = ṭ	थ = th	ळ (ள) = ḷ
ख = kh	ठ = ṭh	द = d	ழ = ḻ

CONTENTS

Chapter I.

Sri Sathakôpa.

The birth of Sri Sathakôpa 2
His early days 3
The early years of Mathurakavi 5
Mathurakavi meets Sathakôpa 6
The Divine Vision 8
The Divya Prabandha 8

Chapter II.

Nâthamuni—the Yôgi 11
The search for the Collect 12
His initiation 14
He returns to his town 15
The Sacred Collect set to music 15
The Yôgi and the King 18
His last moments 19

Chapter III.

Pundarikâksha 23
His last instructions 24

Chapter IV.

Râma Misra 25
Birth of Yâmunâchârya 25
The boyhood of Yâmuna 26
His quarrel with Âkkiyâlvan 26
He is invited to the Palace 27
The two Wagers 28
The Contest 29
The Victory 29
Âlavandâr.. 31

Râma Misra seeks him out 31
The Passport 32
The Master and the Pupil 32
His inheritance 34
He takes Orders 34
His disciples 35
Directed to Kurukâdhipa 36
The last moments of Râma Misra 37

Chapter V.

Yâmunâchârya, the Teacher 37
Âlavandâr and Kurukâdhipa 37
His journey to Trivandrum 38
He bewails his carelessness 39
A strange disciple 39
His great grief 42

Chapter VI.

Râmânuja's birth and early days 43
His previous incarnations 44
His birth 45
Under Yâdava 46
Gôvinda 47
First quarrel with Yâdava 47
His second quarrel 48
Yâdava's plot 49
Gôvinda's warning 51
The divine hunters 52
His miraculous journey 53

Chapter VII.

His Life at Kânchî 55
The conversion of Gôvinda 56
Râmânuja goes back to Yâdava 57
Yâmuna goes over to Kânchî 58
Yâdava and the Evil Spirit 60

Discomfiture of Yâdava 61
Râmânuja drives it out 62
Yâmuna's prayer 63
His last quarrel with Yâdava 64
Yâmuna sends for Râmânuja 65

Chapter VIII.

The Passing of Yâmuna 65
His last words 66
The last moments of Yâmunâchârya 72
Mahâ Pûrṇa at Kânchî 76
Râmânuja's disappointment.. 77
The three vows 78
The future Teacher.. 80

Chapter IX.

The Initiation of Râmânuja 81
Nambi refuses to initiate him 81
Nambi dines at Râmânuja's house 83
The Six Words 85
Mahâ Pûrṇa sent to Kânchî 86
The unexpected meeting 86
His initiation 89

Chapter X.

The Great Renunciation 90
The second offence 90
The last offence 91
He takes orders 93
He tries to get back Gôvinda 95
Âlvân and Aṇḍân 96
The conversion of Yâdava 98
Ranganâtha refused 102
The power of music 103

Chapter XI.

Râmânuja at Srirangam 105
Ranganâtha and Râmânuja 106
Râmânuja enters upon his duties 107
Srî Saila Pûrna's first visit 108
His second visit 110
The reconversion of Gôvinda.. 113

Chapter XII.

Râmânuja and his teachers with Mahâ Pûrna .. 117
„ with Gôshthi Pûrna 117
Initiation of Âlwân 122
Ândân's apprenticeship 122
With Mâlâdhara 126
With Vara Ranga Gâyaka 128
A Doubt 130

Chapter XIII.

Râmânuja: the Teacher 130
His life aimed at 131
Pranatârti Hara: The Daring One 132
Yajñamûrthy the Great 133
The Famous Contest.. 134
The Divine Interference 134
The Victory 135
Yajñamûrthy's conversion 137
Anantâlvân 138
The Master's first pilgrimage 139
At Kânchî.. 140
Before Varadarâja 143
The mysterious guide 144
At Tirupati 144
Srî Saila Pûrna 146
Upper Tirupati 146
Before Venkatêsa 147
The Master receives instructions in the Râmâyana. 147

Gôvinda 148
How to make a bed 148
The Friend of All 149
An odd gift 149
A Deserter.. 150
Back at Ṣrîrangam 151

Chapter XIV.

Râmânuja and his Disciples 151
When to praise oneself 152
Before a house of ill-fame 153
Gôvinda and his wife 153
A strange bridal-night 154
Embâr 155
Which Lord ? 155
Dêvarâjamuni 157
The Ṣrîbhâshya 157
The Master at fault 160
Âṇḍân 162
The strange hand-maiden 164
Mâranêri Nambi 166
The Dumb Ṣishya 167
What to meditate upon 168
Anantâchârya 168

Chapter XV.

His tour throughout India 171
The Divine Pupil 173
Before Sarasvatî 175
The Kashmir Pandits 176
The Master at Tirupati as an umpire.. .. 181
Back to Ṣrîrangam.. 183

Chapter XVI.

Parâṣara Bhaṭṭa—Âlvân the Saintly 184
Âṇḍâl speaks out 185

The birth of Paràṣara 186
A teacher from the cradle 187
The Lord's godson 188
The Little Great Men 189
The Omniscient Pandit 190
His first day at school and the last 191
The Divine Godfather 192
His marriage 192

Chapter XVII.

Râmânuja, the self-exiled—Krimikantha .. 194
Àḷvân the faithful 196
The exile 196
With Nallân's disciples 198
An old disciple 201
The tests 204
Another convert 206
At Sâlagrâma 207
The punishment of Chôḷa 208
Viṭṭhala Dêvâ's conversion 210
An invitation to the Master 212
The Master and the Jains 213

Chapter XVIII.

At Tirunârâryaṇapuram 216
The dream 216
Yet another 217
Tirunârâyaṇapuram 217

Chapter XIX.

Râmânuja, the Saint 234
His trip to Tirupati 236
The eyes of Âḷvân 238
Âḷvân permitted to go back 244
Àḷvan goes back 247
The installation of Pârâṣara 252

The Master's image 253
The future Teacher.. 254

Chapter XX.

The passing of Râmânuja 254
His exhortations 256
The 72 golden words of Râmânuja 257
He begs forgiveness 266
His last moments 266

Chapter XXI.

The Visishtâdvaita Philosophy 270
Parabrahman 271
Achit 283
Evolution 283
Involution 286
The Worlds 286
Chit 287
Karma 288
Naraka 289
Svarga 290
The Gods 290
Moksha 291
The four means to attain this glorious end .. 292
Prapatti 295

Chapter XXII.

Râmânuja's Disciples 297
Ândhra Pûrṇa 299
Âṇḍan the Younger 301
Marudoor Nambi 302
Nambi Trivaludi Vaḷanâḍu Dâsa 302
Piḷḷai Tiruvaludi Vaḷanâḍu Arayâr 302
Embâr 303
An exception 304

Chapter XXIII.

Behind the veil 304

Chapter XXIV.

The Elect 315

Chapter XXV.

The Spiritual Hierarchy—The Guruparampara .. 316

Mantra parampara 316

Mantrârtha Guruparampara 317

Ṣrî Bhâshya Guruparampara 317

Bagavad Vishaya Parampara.. 317

Âṣrayaṉa parampara 317

Grantha parampara.. 317

SRÎ SATHAKÔPA.

CHAPTER I.

THERE lived at Srî Nagari, on the banks of the Tâmraparni, in the Tinnevelly District, a family of Sûdrâs, who, for generations back, were ardent devotees of Mahâ Vishnu. The first representative of it, of whom anything is known, was one Srî Vibhûti Nâtha. One of his descendants was Kâri. His father, Porkâri, in search of a good wife for his son, sought and obtained the hand of Nâtha Nâyikâ, the daughter of Kamalaidhita Vaksha, a resident of Tiruvanparichâra, in Malabar. The marriage was a happy one, but the happiness was saddened by the couple not being blessed with what all Hindus so earnestly long for—a son to perpetuate the line.

Once, on his way back to Srî Nagari, from a short visit to his father-in-law, Kâri, with his wife, halted at Tirukkurungudy to offer their worship at the shrine of

---

[1] The genealogy of Sathakôpa :—

Vibhûti Nâtha
|
Dharmadhara
|
Chakrapâni
|
Achyuta

Pâtâla Lôchana
|
Porkâri
|
Kâri = Nâthanâyikâ ([illegible])
|
Mâra or Sathakôpa. (*Prap.*)

Lord Kurangêsa. In the presence of the All-Father, the desire of their hearts came out unbidden, and they uttered a prayer—" O ! Thou Searcher of Hearts, may we be blessed with a son "—when, wonder of wonders! the Mighty One deigned to express himself through the high priest and said—" So be it. We ourselves would be born in your family. " They were speechless with joy and amazement, and could scarcely believe their good fortune.

But all doubts were set at rest, when Nâtha Nâyikâ was *enceinte* (in the way to become a mother), and they joyfully looked forward to the fulfilment of the will of the Lord.

The Birth of Srî Sathakôpa.

Meanwhile, in the Supreme Heaven, Vaikuntha, the Great Father, saw that the time was come for Him to incarnate once more on the face of the Earth and restore the Good Law. He turned his eyes towards the Mighty Angels that always stand near His Throne, and directed Vishvaksêna,[2] the leader of the Divine Hosts, to go down upon Earth and take his birth in the family of Kâri.[3] And

---

2 He is the amsa of Nârâyana and Sênêsa (*V. G.*); of Kausthubha, the gem on the breast of Nârâyana, (*Pal*). One can be born of the amsas of many beings. Lakshmana and Balarâma were born of the amsa of the Lord and Sêsha; Hanumân was the amsa of Vâyu and Rudra, etc. (*L.A.*)

3 The following are the authorities that bear upon the birth of Srî Sathakôpa :—

(*a*) Sênêsa, the Lord of the Divine Hosts, would come down upon Earth about the beginning of Kali Yuga to restore the Good Law and lead men on the Path of Devotion to the Great Father.—*Bhavishyat Purâna.*

(*b*) The youth would remain silent, even as one dumb, till he be sixteen years of age. He would seat himself under the Holy Tamarind, lost in contemplation of the Divine Presence, and revelling in the delights thereof.—*Bhârgava Purâna.*

so it was that, on the 43rd day from the birth of the present Kali Yuga, the Great Saint[4] came down amongst us. Ananta, another of the Mighty Ones, slightly preceded him, and was visible to mortal eyes as a Tamarind Tree, near the precincts of the temple of Âdinâtha, in that place.

His Early Days.

Şaṭhakôpa was as unlike any other infant in his worldly ways, as he was found to be, later on, in his spiritual life. He stoutly refused all material sustenance, but preserved a health and freshness that appeared quite extraordinary. His parents were entirely unable to account for this strange phenomenon. They refrained from speculating upon what seemed to them some holy mystery, and humbly bowed in submission to the Divine Will. On the twelfth day they placed the infant in the presence of the

---

(*c*) When the terrible Kali Yuga sets in and the True Faith is defiled by atheists, there will come down upon the Earth, one born of the ray of Vishṇu.—*Pâdma Purâṇa.*

(*d*) *Listen*, ye sages, to a mighty mystery I will unfold to your eyes. Ananta, my couch, will, in a future age, go down upon Earth as a Sacred Tamarind Tree, and I will gladly follow him there as a Bhakta of mine, by name, Şaṭhakôpa. I will throw open the gates of Salvation to all, irrespective of caste, creed or sex, by revealing to them the secrets of the Vedâs in the language of the masses.—*Brahmâṇḍa Purâṇa.*

(*e*) A spark of the Divine Fire that emanated from the Kausthubha fell down upon the Earth and assumed the resplendent form of Şaṭhakôpa.—*Mârkandêya Purâṇa.*

(*f*) At the beginning of Kali Yuga, Sênêşa will come down upon the Earth to restore the doctrine of devotion to the Lord.—*Vriddha Pâdma Purâṇa.*

[4] The date of his birth :—

Era—the 43rd day from the beginning of Kali Yuga.
Year—Pramâthi.

Lord Âdinâtha and had him named 'Mâra';[5] after which, they laid him in a cradle under the Sacred Tamarind. They could not bring themselves to believe that theirs was an ordinary child, but regarded him as some Great Being, who had taken human form for some grand purpose. Sixteen revolving years still found the boy seated in the same place, in deep Samâdhi, silent, motionless, and entirely oblivious of the throbbing world around him. May be, he revelled in the glorious bliss of the Divine Presence that gave him no eyes for objects material. May be, his silence proceeded from his utter inability to express in human speech the Great Mystery—a task from which the Vedâs themselves had recoiled in despair. May be, he could find no qualified hearer. Be it as it may, his parents misconstrued this extraordinary behaviour on their child's part as a punishment visited on themselves by the Lord, for some unknown sins of theirs. For, are not the sins of parents visited upon their children, even to the seventh generation?

Month—Vaiśâkha.
Date—12.
Day of the week—Friday.
The day of the fortnight—The full-moon.
Constellation—Viśâkha.
Lagna—Karkaṭaka.
Year—Bahudhânya.—(*Pal.*)

[5] The names of Mâran or Śaṭhakôpa:—

(*a*) His life had so little in common with that of the rest of the world that he was named மாறன்.

(*b*) An infant, when in the womb, can see far into its past and future; but at the moment of its birth, it is touched by the psychic current Śaṭha, and a veil of oblivion is thrown over its consciousness. Then it begins to cry and behave like mortals. But Mâran defied its power, and by pronouncing the mystic syllable—Aum,—put it to flight. Hence the name Śaṭhakôpa.

The Early Years of Mathura Kavi.[6]

Long before this, another Great Soul had taken human shape to form one of the Stones in the great Living Wall of the "Guardians of Humanity." One of the highest of the Divine Hierarchies in Vaikuṇṭha, Kumuda[7] by name, had incarnated at Tirukkôvaloor, in a Brâhman family. The world knows him as Mathura Kavi (the Sweet Singer) and he was the bright Aruṇa to the radiant Sun Ṣaṭhakôpa. His fleshly encasement could but thinly veil the Divine capabilities of the advanced soul that inhabited it; and Supreme Wisdom and Dispassion manifested themselves very early in his life.

(c) The Lord favoured him above other Âlvârs and called him 'Our Âlvâr.'—Hence the name Nammâlvâr (நம்மாழ்வார்).

(d) The Lord Âdinâtha presented him with a garland of Vakuḷa flowers from his own neck. Hence the name Vakuḷâbharaṇa.

(e) The sectarians of all ages fear him, as an elephant the sharp iron goad. Hence the name Parânkuṣa.—(*L. A.*)

6 Ṣaṭhakôpa's pupils were Mathura Kavi and Nâthamuni.

The date of Mathura Kavi's birth :—

Era—883, 878 years from the beginning of Dwâparayuga.

Year—Îṣwara.

Month—Chaitra.

Fortnight—Fifteen.

Week—Friday.

Constellation—Chitra.—(*Prap.*)

Era—863,879. Fortnight—14. (*V.G.*)	Year—Vikrama. Fortnight—10. Date—5. (*Per.*)

7 He was the amṣa of Kumuda, one of the angels around the Throne.—[*T. G.* (1880).]

Of Kumuda and Garuḍa.—(*Pal.*)

His father's name was Nârâyaṇa, and he was a Pûrvaṣikha Brâhmaṇa.—*Prap.*

The following passage bears upon his birth :—

On the banks of the sacred Tâmraparṇi, there will be born of Brâhmaṇa parents, one, Mathura Kavi by name, of the amṣa of Garuḍa, an ardent devotee of Ṣaṭhakôpa. (*Pâdma Purâna—Pal.*)

Mathura Kavi Meets Sathakôpa.

Many a long year afterwards, Srî Sathakôpa was born, and when he was sixteen years of age, Mathura Kavi was on a pilgrimage to the Shrines of Hindustan and was even then at Ayôdhyâ. One night, he saw, proceeding as it were from the south, what appeared to him an immense blaze of light, calm and steady. He very naturally concluded that it might have been from a conflagration in some village near or in the woods. But the same light presented itself to his eyes the second and the third night too. His curiosity was awakened, and he set about to fathom the mystery. So he travelled south, sleeping through the day, and walking all night, guided by the pillar of Light, but failed to locate it in every holy spot he passed through. He reached Srîrangam, hoping to find there the solution of the mystery, but still the light shone farther south. On, on he travelled, until he came to Kurukoor (Kuruhoor) or Srî Nagari. There it was, but when he went further south, he saw it to the north. He came back to the place and easily traced it to the Sacred Tamarind.

There he found a young lad (youth) sitting in Padmâsana, in deep contemplation, his eyes closed and his body erect and motionless. The blaze of light proceeded from his head and heart, radiated from him on all sides, and extended far, far as the eye could reach, and was lost in space illimitable. He stood speechless before him, wrapt in wonder and admiration. A curious fancy took possession of him—almost a fantastic one. "Is this strange being mortal ? One of us ? Has it a consciousness like any other ? Is he pervious to external sensation ?" On the spur of the impulse, and entirely forgetting that he was committing a sacrilege by his act, he let fall a slab of stone right in front of Saṭhakôpa. His experiment was successful. The Master suddenly opened his eyes ; may be, the noise roused him ; may be, he thought that the time was come for him to initiate the pupil whom he had thus drawn to him from afar. Mathura Kavi was taken aback at his own temerity ; but he reassured himself and resolved to see the matter through. "When in doubt, play the trump," and Mathura Kavi naturally acted upon the time-honoured advice. So he ventured a question—rather the expression of a doubt—" The small one born of the dead, what does it live upon ? Where does it rest ?"[8] Truly a question more in the line of the Egyptian Sphynx. What he really meant was only this. The dead is Achit—matter that is dead or devoid of consciousness. The small one is the Ego, atomic in its shape and smaller than the smallest ; its being born of the Dead, indicates the encasement of the Ego in its material vehicles. What go to make up the materials of its experience during its incarnations ? Where does it rest ? Through what instruments does it gain this experience in the various spheres of material existence ? The daring questioner was not kept long waiting. Forthwith flashed the answer, short and sweet—" It feeds upon *It* and lies *in It*"—a reply nowise less mystical than the question. Anyhow the doubts of the questioner were cleared ; he understood Saṭhakôpa to mean—" It grows by assimilating the experiences of pleasure and pain gathered through the material vehicles and remains attached to the same through the links of Karma."

Mathura Kavi's eyes were unsealed ; the flood-gates of his memory were thrown open ; he saw into the far past

---

[8] Another reading :—

If the Small be born of the Great, (*i.e.*,) if the atomic Jîva be endowed with infinite wisdom, what will be the objects of its cognition and wherein would it rest ?—(*L. A.*)

and recognised his Teacher through an endless series of lives. He lay at his feet, sobbed with joy, and prayed to be allowed to serve him for ever. The Master raised him up and welcomed him to his heart. Thereafter Mathura Kavi was ever the shield and shadow of Srî Sathakôpa.

The Divine Vision.

About this time, the Lord graciously desired to bless Sathakôpa with a sight of His Presence.[9] The Celestial Bird, Garuda, anticipated, as it were, His wish, and stood before Him. And so He appeared to the wondering Srî Sathakôpa's eyes, seated on Garuda, with the Great Mother beside Him, and conferred upon him the Divine vision from which nothing is hidden. Sathakôpa was thus enabled to stand face to face with the Mighty Presence ; he gazed upon the awful majesty of the Mighty Isis without her veil; he realised in himself simultaneously the infinite nature and powers of the Supreme Purusha. He revelled in the ineffable Bliss until he was permeated with it; until he lost himself in the illimitable ocean of Divine Love and Harmony.

The Divya Prabandha.

In the midst of his ecstatic beatitudes, there shot a pang across his heart. " Shall I be happy, and hear the world cry? Shame upon me if it were so." He was the Lord of Compassion before all, and held his wisdom and powers only in trust for the great orphan—Humanity—whom he desired to lead on the Path he himself trod with such happy results. The age had become degenerate, and Samskrit was no longer the language of the literary and the sacred classes. He was one of those Saviours of Humanity that wanted to throw open the doors of wisdom

---

[9] Lakshmi requested the Lord to provide means for the easy regeneration of all classes of men. Thereupon Sênêsa was directed to initiate Sathakôpa into the Divine mysteries.—(*V. G.*)

wide to all, without any distinction of caste, creed or sex; he was a real "Friend of Man." He tried the novel experiment of giving out to the masses the Divine Mysteries in Tamil—the language of all in Southern India, high and low, man and woman. The Tiruviruttam, Tiruvâṣiriyam, Peria Tiruvantâdi,[10] are, respectively, an epitome of the Teachings of the Rig, Yajur, and the Atharva Vêdâs; and Tiruvâimoli, the best kown and the most popular of his works, is an expression of the Grand Truths echoed in the Sâma Vêdâ—the most esoteric of the four. "Of the Vêdâs, I am the Sâma," says the Lord. It consists of 1,102 stanzas, divided into ten chapters; and is the clearest and the most succinct exposition of the eternal truths of the Vêdâs. The five Great Truths of which all the Vêdâs and, the Ṣâstrâs are but an amplification, and the Sacred Two Truths, the Holiest of the Holy, that faintly voice forth the final mystery of Surrender to the Divine Will, find their clearest expression in it.

Thereafter, the various manifestations of the Lord in the Sacred Shrines all over Âryâvarta, presented themselves before the opened eyes of the Master under the Holy Tamarind; the Spirits before the Throne and the Divine inhabitants of the White Island (Ṣwêta Dweepa) came to pay him their respects and do him honour. For five and thirty years did this Great Being[11] inhabit his tabernacle of

---

10 Tiru Viruttam (திருவிருத்தம்)	..	..	100 stanzas.
Tiru Vâṣiriyam (திருவாசிரியம்)	..	...	7 do.
Peria Tiruvantâdi (பெரிய திருவந்தாதி)		..	87 do.
Tiruvâimoli (திருவாய்மொழி)	..	..	1,102 do.

11 His superior excellence lies in the fact that he was endowed with all perfections even from his very birth, and had not the slightest touch with the world and its ways, quite unlike the other Âlvârs, who were blessed at some period of their lives or on some occasions only. Hence he is described as the soul of the group and the other Âlvârs as his body:—

Bhûtattâlvâr.. ..Head.

flesh,[12] sowing the seeds of Divine wisdom that were to grow later on into the mighty system promulgated by Ṣrî Râmânuja, under whose shade rest, in peace and joy, countless Egôs, heartsore after trials untold and footsore after the long journey through lives innumerable.[13]

Poigaiyâlvâr and Peyâlvâr	..Eyes.
Periâlvâr ..	..Face.
Tirumaliṣaiyâlvâr	..Neck.
Kulaṣêkharâlvâr and Tiruppâṇâlvâr	..Hands.
Toṇḍaraḍippoḍiyâlvâr	..Breast.
Tirumangaiyâlvâr	..Navel.
Mathura Kaviyâlvâr	..Feet.

The Sandals of the Lord are named Ṣaṭhakôpa after his favourite Âlvâr.—(*L. A.*)

12 Âḷavandâr : 'the Lord himself incarnated as Nammâlvâr.'

Embâr : a Jîva, bound to the wheel of cyclic existence, was raised by the mercy of the Lord to the Dual Greatness (in this world and the next).—(*Var.*)

13 Mathura Kavi survived his master for 50 years and travelled about the Land singing the Sacred Collect and celebrating his Master's glory. He composed a short poem of eleven stanzas on his Master, beginning with கண்ணிநுண் (Kaṇṇinuṇ). He set up his image at Tirunagari and celebrated festivals in his honour with great pomp and splendour. On one of these occasions, some of the disciples of the Tamil Sangam at Madura took objection to the proclamation of the titles of Ṣaṭhakôpa. "Your Âlvâr is but a devotee and not the Lord. He was never admitted to the Sangam, nor were his works placed on the Board. How could you then call him the Revealer of the Vêdâs in Tamil ?" Mathura Kavi was pained to the heart, and, having neither men nor money to back him up, sought refuge at his Master's feet. "Grant me, Lord, to put down these ungodly men and make thy face bright." The next day, an aged Brâhmaṇa came to him and said, "It seems to me that if you write a stanza of the Sacred Collect, say the first foot of [Tamil text] on a bit of a palm leaf and place it upon the Board, Ṣaṭhakôpa will look after his own." Mathura Kavi adopted the expedient ; when, lo ! the Board sank into the water with all the poets upon it. It rose again immediately, bearing the single palm-leaf. The dismayed crew struggled on to the banks as best they

CHAPTER II.

Nâthamuni—the Yôgi.

Long, long afterwards, there lived at Vîra Nârâyaṇapura, the capital of a petty Chôla prince, a Brâhmaṇa, named Îṣvara Bhaṭṭa. And unto him was born a son, Nâthamuni,[1] and a grandson, Îṣvara Muni.

One day, they were all in the Sanctuary of the Lord in that place, when, by a curious coincidence, the three prayed to the Lord to be given permission to make a pilgrimage to the various Holy Spots over which His Blessed Feet trod during His many incarnations. It was graciously granted, and they set out on their holy tour.

They were so much charmed with the natural beauty of Gôvardhana and the pure spiritual magnetism that pervaded it, that they decided to settle themselves there.

---

might, and their eyes were opened to the heinous act of sacrilege they had committed against the Great Being. They were now convinced that he was a Ray of the Lord and was a Master of Infinite Wisdom. Their pride was humbled, and every one of them sought to be the first to obtain forgiveness at the hands of the Great Saint. Every one sang out a verse in his praise; but, lo! whatever they might have meant, there came out of their lips the following words:—

"Where is Vaikuṇṭha? Is it the Ocean of Milk or Tirunagari? What shall we call the Lord? Nârâyaṇa or Parânkuṣa? What is there about his neck? A garland of Tulsi or Vakuḷa flowers? How many arms has he? Four or two?" They were struck dumb with awe and wonder. "What is this? Verily, great is Ṣrî Ṣaṭhakôpa, and his ways are mysterious. What is a fly before Garuḍa, the Lord of Birds? Can the glow-worm outshine the Lord of the Day? Would the dog compete with the fierce tiger, the fox with the monarch of the woods? Dare the horrid Bhûta dispute the prize of Beauty with the celestial nymph Ûrvaṣi? What is all the poetry in the world before the thousand verses of Ṣrî Ṣaṭhakôpa?" And they vied with one another in adding fresh titles to the Great Saint. —(*L.A.*)

It was the Great poet Kamban and his 300 colleagues that opposed Mathura Kavi.—[*T. G.* (1880). *Prap.*]

[1] The date of Nâthamuni's birth:—

Era—3,684 of the Kali Yuga; year—Ṣôbhakṛit;

Years passed over their heads. One night, the Lord Râjagôpâla appeared to them in their dream and said, "I want you back at Vîra Nârâyaṉapura, as soon as you can come." They submitted the question to the Lord there and were agreeably surprised to hear that they were to go back. They retraced their way, breaking their journey at many a holy shrine and sacred spot. The Vaishṉavâs of Vîra Nârâyaṉapura joyfully welcomed the returned pilgrims; and as they had already been directed, by the Lord, to make all provisions necessary for the material wants of the family, father, son and grandson found themselves free to devote themselves entirely to the service of Ṣrî Râjagôpâla.

The great learning and deep erudition of Nâthamuni, and his utter purity of life, very soon attracted to him disciples from far and near.

The Search for the Collect.

One day, some Vaishṉavâs, from the west, visited the place and recited before the Lord Râjagôpâla, the decade of the Holy Collect, beginning with Ârâvamudê (ஆராவமுதே). Nâthamuni listened with rapt attention and, at the end, said to them,—"It seems that this decade is one of the Sacred Thousand. Do you happen to know it entire?"

"No, only this, and nothing more."

"Are copies of the Collect available in your parts, or are there any who will kindly undertake to teach it?"

Month—Âni; Date—7; Week—Wednesday;
Fortnight—13 (waning moon); constellation—Anusha;
Amsa—Gajânana, one of the Ministers of Vishvaksêna. —(*Prap.*)

Era—3264 of the Kali Yuga.—(*Per.*)

The following passage foretells his birth:—"There will arise one Nâtha, a great Yôgi, who by his Yôgic power will restore to the world the long-lost Sacred Collect of Ṣrî Ṣaṭhakôpa."—(*Vriddha Pâdma Purâna*: *Pal.*)

"Unfortunately no. We have heard of none who know more than this."

Nâthamuni decided to proceed to Srî Nagari[2], naturally expecting that the birthplace of Srî Sathakôpa would furnish him with copies of his works and expounders thereof.

But he met there one Parânkusa Dâsa, one of the disciples of Mathura Kavi, who said to him—"It is long since we had any one among us, who knew the sacred verses. They are lost to us.[3] But my Master has taught me the mystic decade beginning with Kanninun (கண்ணிநுண்.) and if any one, with a pure heart and earnest mind, stand before the image of Srî Sathakôpa and recite this poem 12,000 times, he will find favour in the eyes of the Holy One and be blessed with a sight of his glorious presence."

"Then," said Nâthamuni, eagerly, "I pray you, out of your great compassion, to set me on the way."

Parânkusa Dâsa gladly did so, and Nâthamuni found no difficulty in carrying out his directions.

---

2 He learnt the decade from the Vaishnavâs, and, proceeding to Kumbhakonam, prayed the Lord Sârangapâni to instruct him in the Sacred Collect, but the latter directed him to Tirunagari to learn them from Sri Sathakôpa himself.—(*Prap.*)

3 Said Parânkusa Dâsa:—"I will relate to you how the Sacred Collect came to be lost to us. It embodied in itself the essence of all Vêdic lore, and threw the doors of salvation open to all classes according to the stages of their spiritual progress. So there was never any one who studied it reverently but was taken to the Lord at its close. In course of time, people came to look upon it as dangerous and unlucky, and fatal to those that engaged in its study, and gave it up in consequence. Nay, some went even so far as to advocate the entire destruction of all the available copies of the work, alleging that it would draw down danger and misfortune upon every house that had it. They were carefully collected and thrown into the river Tâmraparni; when, lo! one of the leaves swam against the current and the beholders were so much struck with the marvel, that they concluded it must contain some mighty

His Initiation.

The Divine Mother, deeply touched by the single-heartedness and devotion of the man, directed Saṭhakôpa to instruct him in all knowledge, human and divine. Then Nâthamuni felt a Mighty Presence near him and a voice* was heard to say—"Servant of the Lord, what desirest thou, that seekest me so earnestly?"

"May I find favour in Thy sight and be instructed in the Holy Collect?"

Srî Saṭhakôpa endowed him with divine vision and taught him the Three Secrets, the Holy Collect, the Essence of the various schools of philosophy and systems of religion, and the Mysteries of the eightfold Path of Yôga. Nâthamuni resided there for a time, devoting himself to the service of the Lord Âdinâtha and Srî Saṭhakôpa.

secret, and preserved it. And it was the decade dedicated to the Lord Sârangapâṇi—the only survivor of the Sacred Collect."-(*Prap.*)

* If Nâthamuni received all his teachings from Saṭhakôpa, whose voice alone he heard, how is it we hear that Nammâlvâr gave him the image of the Future Teacher? The story runs thus:—

Said Nâthamuni to his Teacher,—"Lord, among the stanzas of the Sacred Collect, I find one (iv-2-1) that speaks in veiled words of some great future incarnation. Deign to raise the veil upon it, even so little." That very night, Srî Saṭhakôpa appeared to a sculptor of the place in his dream and said,—"Carve thou an image like the person thou seest before thee and take it to one Nâthamuni whom thou wilt find under the Sacred Tamarind."

The image was reverently handed down through Nâtha Yôgi, Puṇḍarîkâksha, Râma Misra, Yâmunâchârya, Gôshṭhi Pûrṇa and his daughter Dêvaki. But when Râmânuja went to Gôshṭhi Pûrṇa to seek initiation into the Great Truths, the image mysteriously disappeared. It was absorbed into his body, and he was the personage pointed out in the second verse.

Another legend is to this effect:—

Once upon a time, Nârâyaṇa turned to the sage Harita and said,—"During the Kali Yuga when the Ârya Dharma is in danger of being overwhelmed by the waves of Materialism that disbelieves and Superstition that misbelieves, there will incarnate in your line one

He Returns to His Town.

One night, he was directed by Lord Râjagôpâla, to come back and recite before him the Sacred Collect. He obtained permission of his Master and returned to Vîra Nârâyaṇapura, stopping at the various Holy Spots described in the Sacred Collect, and reciting in every temple the verses dedicated to the Lord of the place.[5]

Soon after, Srî Râjagôpâla appeared to him in a dream, and recited the Collect along with him.

The Sacred Collect set to Music.

" Set these verses to divine music ; " said the Lord, " all men would more easily remember them. Besides it would give me infinite pleasure to hear the immortal words of Saṭhakôpa sung in my temples."

---

of my servants, a Great Being who will compose a Bhâshya on the Vyâsa Sûtras. Millions untold will he bring into the fold and lead upon the path that leads to my feet."

Yet, another tradition :—

Some of the disciples of Râmânuja reverently approached him, and, prostrating themselves at his feet, said to him,—" In the Yâdavâchala Mâhâtmya there occurs the following passage : ' Ananta is the first manifestation, Lakshmaṇa the second, and Balarâma the third ; yet will the fourth come on in Kali Yuga.' To whom does it refer ? " The master put them off for a long while, but, finding them all the more importunate, he took them aside and whispered into their ears,—" It is I and no other."—(*Prap.*)

[5] The elders of Tirunagari soon recognised that Nâthamuni was dear to the Lord ; so they reverently went unto him and said,— "In days past, the holy Parakâla (பரகால) instituted an annual visit of the image of Srî Saṭhakôpa to Srîrangam during the month of Mârgaṣirsha. For ten days, from the eleventh day of the bright fortnight, the Sacred Collect was to be recited before Ranganâtha. He called it the " Festival of the Sacred Recital. " In course of time the visits ceased, and, sadder still, the Sacred Collect itself was lost to the world. All hail to you, thou restorer of the great treasure ! We look up to you to restore the annual visit and the " Festival of the Sacred Recital." Nâtha resolved to complete the pleasant duty he had undertaken ; he proceeded to Srîrangam, brought round the Temple authorities to revive the festival in

Nâtha called to his assistance his two nephews[6] (Bhadrâksha and Râma Miṣra—) and set the stanzas to divine music[7], as he thought secular music was utterly inadequate to give expression to such high and sacred themes.

---

all its glory, and amplified it by his instituting the recital of the first thousand and the Tiruvâimoḷi, during the first ten days of the month and the Iyarpâ (இயற்பா) on the twenty-first. He next proceeded to Kumbhakoṇam, where he founded the shrine of Ṣrî Ṣaṭha-kôpa, and there also he introduced the Festival of the Sacred Recital without clashing with the Sankramaṇa festivals. As a humble mark of his gratitude to the Lord Sârangapâṇi, through whom he was enabled to recover the Sacred Collect, he named him 'Aparyâptâmrịta' [*Divya Soori*—(*Prap.*)] (*V. G.*)

6 He directed his nephews to settle themselves at Ṣrîrangam and recite the Collect before Ranganâtha.—(*V. G.*)

7 Once upon a time two courtesans, one skilled in lay music and the other in the celestial, sought the audience of the Chôla king to determine their rsepective superiority. He called together the musical experts and directed the courtesans to sing before them. The umpires decided in favour of the representative of lay music, and the king sent her away with great honours and valuable presents. The other, cut to the heart at this want of appreciation on their part, said to herself,—" Verily, the divine music is not for the men of the world. It is of the Gods, and they alone are qualified to enjoy it. Henceforth I shall not degrade the noble science and myself by singing it before mortals. " She then went round the Sacred Shrines and sang before the Lord. In the course of her tour she came to Vîra Nârâyaṇapuram and was agreeably surprised to find in that far away corner one who could best appreciate her art, nay, was qualified to be her master in it. Nâthamuni was so much charmed with her performance that he directed the honours of the temple to be paid her—a rare honour indeed. She touched his feet with her head and departed. Proceeding straight to the Chôla king, she triumphantly told him that there did exist upon Earth a person who could appreciate her art. The king, greatly amazed, at once invited Nâthamuni to his palace with all honours. " Is it true, revered Sir, that this woman is skilled in what she calls divine music ? To us it is but unpleasant discord." " Nay, nay, Your Majesty, I could prove it to you easily enough." He then had the two women sing before him ; all present were enraptured at the performance of the lay singer. But Nâthamuni was the only one to whom the divine strains spoke of things high and mighty. The king was preplexed and said to the Yôgi—" Lord, deign to explain to us wherein lies the superiority of what you call the music of Gods. " " He who pretends

Very soon the Sacred Collect, in its new and attractive musical garb, made the round of the land and was sung in every temple.

Of his numerous disciples, the best known were Puṇḍarîkâksha and Kurukâdhipa, [8] who were to become so famous later on.

---

to know anything of it should be able to give out the weight of any metal by the sound that proceeds from it." The king was minded to test the truth of what he secretly thought was but an idle boast. So he took Nâthamuni at his word, and placing before him 340 cymbals of various metals and weights, said to him — "Learned Sir, you would not take it as an offence if I request you to ascertain the weight of these cymbals by noting the sounds proceeding from them." Nâthamuni, who had already guessed what was passing in the mind of the king, smiled pleasantly and replied—"Be it so, Your Majesty. Yet, to save time, I would like that they all be sounded at the same time." "Now it is bravado, pure and simple," thought the king; "I have him in a tight place, and no doubt of it." He gave a sign, and the 340 cymbals, large and small clashed together, making a Babel of jarring notes. Then, turning towards Nâtha, the king said, a covert smile of anticipated triumph playing upon his lips,—"Shall I ask the weights of the cymbals to be taken down as you give them out?" "Even so," replied the Brâhmaṇa, and proceeded in a calm and indifferent tone to name the weights of every cymbal quicker than the attendants could write it down. The king waited till the figures were verified; when, lo! they were exact to the turn of a hair. He threw himself at Nâthamuni's feet and implored his forgiveness for doubting his greatness and testing his abilities. He could not prevail upon the Yôgi to take anything from his hands, and saw him depart with a heavy heart.—(*Prap*).

He directed a cymbal to be placed on a granite pillar hard by, and all were surprised to see that when the woman had ceased singing they were unable to take it off. The hard granite had melted while she was singing; when she ceased, it grew solid again, and the cymbal was naturally imbedded in it. He caused her to sing again; all present perceived the granite melt again, and the cymbal was easily taken out of it. "This is the music of the Gods," explained the Yôgi.—(*V.G.*)

[8] Month.—Makara.
Nakshatra.—Viśâkha.
Place of birth.—Kurukoor (Kuruhoor).
Residence.—The Samâdhi of Nâtha Yôgi.
Daily worship.—Śrî Râma.
Term of life.—151 years.

The Yôgi and the King.

In course of time, the great fame of his knowledge reached the ears of the ruler of the country and induced him to pay a visit to the Yôgi. The latter was in deep Samâdhi at that time; so the king contented himself with offering him reverence from a distance and was going back, when, to the surprise of all, Nâthamuni sprang up and ran after him. His disciples protested against this unseemly breach of etiquette and reminded him that it ill-became a high born Brâhmaṇa to run after one of an inferior caste.

"Is it even so?" replied the Yôgi, in evident surprise; "to me they were Srî Krishṇa and his Gôpîs. Else why should I have done so?"[9]

One day he asked his disciples Puṇḍarîkâksha and Kurukâdhipa to learn from him the science of Yôga.

"Not I, my Lord," replied the former; "who would ever think of marriage with a corpse at his door? I have yet large Karmic debts to pay off, and shall take it up sometime before I quit this body, when it will be pure enough and respond to the intensely powerful spiritual vibrations set up by the practice." But the

---

[9] "The Lord Srî Krishṇa," replied the Yôgin, "and his favourite Gôpîs were with me all the while; we were discoursing upon things sweet and high, when, all on a sudden, he disappeared; and, it seemed to me, went this way. What could I do but follow him?"—(*Prap.*)

"The Sacred Scriptures say," rejoined the disciples, "that the Yôgi is above the Vêdas and bows not unto their injunctions and prohibitions. His Karmic debts have all been paid, long, long ago, and he remains in high Samâdhi. Lord, art thou such a one? And art thou resolved to turn thy back upon suffering Humanity and the service of the Lord?"

"The Great Vâsudêva forbid" exclaimed the Yôgi. "I am but a humble servant of the Lord, and you have rightly set my erring feet on the Path of Devotion." Thereafter he confined himself to teaching the good Law and instructing his disciples.—(*V. G.*)

other had no such objections, and the Master imparted to him the secrets of the Science of Yôga. He directed Puṇḍarîkâksha to take upon himself the teaching of the Law and the exposition of the Sacred Verses. He then called his son Îṣvara Bhaṭṭa unto him and said—" A son would be born unto you, whom you will name Yâmuna; and my disciples will hand down to him whatever I have deposited with them. " He then went back to his Samâdhi, wherein he remained for long years.

His Last Moments.

The ruler of the province, came out a-hunting to that part of the country, and was returning to his capital. At about the same time, the Yôgi came out of his Samâdhi and went back to his residence, when he was told by his daughter that two hunters and a woman had been there, along with a great monkey, and had asked for him.[10] It at once flashed upon his mind that they were no other than Ṣrî Râmachandra, Lakshmaṇa, Sîtâ and Hanumân, and that it was a call for him to come back to his glorious seat in Ṣrî Vaikuṇṭha. He ran after them and, directed by the passers-by, traced them as far as the eastern gate of the capital, where they were lost to view. The disappointment was more than he could bear, and he fainted away;[11] then from his mortal body there arose a glorious shape, that soared aloft, joyfully

---

10 "Tell him to hasten after us," said they, and departed.—(*V.G.*)

11 When he was seeking them far and wide, the Lord presented himself before his servant as the Terrible Man-lion. But Nâthamuni would not be consoled. "Miserable sinner that I am," cried he, "my Lord sought me out, me, even me; and He, the Mighty One, whose very Presence dispels the dark clouds of sorrow and ignorance. Of a truth, I have by my own merit raised myself to the unenviable eminence of being the only man whom the Omnipresent Lord sought and found not." He fainted away with grief, and as he lay there, the glorious vision that he so much yearned to see was vouchsafed to him. And his eyes never opened upon anything of this earth thereafter.—(*V.G.*)

welcomed by innumerable Celestial Presences—ever higher and higher until it was lost in an Ocean of Radiance.[12]

His son[13] and disciples[14] found his shell lying where he left it, and reverently took it back to Vîra Nârâyaṇapura,

---

Sîta managed to live away from her beloved Lord for ten long weary months. She was the joy of his heart and knew what it was to live in the company of the Divine Lover. But Nâtha Yôgi, who never had even a glimpse of him, so much took to heart his having missed the glorious opportunity that he could not survive it for as many hours.

12 The date of his death :—the eleventh day of the bright fortnight in the month of Pushya.—*(Per.)*

He lived 340 years—(*V. G.*) | He lived 330 years.—(*Prap.*)

13—14 His son was Îṣvara Bhaṭṭa, Aṃṣa of Priṣnigarbha (Vishṇu) and his wife Aravindappâvai (அரவிந்தப்பாவை) the daughter of Vankipurattâcchi வங்கிபுரத்தாச்சி.

Once she wanted her daughter to come and stay with her some days; and Puṇḍarîkâksha was directed by his master to accompany her. The old lady pressed him to stay for dinner, and directed her servants to take every care of him. But they, looking with a disdainful eye at the low-born (as they thought) forelock-Brâhmaṇa (சோழியன்) and mistaking his utter humility, seated him in the court yard of the house (an honour rarely shown to Brâhmans, but the exclusive privilege of Ṣûdras) and served him with the watered remains of the previous day's meals. Puṇḍarîkâksha partook of it with unfeigned delight, and respectfully took his leave. On his return, the great joy of his heart reflected in his features, failed not to attract the attention of his master. Turning his eye inwards he very soon acquainted himself with what had transpired. "Well, my son," said he, with an innocent look. "I hope they treated you well." "Nay, my Lord," replied he, in tones vibrating with intense joy, "they did me too much honour and made me feel my unworthiness but too keenly. Verily, they have made me the envy of the three worlds." "How so, my son ?" "The Sacred Books say that food from the hands of a servant of the Lord is pure beyond all praise. It was given me to be blessed with the remains of such a meal, further purified with holy water. Indeed, my Lord, I feel I shall grow vain of the great honour."

The Yôgi was overcome with the sight of such unique devotion on the part of the man towards his master; and what was more striking, towards everything in any way connected with him. Tears of joy coursed down his cheeks; he clasped him to his heart and

where it was cremated with the rites of Brahma Mêdha—who more deserving of it than he, the disciple of

---

cried out—" I am indeed unworthy to call myself thy master. You have made me your slave, body and soul. I am but a poor Brâhmaṇa, and can do no more than request you to accept whatever I have to give. May the All-Father reward you as you deserve, for you need it not at the hands of man." He placed his Sacred Feet on the head of his disciple, and remained lost in thought. "Lord, Lord," sobbed out Puṇḍarîkâksha, overcome with emotion, "ill do I deserve this highest honour. Grant me that thy Lotus feet ever adorn this humble head of mine, ever and for ever."

"They are a goodly pair," remarked the bystanders, "and fit each other beautifully like the Lord Nârâyaṇa and his divine consort. We are at a loss which to admire more—the devotion of the disciple to his master, or the love of the master towards his disciple."

The old lady came to know of this and hastened to throw herself at the feet of the holy man, and implore his forgiveness for the heinous sin she had unwittingly committed against him. "Alas," cried she, "little have I gained by having such a great Yôgi as my son-in-law, whom all the world look up to as their Teacher and Guide. I am too much a woman of the world to profit any way by the glorious truths that fall from his lips. Yet, the Holy Books say that a good son uplifts ten generations and a good daughter a hundred. I bless myself in having such a daughter, through whom I can claim some relation with the great Teacher.—(*V. G.*)

He wrote the following works—Nyâya Tatva; Yôga Rahasya; Ṣrî Purusha Nirṇaya.—(*Pal.*)

Of his many disciples, the most famous were:—Puṇḍarîkâksha (உய்யக்கொண்டார்); Kurukâdhipa (குருகைக்காவலப்பன்); Ṣrî Krishṇa Lakshmî Nâtha (திருக்கண்ணமங்கையாண்டான்).

The last came of the village of Krishṇamangala (திருக்கண்ணமங்கை) and was a married man. Nâtha Yôgi initiated him into the mysteries of the True Faith, and directed him to return to his village and lay out a flower garden for the use of the Lord Bhakta Vatsala in that place. Krishṇa followed his master's behests and devoted himself so completely to the service of the Lord that he progressed fast in holiness and purity.

One day the Lord bethought Himself that the various measures taken by his servants towards the regeneration of humanity were solely confined to the expounding of the Sacred Scriptures; but it required something more than teaching and precept to touch the hardened hearts of worldly men. The principles must be lived out, exemplified in daily life, that would surely bring conviction to the

Saṭhakôpa and the great Yôgin? Kurukâdhipa remained in Yôgic Samâdhi on the spot sanctified by the presence of his revered Guru.

---

minds of the unbelieving and attract them to the Way and the Life. And he decided to make Sri Krishṇa an instrument of his work.

One day, two hunters went into the temple to offer their worship to the Lord and left their shoes outside in charge of their faithful hounds. Very soon the animals began to quarrel, and the quarrel developed into a set fight. Their owners rushed out at the noise, and, by their cries, encouraged the already infuriated hounds. A large crowd of sightseers quickly gathered round them, watching with deep interest the strange combat.

In the end, one of the dogs was so frightfully mangled by the other that it fell to rise no more, and its owner, maddened with rage at the loss of his favourite hound, drew his sword and cut off the head of the victor. Forthwith flashed the sword of its master upon him, and long and fiercely did they fight until both of them lay on the ground, bleeding to death of their countless wounds. Meanwhile Sri Krishṇa was an unwilling spectator of the whole, being prevented by the dense crowd from proceeding to the temple to lay his daily garland of flowers at the feet of the Lord. The scene affected him curiously and with a strange power; all at once he flung aside the garland and cried—"Lo! these poor animals, irrational and devoid of the divine spark, have cheerfully laid down their lives in the service of their masters, out of pure attachment and gratitude. And they, in their turn, have sacrificed themselves to avenge an injury inflicted upon an animal whom they called their own, and who looked up to them for protection. And shall I conclude that the All-Father and the Great-Mother, are less attached to Their children and more callous to their sufferings? Far from me be such an unholy thought. Right here I renounce every worldly tie, and take my refuge in Thy Infinite Mercy. Lord, Thy will be done."

He was a changed man from that moment, and his ways were stranger still. In imitation of the hounds that brought about his conversion, he reduced himself to a state of nature and ran about on all fours. At the dawn of the day, he went out of the village to clean his body and ran back to the temple, where he lay thereafter under a tree within its walls, silent, motionless and rapt in meditation. *His Master* took care to see that he was supplied with the very little food he required. The strange spectacle attracted numerous crowds from all parts of the land. Some gazed at him idly with a curious eye, or pitied or criticised him; while others offered him their reverence from a distance. One night, the people of that place, man and woman, young and old, had a dream in which the Lord Bhakta

CHAPTER III.

Puṇḍarîkâksha[1]

the oldest of his disciples, and the best beloved, succeeded him as Teacher, and continued the line of instruction to deserving disciples. Of them, one Râma Miṣra was most devoted to him, and served him faithfully up to the last. Âṇḍâḷ, his master's wife, died, and Râma Miṣra cheerfully undertook to perform all the household work.

One day, his master's daughters proceeded to the river for a bath, and Râma Miṣra accompanied them. On their way back, they had to walk over a dirty place;

Vatsala appeared to them and said—" Tomorrow, at such an hour of the day, fail not to present yourselves at my temple, for I mean to take unto myself that most beloved servant of mine, even Ṣrî Krishṇa."

A dense crowd thronged the yards of the temple and spread far and round, long, long before the appointed time. That morning, Krishṇa went out as usual, but instead of returning to his place under the tree, he made the circuit of the sacred courtyards one after another, the vast crowd walking behind with silent awe and reverence. He made his way to the Holy of Holies, even to the foot of the Throne, and lifted his eyes to the Lord, as if awaiting his commands. The next moment, a dazzling radiance filled the place and blinded their eyes, and when they opened them again, there was the image of the Lord Bhakta Vatsala, with the eternal look of holy calm upon its countenance, silent as Death, serene as the sky and unfathomable as Infinity. But they saw *him* not—the living exponent of the Doctrine of Surrender to the Divine Will, whom the Lord had gathered unto His bosom.—*(Prap.)*

1 Puṇḍarîkâksha's birth :—Era—3,927 of the Kali Yuga.
Year—Parâbhava ; month—Chaitra.
Week—Wednesday ; fortnight—1 (Bright).
Constellation—Krittika.
Amṣa—Sêna.
Term of life—105 years.
Place of birth—Ṣvêtagiri (திருவெள்ளறை) north of Ṣrîrangam.
Place of death—Ṣrîrangam.—[*T.G.* (1880).]
Week—Friday.
Fortnight—15.—(*Prap.*—*Per.*)
Amṣa—Vishvaksêna.—(*Prap.*)
" Jayatsêna.—(*Per.*)

Râma Miṣra would not hear of their soiling their feet but laid himself down across it and made them walk over his body. His master chanced to hear of it, and was so much touched with his absolute devotion to his teacher and to every one in any way connected with him, that, calling Râma Miṣra to his side, he placed his Sacred Feet on the head of his beloved disciple[2]—the greatest mark of affection on the part of a master, and one whose spiritual effects are as deep and far-reaching as the act itself seems trite and common-place.

"What can I do for you, my son?" asked the teacher, with tears of joy starting from his eyes. Râma Miṣra hung his head in great confusion, and humbly replied—"My poor services have been rewarded beyond my highest hopes. What more do I lack?"

"Nay, my dear," replied the master, "not so; accept from me, a poor Brâhmaṇa, all that is mine to give. I will even instruct you again in the Two Sacred Truths—the master-key to all Wisdom and Power."

His Last Instructions.

When the time drew near that his master was to depart from among men, Râma Miṣra approached him reverently and said—"Whom hast thou selected, Lord, to take thy place?"

"Whom should I choose," exclaimed the master, "but thyself, the child of my heart, who had served me thus long and faithfully? You will gather all my disciples around you and continue the work. At no distant date, Îṣwara Bhaṭṭa will beget a son, whom you will name Yâmuna. My great master, of happy memory, enjoined upon me the pleasant duty of instructing him in the

[2] Said he,—"My master once deigned to reward me in this way, when he thought himself pleased with something I did; and I but follow his example."—(V.G.)

sacred lore. But alas! unfortunate that I am, it is not given me to thus contribute my mite to the sacred cause. May be, you might be more blessed. I have taught you all I know, all that was given me by my Guru. Watch over the future teacher; get access to him at any cost, and impart to him faithfully what you have received from me. He will be a mightier man than any of us. Fail not."

He then seated himself in the Padmâsana posture, and, placing his master's sandals before him, concentrated his soul on his Holy Feet, and rose out of his mortal body that was duly cremated by his disciple.

CHAPTER IV.

Râma Misra[1]

faithfully carried out the instructions of his Guru, and followed in his footsteps.

Birth of Yâmunâchârya.[2]

Meanwhile news reached him that a son was born to Îṣvara Bhaṭṭa; he hastened to Vîra Nârâyaṇapura, where

---

1 Râma Miṣra's birth :—
Era—3932 of the Kali Yuga.
Year—Virôdhi; Month—Mâgha.
Week—Monday.
Fortnight—14 (Bright).
Constellation—Mâkha.
Amṣa—Kumuda.
Place of birth—Maṇakkâl, near Ṣrîrangam.
Place of death—Ṣrîrangam.
Term of life—105 years—[*T. G.* (1880)].
Amṣa—Kumudâksha.—(*Prap*).
Week—Wednesday.—(*Per*).

2 Yâmunâchârya's birth :—
Era—4017 of the Kali Yuga.
Year—Dhâtu; Month—Âshâḍha.
Week—Wednesday; Fortnight—Full moon.

he found the prophecy of his master more than fulfilled in the infant he found there. On the twelfth day from his birth, he had him named Yâmunâchârya, as his teacher had directed him to do; and after congratulating the father on the birth of his glorious son, he joyfully returned to Ṣrîrangam.

The Boyhood of Yâmuna.

The boy grew apace, a marvel of loveliness and intelligence. His memory was so keen and his grasp of a subject so great that he had no occasion to be taught anything twice over. In a very short time, he mastered all the branches of secular learning; and his father had the pleasure of seeing him married before he died—an event that occurred not long after.

His Quarrel with Âkkiyâlvan.

He was then placed under one Mahâ Bhâshya Bhaṭṭa, a famous Pandit of the time, to study the various systems of religion and philosophy. In common with the others of his class, the Pandit used to pay an annual tribute to one Âkkiyâlvân, the Royal Chaplain, and the terror of all the learned men, far and near. One day his servants came to demand of him his yearly tribute; but the Pandit was not behind others of his class in the possession of the only quality they had in common—extreme poverty. He was gloomily thinking over his inability to pay the very small

---

Constellation—Uttarâshâḍha.
Amsa—Simhavahana.
Place of birth——Vîra Nârâyaṇapura.
Place of death—Ṣrîrangam.
Term of life—125 years.—[*T. G.* (1880)].
Era—3657 of Kali Yuga.
Month—Kârtika.
Week—Friday.
Parents—Îṣvara Bhaṭṭa and Ranganâyaki.—(*Prap.*)

sum of money, and of the probable consequences that would follow, when Yâmuna came up to him and said,—" What is it, that lies so heavy on my Lord's heart ?"

" Nothing my dear boy, " replied the Pandit, " but the demand of that haughty man Âkkiyâlvân for his annual tribute. I fear I shall not be able to send it. "

Yâmuna laughed long and shrill. " What ! you to allow this trifle to cloud the serenity of your mind ! Then, have I been your servant to no purpose ?"

He thereupon turned to the messengers and said with a laugh of derision—" Tell your master from me that Mahâ Bhâshya Bhâṭṭa's pupil denies his right to any tribute and thus tears his order to pieces. "

When the news was carried to him, Âkkiyâlvân was beside himself with rage. " Is he a mere composer of rhymes or a proficient in the Ṣâstras ? "—he sent back word. Yâmuna's reply almost took his breath away. " No mere poet am I, nor a mere Ṣâstrin, but I am a terror to every one that dare oppose me in disputations. "

He is invited to the Palace.

" This is passing strange, " thought the Pandit, and informed the king of it. The latter commanded Yâmuna's immediate presence before him, but his mandate fared no better. " There is something in all this, " said the king to himself. " Great indeed must be his merit, or his audacity, who should dare trifle with me thus. Well, I shall assume the best. " A palanquin and the other appurtenances of honour were sent to fetch him ; and Yâmuna, satisfied at last of having made himself felt, set out for the palace. Meanwhile he sent a messenger to the king to proclaim in his presence—" The Great Yâmunâchârya, the terror of all that dare to oppose him in argument, is on his way here. Your Majesty would do well to search the whole of India, from the snow-capped Himalayas to the shores of the Southern Sea, sanctified by the feet of Srî Râmachandra, to furnish him with a pandit worthy to hold debate with him in any branch of knowledge, lay or spiritual." In due time he reached the palace, and the Royal Pandit was all eager to engage him in argument then and there. But Yâmuna was too clever to be taken at a disadvantage. "Nay, not so" said he to the king; "if we were to argue before Your Majesty, you would not be able to find out who won; and neither of us would willingly acknowledge that he had been defeated. So let the learned men of the place be assembled, and an umpire chosen." It took no time, for all the town was there to witness this strange intellectual combat between that slip of a boy and Âkkiyâlvân, the hero of many a hard-won fight.

The Two Wagers.

The queen, who was watching with a curious interest the strange scene, said to the king—"My heart yearns towards the bright boy. If he be worsted, as I know he cannot be, I consent to be thrown to the wild dogs; but if he wins, you should promise me to give him half of your kingdom."[3] The king, whose faith was strong in the invulnerability of his Pandit, readily accepted the challenge and fondly expected it would be only a walk-over for Âkkiyâlvân. By that time the vast audience-hall was densely packed with eager crowds of Pandits, Sâstrins, poets, philosophers and sight-seers. The king took his seat, and the proceedings began by Âkkiyâlvân challenging his opponent:—"Let me first try you in lay

[3] Said the queen—"If the bright-eyed boy be worsted (as I am sure he will never be), I consent to become your slave for six months." "And I," exclaimed the king, "am so confident of our Pandit's success, that I promise you half of my kingdom, if you stripling should win."—(*Prap*).

knowledge. You shall state three propositions,[4] positive or negative, which I will disprove; and the winner is to strike at the other's head with his foot." "Please yourself," replied Yâmuna, "it does not matter to me a bit."

The Contest.

"Now, look here, I affirm the following:—Your mother is not a barren woman; the king is all-powerful; and the queen is a pearl of chastity—disprove them if you can." The Pandit never bargained for this. How could he, with any sense of decency, prove that his mother was barren, or that the king was powerless, or, worse than all, that the queen was unchaste? He hung his head in shame and confusion, and preserved undignified silence. The first blow is half the battle. In the argument that followed on religious and philosophical subjects, he fared no better, and with a beating heart awaited the fulfilment of the wager. He lost his nerve, while his bluff and insolence, that had seen him through many an intellectual combat with meaner opponents, now deserted him entirely.

The Victory.[5]

Then Yâmuna rose and said—"Fair Sir, I need not point out to you that by the rules of the challenge your

---

[4] The D. C. omits the question about the queen.

[5] Yâmuna: I affirm that your mother has a son. Deny it if you can.

Pandit: (to himself) What! If I were fool enough to try to prove that my mother did not bring me forth, the very dogs in the street would howl at me. Verily, this is the worst bargain I ever struck, and I have caught a Tartar, no doubt of that.

Yâmuna: Try this at least. You king is a righteous ruler. Deny it by the force of your logic.

Pandit: (to himself). Worse and worse. Should I even get up a lie to prove the king a wicked ruler, would he not spit in my face and cry out—"You ungrateful wretch! I picked you up from the streets and raised you to honour and

honour is forfeit, and nothing stands between you and the chastisement you so richly deserve. But you may thank your grey hairs, and the position you hold as Pandit to the king, that I spare you the indignity. I may here suggest to you that you would do well to employ the few years that you have to live, in learning to know yourself better and in using your talents and position to benefit and honour others of your class, and not to insult or oppress them."

The thousands there assembled rose as one man and shouted themselves hoarse with applause at Yâmuna's extraordinary abilities and unheard of magnanimity. They would be satisfied with nothing short of showing

---

affluence; and this is the return you make—you try to prove to the assembled multitude here, that I am a scoundrel, and have been systematically oppressing them. Off with his head."

Yâmuna: What! silent yet? I sincerely hope you will fare better this time at least. Now, this is the third proposition and the last—The queen yonder is a pearl of chastity. Kindly disprove it.

Pandit: (springing off his seat in great fright): Horror of horrors! Where have I got to? I am playing with edged tools and fire. Is it the punishment of the Lords of Karma who avenge, through this stripling, my past haughtiness and arrogance towards learned men? I am to prove the queen unchaste, is it? Should I even breathe a word of disrespect towards that gem of a woman, I would be torn to pieces the next moment. (Hangs down his head and reflects). What have I to do with these trappings and trinkets? They but proclaim all the louder my ignorance and wicked heart. (He tears off the numerous hard-won trophies of past victories, places them at the feet of Yâmuna, and touches his feet.)

King: Fair Sir, you have won, and that by a long distance. But, may I request you to answer the questions you set him. The task seems well-nigh impossible.

Yâmuna (with a smile): Nay nay, Your Majesty indeed magnifies the difficulty. Look here. He is the only son to his mother. Is it not so, Pandit? Well, and the Sacred Laws lay it down that an only son is no son at all. So

him the highest honour that is ever accorded to a Brâhmaṇa. They seated him in a magnificent chariot, and Brâhmaṇas, young and old, drew it along the streets of the capital with great eclat.

Âḷavandâr.

The queen went out to meet him, and, with tears of joy running down her cheeks, embraced him warmly, exclaiming—"Oh! you have indeed come to save me." And he was ever afterwards known as 'Âḷavandâr' (he that came to save).[6] The king took his defeat as a gentleman, and, with a very good grace, gave him half of his kingdom, and installed him as the ruler thereof.

Râma Misra Seeks Him Out.

All this time, the aged Râma Miṣra had been carefully watching the growth of young Yâmuna, and was waiting for a fit occasion to introduce himself and discharge the duty laid upon him by his master Puṇḍarîkâksha. The news of Yâmuna's victory and instalment as a ruler filled him with deep joy, and he came over to see him. But it was no easy matter to get access to the young Brâhmaṇa ruler; for, Yâmuna lived in state, and in such lordly

she is barren, to all intents and purposes, at least in the eye of the Law.

Again, how could you be called a righteous ruler, especially when you are responsible for the misdeeds of the millions under you, whom you think for and whose ideals you set up?

Lastly, know you not that every woman is married to many other husbands before she touches the hand of her earthly partner? Listen to the Ṣrutis—"Sôma knew her first; the Gandharvas knew her next, and Agni last. Sôma gave her to the Gandharvas, the Gandarvas to Agni, and from Agni I receive." So every woman is, according to the Ṣrutis unchaste; and the queen is no exception.—("*Vinôdarasa Manjari.*")

6 Âḷavandâr (ஆளவந்தார்) = Rakshâgata Guru.

seclusion as eastern potentates generally affect. So, after waiting for many days, he hit upon a curious plan to make himself felt.

The Passport.

He made friends with the servants of the royal kitchen, and very soon ascertained that Yâmuna's favourite dish was a preparation of தூதுவளைக்கீரை. For six months he went on supplying the kitchen with the precious vegetable, hoping thereby to gain Yâmuna's favour. But it was in vain; so he tried the other way, and withheld from the royal kitchen the usual supply. Yâmuna missed his favourite dish, and asked the cooks—" How is it that for the last four days I am not served with the vegetable I so much relish?"

" An aged Brâhmaṇa," replied the steward, " had been supplying us every day for six months, but somehow or other he has stopped it for the last four days." Yâmuna thought for a moment and said—" The next time he comes here, bring him up to me straight." Curiously enough, Râma Miṣra made his appearance at the kitchen the very next morning with the vegetable, and was forthwith taken to their royal master.

The Master and The Pupil.

The moment Yâmuna cast eyes at Râma Miṣra a sort of veil seemed to be removed from before his inner vision; he recognised in him his master, received him with every mark of respect and reverence, and humbly said—" I beg to be pardoned for having unconsciously kept you waiting for so many weary months. May I request to know what I can do for you? Wealth, lands and anything that I have are at your service."

" Nay, I want none of these. Some valuable treasure has been left in my care by your grandfather to be delivered over to you at the proper time. [7] I know where it is, and I only request to be allowed to have free access to you every day until you take charge of it."

"I am ever at your service," replied Yâmuna, and arranged it accordingly.

From that time, Râma Mişra came to Âļavandâr every day and instructed him in the inner meaning of the Bhagavat Gîta, the Bible of Humanity for all time. The desire to realise in himself the sublime state of spiritual perfection so glowingly described in it, grew strong in him day by day, and he ventured to ask—"Is it given me to lay myself at the feet of the Lord and serve him, ever so humbly?"

"Why not?" replied the Teacher. "All are welcome. Verily, the eyes of the Holy Ones are grown dim with watching for a glimpse of the Pilgrims on the Path." He then took him apart and duly initiated him into the Grand Mystery of the Last Verse (Charama Şlôka)—the sublime secret of self-surrender. Within a very short time the smouldering spark of Vairâgya burst into a blaze, and

---

7 "What kind of a treasure is it?"

"Unlike the treasures in the palaces of kings and emperors, it is proof against fire, water and other destructive agencies of nature."

"How can I see it?"

"Magical unguents can enable you to see the material treasures of the world. But this is of a peculiar nature. One should free his sight of any such preparations to see it."

"How can I get at it?"

"Oh! You need not offer any sacrifices to it, either of animals, or of men. There is a leaf with very occult properties, which you have only to lay upon it, to make it your own."

"Well, where is it?"

"In a spot between two rivers; it is guarded by seven strong fortresses, one within the other, and is placed on a magical Yantra. A huge serpent is coiled around it, and once in twelve years there comes from an island in the southern seas, a Râkshasa, to see if it is safe."

Yâmuna longed to have done with the world and its hollow pleasures, and devote himself purely and solely to a life of devotion to the Lord. Râma Miṣra, who was keenly watching the spiritual growth of his disciple, now satisfied himself that Âḷavandâr had set his foot irrevocably on the Path of Renunciation and his face against the Path of Enjoyment and Activity.

His Inheritance.

He took him to Ṣrîrangam, the holiest spot in all India, and the favourite abode of Nârâyaṇa. He brought him even unto the Sacred Presence, and, pointing to the Divine Image, said—"This," my dear son, "is the priceless treasure your predecessors have left you, and this I have been deputed to lead you to." Âḷavandâr gazed on the Ineffable Beauty that had enthralled the vision of many a sage and devotee before him, and stood rapt in ecstasy.

He Takes Orders.

For his life he could not tear himself away from the place. Then and there he formally renounced the world, and took the vows of a Sanyâsin. Are not wives, children, friends, houses, lands and wealth but so many impenetrable veils that hide the lotus feet of the Lord from the longing eyes of his devotees ?[8]

---

8 "Behold, " said he to himself, " I was a miserable worldling, and was far on the way to spiritual death. This holy man sought me out, me the sinful one, waited upon me for six months, got access to me by the most curious channel imaginable, stayed with me day after day, teaching me with infinite patience and anxiously watching over my spiritual growth, and in the end offered to place me in possession of the treasure of my forefathers. I very naturally thought that it was some buried hoard of jewels or coin. But now I find that it is no other than the Great Father. Verily, the most precious of all treasures. I then wanted to ascertain whether it was gold or silver or jewels. He replied that it was proof against any destroying agency —the Eternal Lord. I then desired to know if any magical preparation exists, which, if applied to one's eyes, would enable him to find

He spent his days in the holy spot,[9] ever intent upon serving the Lord and entirely engaged in handing down to deserving disciples the knowledge entrusted to him by his master.

His Disciples.

They were many, but the following names stand out conspicuous by their learning and holiness:—Mahâ Pûrṇa, Gôshṭhî Pûrṇa, Ṣrî Ṣaila Pûrṇa, Mâranêri Nambi, Kânchi Pûrṇa, Daivavâriyâṇḍân and Mâlâdhara.

---

where it is buried. He answered by a pun upon the word Anjana (Collyrium, and also worldly taints). One should have his eye free from any Anjana to see it. Only the opened eye of spirit, free from any Anjana or worldly taint could see the glory of the Lord. As buried treasures are generally recovered by offering some sacrifice to the spirits that watch over it, I asked him to tell me the process of getting at it. He mentioned a leaf of some plant, with occult properties. Sure enough it is the Sacred Tulasi and no other. Of course, the treasure is between two rivers, the branches of the holy Kâveri. The seven court-yards of this temple guard it like seven fortresses. The magical Yantra is, verily, the Vimâna, of the form of Praṇava. The huge serpent is Âdiṣêsha, the symbol of Infinite Wisdom. And the great Bhakta, Vibhîshaṇa, comes once in twelve years to offer his worship to the Lord of the Temple. This treasure was left me by my grandfather Nâtha Yôgi. It is now plain as anything, that he wanted me to stay here and serve the Lord for ever. Lo! What disinterestedness! My master found me a miserable worm grovelling in the mires of sensual life, and raised me into the regions of Eternal Life and Light. What are wives, children, friends, fame, wealth and the thousand and one deceitful phantoms of worldly pleasures before this Sweet and Holy life? Ere I am a second older, I shall devote myself solely and entirely to it."—(*Vino*).

9 Yâmuna's holiness and great fame failed not to reach the ears of the king and the queen. And induced by the latter, who was the first to find out the great Teacher, by spiritual instinct as it were, they came over to Yâmuna and requested to be taken as his disciples. Yâmuna was only too glad to do it; and they entered the Fâith and were known among the elect as Ranga Chôla and Ranga Nâyaki; and along with them the once haughty Âkkiyâlvan, but now the foremost of Yâmuna's admirers. At his initiation, he received the name of Nâthamuni Dâsa. Yâmuna's half of the kingdom was made over to Ṣrî Ranganâtha, and remained so down to the time of Krimikaṇṭha Chôla who took it back. Then his two sons came and lived with him at Ṣrîrangam—(*Prap*).

Directed to Kurukâdhipa.

One day Râma Miṣra went to Âḷavandâr and said —"There is only one more duty for me to discharge by you. Your grandfather has entrusted Kurukâdhipa, one of his disciples, with a secret to be communicated to you, and I would like you should receive it from him.[10]

"But how is it," asked Yâmuna in surprise, "that you have it not?"

"Your grandfather, of happy memory, wanted his disciple and my master, Puṇḍarîkâksha to learn it from him; to which my master replied—"Who would think of marriage with a corpse at his door? I am not yet prepared to take up that course. I think I will be pure enough for it when I cast off this body of mine."

"Then", rejoined Âḷavandâr," I shall be only too happy to sit at the feet of the great Yôgi and learn."

Ranga Gâyaka :—Year—Pingaḷa ; Month—Vaiṣâkha ; Nakshatra —Jyêshṭha ; Term of life—115 years ; Amṣa—Ṣankhakarṇa.

Ranga Gâyaka was extremely devoted to Âḷavandâr and his greatest delight consisted in singing the Collect and meditating upon its import. Âḷavandâr was very much struck with the masterly way in which he sang it, and directed him to proceed to Ṣrîrangam and sing before the Lord, as the nephews of Nâthamuni had done.—(*V.G.*)

Vara Ranga was not the son of Âḷavandâr, but only of the same gôtra. Yâmuna had only one son, Piḷḷaikkaraṣu Nambi.—(*Pal.*)

He had four sons: Choṭṭai Nambi, Daivattukkaraṣu Nambi, Piḷḷai Araṣu Nambi and Vara Ranga Gâyaka [illegible]. They all became disciples of Râma Miṣra along with their father.—(*V.G.*)

10 Once, when Râma Miṣra was explaining the stanza [illegible] Yâmuna eagerly asked—"If the Lord is so easy of access as that, there must exist some process of seeing him face to face. Initiate me into it, if thou thinkest I deserve it." "I know it not, because I never aspire to such high honour. I prefer to be the meanest of his servants here; I am fit for nothing else. That is the goal I have set before myself, and that is the subject of all my meditations. As for you, Kurukâdhipa is your man. He will put you on the way."—(*Vârt.*)

The Last Moments of Râma Misra.

Now Râma Misra was getting old and infirm; having discharged, to his heart's content, the duties laid on him by his master, and having left behind him an able teacher, he be thought himself of 'shuffling off this mortal coil.' So he called unto him Âlavandâr and said—"You are doubly related to the great Yôgi Nâthamuni. Let his sacred feet be your guide and goal. Abide in this holy spot and consider that you have discharged your duty by me only when you have left behind you a worthy successor to take up your work." He then concentrated his whole soul on the feet of his master Pundarîkâksha, cast off his body, and took his place by the side of the Lord. Âlavandâr and the other pupils were plunged in great grief; but very soon they realised the futility of their sorrow, as they well knew that though absent in body, he was always present with them in spirit. Then Yâmuna, as his oldest and most beloved disciple, cremated him duly with the rites of Brahmamêdha.

CHAPTER V.

Yâmunâcharya, the Teacher.

Some time after, Âlavandâr resolved to approach Kurukâdhipa, and with his pupils went to the place where the Yôgi was seated in Samâdhi.

Âlavandâr and Kurukâdhipa.

The majesty of his appearance struck them with awe and reverence, and they stood silent behind the walls of the building, afraid of disturbing his Samâdhi. All on a sudden the Yôgi turned round and said—"Is there any one here of the family of Chottai?" Yâmuna came forward, and prostrating himself before him, replied—"Here is Yâmuna lays his head at your feet." Kurukâdhipa gave him his blessing and raised him up. But Âḻavandâr's curiosity was so great as to make him forget his object for a time. "My Lord will pardon me for asking him a question. How is it that he was aware of his servant's presence here?" "Nay, my son, the explanation is very simple. The Supreme One, when He blesses me with His Divine Presence, is usually quite oblivious to every other thing; so much so that even the Divine Mother has no power to attract His attention from me. But just now, He placed His hands on my shoulders and looked beyond me more than once. I naturally guessed that no other than a member of the family to which my revered master Nâtha Yôgi belongs, has the power to divert His attention that way. You see now how I knew of your arrival." Âḻavandâr touched the feet of the Yôgi and humbly said—"May your unworthy servant crave the boon of being initiated into the mysteries of Yôga?" The Yôgi thought for a moment and replied—"My son, I can deny nothing to the grandson of my master. Nay, it is a duty laid on me by him. I will initiate you when I am about to leave this body. It might come off on such a date in the month of Pushya. Fail not to be here then." Âḻavandâr readily promised to do so and took his leave of Kurukâdhipa.

His Journey to Trivandrum.

On one of the days of the Sacred Recital, Ranga Gâyaka, while reciting, with the appropriate gestures, the decade beginning with கெடுமிடராயவெல்லாம் (x. 92. 1) came to the stanza நடமினோநமர்களுள்ளீர் (x 92. 8)[1] He gazed fixedly on Âḻavandâr and sang the stanza more than once. Then Âḻavandâr thought to himself that he had too long omitted to offer his worship at the sacred shrine of Padmanâbha; and, having got permission of the Lord,

[1] It directs the godly to proceed to Trivandrum to worship Srî Padmanâbha.

Ranganâtha, he proceeded to Trivandrum, leaving behind him Daivavâriyâṇḍân in charge of the maṭḥam.

He bewails his Carelessness.

He stayed at Trivandrum for some time, when one day he bethought himself of the promise he had made to Kurukâdhipa ;[2] and to his surprise and dismay he found that it was the very day he was to have presented himself before the Yôgi. His grief at this oversight almost broke his heart. He cursed himself for having been careless in an affair of such great moment, and bitterly bewailed his bad Karma that kept him back from such a priceless gift. " Miserable sinner that I am," cried he, " what right have I to be so blessed ? Indeed, I am the prince of disciples and very well deserve to be entrusted with such a grand secret—I that have broken my promise to the Holy One and stupidly forgotten that which any other in these three worlds would have given his life and everything he holds dear, to acquire. Oh ! that I had the wings of Garuḍa ! Oh, that an aerial car like the Pushpaka were at my disposal ! But a truce to these vain regrets. Let me go back to the Holy Feet of Ranganâtha where one can find peace and light."[3]

A Strange Disciple.

Meanwhile Daivavâriyâṇḍân could not bear to be long away from his beloved master and fell ill. He grew so

---

2 On his return from Trivandrum he halted at Madura ; and the lovely bowers on the banks of the Vaigai seemed to him the fittest spot for the practice of Yôga. This recalled, by the association of ideas, his promise to the Yôgi.—(*Prap.*)

3 When he bewailed his carelessness in having failed in his promise to the Yôgi, the Lord appeared to him and said—"It was I that did it, and with a purpose. Confine yourself to the same goal as your master, Râma Miçra."

weak, that his friends despaired of his life, and called in wise physicians who said—"The illness is purely of the mind, of the heart. He longs after something, which, if he gets not soon, he will die." Then they asked Âṉḏân—"What is it that you are pining after?" "What can I long for," replied Âṉḏân, "but a sight of my beloved master?" "Then," said the physicians, "there is only one thing that can cure him—he should be taken to where his Guru is." Accordingly they had him conveyed by easy stages to Trivandrum; he grew better every day and was so much recovered as to be able to walk. When they were a few miles from the place, they heard that Âḻavandâr was on his way back to Ṣrîrangam and hastened to meet him. No sooner were Yâmuna and his disciples in sight, than Âṉḏân ran towards his master, who was dearer to him than his life, and fell at his feet sobbing like a child. Âḻavandâr, unaware of the facts of the case, was deeply offended with his pupil for taking upon himself to quit his post without permission. "You were right, Âṉḏân," said he, "and I am a fool to be angry with you. Ṣrî Râmachandra asked Bharata to wait fourteen years for him, until he should come back; Bharata knew that his brother was divine and that nothing might stand between him and the object of his desire. Alas! what am I?—a poor, insignificant mortal, that knows not what might befall me the next moment, a very worm that cannot move out of the path to escape being trodden to death. How can you expect me to keep my word to you? You did very well and wisely too. I thank you very much for coming over to see me and so enabling me to fulfil my promise to you." Truly, Âṉḏân had never bargained for such a reception as this. His illness, from which he was then only recovered, came upon him afresh, and he lay there unable to rise, thinking, "Truly, it were well had I remained behind and died." Â̱lavandâr, seeing that Âṉḏân still continued to lie there, understood it as a sign of refractoriness, and said in angry tones—"What! do you mean to lie there until I make you as mighty and as independent as Sri Râma? What an excellent pupil! Good Sir, I am highly obliged to you for this lesson." Âṉḏân was pierced to the heart by these cruel words, and, with a superhuman effort, stood up trembling before his angry master. Then the other disciples acquainted him with the real state of the case; whereupon he was silent for a moment and then said—"Wonderful! Is it even so? And I have cruelly misunderstood you. Could you ever forgive me, my dear, for my inconsiderate roughness to you. But, truly, Âṉḏân, I was never angry with you; I could not bear the thought that you, of all my disciples, should be considered as wanting in the observance of your duty. Really, as I said before, you have taught us all a lesson, and one I would not forget in a hurry." Then he folded him to his heart, held him at arm's length to look at him better, and said—"My dear, you seem to be very ill indeed. Now that you have come so far, go to yonder sacred shrine and offer your worship at the holy feet of the Lord Padmanâbha." "Nay, my Lord, I have already done it." "How so, my son?" "My Lord Padmanâbha met me on my way to His shrine, and even now I stand in His Gracious Presence. I have found favour in his eyes, in as much as he had deigned to touch, with His Holy body, this unworthy carcass of mine. Oh! what have I done to be so blessed above all other mortals?" Â̱lavandâr remained silent, overcome with the sight of such perfect devotion and such single-hearted affection. He blessed him again and again, and held him thenceforth in greater love and estimation, if possible, than before. They all returned to Srîrangam, where Â̱lavandâr spent his time in unremitting devotion to the Lord and untiring dissemination of the knowledge entrusted to him by his master.[4]

His Great Grief.

But his heart knew not peace; he was a prey to an ever-gnawing grief. He was growing old and weak; there was no one upon whose shoulders he could lay his burden and seek rest; he had not discharged the duty laid on him by his master; and his anxious eyes wearily

---

[4] One day, Yâmuna was explaining the meaning of the verse—[Tamil text] (II.23, 1.), when Saila Pûrna, one of his disciples was so much carried away with the spirit of service to the Lord taught in that stanza, that he stood up at once, and said respectfully—"May I request permission to proceed to the Holy Mount and serve the Lord?" The offer was gladly accepted. "He should have realised the inner spirit of the Doctrine of Service in no small degree," thought the Teacher to himself, "and his natural devotion should have been something wonderful. Else could he never have been seized with such an eager and uncontrollable desire. May be the Great Law will find its exponents in his line; may be the Future Teacher will rejoice in such pure heredity."

On another occasion, while commenting upon the stanza [Tamil text], he suddenly stopped short and was lost in thought. "Who might be the Great One hinted at so obscurely in these lines? He has either come and gone, or is yet to. Srî Sathakôpa never fails in his forecasts; from him nothing is hidden; from him nothing is concealed." His disciples, rightly guessing the trend of his reflections, humbly submitted that he and no other was the fulfilment of the prophecy, "for, said they," "thou are verily the Lord of all Perfections." Yâmuna smiled, a pitying smile—"Far be it from my humble self, the meanest of the mean, to arrogate to myself such a supreme honour. The lines refer to the incarnation upon earth of a Great Being, the Saviour of men and the restorer of the Good Law. And I am certain that it applies not to any teacher of the past, and much less to myself. For, have the results predicated come about? Has Kali disappeared from earth? Are the hells empty and is the God of Death in blank despair? Has the Krita Yuga come again upon earth? No. Then the Teacher is to come, and I can only tell you that the time is not far off. It is not given me to know whether I would live to see the happy day or no. May be some of you might have that privilege and pleasure. Then will you realise the true import of the stanza [Tamil text], of the dark passages in the Hârita Samhita and the Yâdavâchalamâhâtmya."—(*Prap.*)

watched for the signs that would precede the appearance into the world of the Future Teacher. But, thanks to the unerring justice of the Lords of Karma and the illimitable mercy of the Supreme One, he had not long to wait.[6]

CHAPTER VI.

Râmânuja's Birth and Early Days.

Sri Saila Pûrna, one of the disciples of Âlavandâr, had two sisters ; the elder of them, Kântimati, was given in marriage to Âsûri Kêsava Sômayâji of Sri Perumbûdûr, and the younger, Dyntimati, to Kamalâksha Bhatta of Valalamangalam.

[6] There lived at Srîrangam, two Vaishnavas, the disciples of Yâmunâchârya, who were so much attached to one another, as to be commonly known as "The Inseparables." One day Yâmuna saw one of them return alone from the river and said—"He has known his self, when he has realised in himself the state of the Krauncha bird."

[The Krauncha is remarkable for its strong attachment to its mate. Its home is on the Talipat palm, where it builds its nest, of rough and sharp thorns outside and soft grass and feather within. They are never found apart from one another, at any time of the day or the night. They cannot see in the dark ; and they sleep with their bills intertwined lest they should be unconsciously separated. If, by accident, one stays away from the other, it calls out twice or thrice in a peculiar heart-rending tone of voice, and its mate generally manages to guide itself to its beloved. If it does not, the poor Krauncha does not survive the separation. It is a favourite symbol of love with the Samskrit poets. Yâmuna only meant that such a strong love and devotion to the servants of the Lord was the surest path to the knowledge of Âtman.—*Compiler.*]

One day, Yâmunâchârya was about to enter the Sanctuary to offer his worship to the Lord, when he saw a woman inside and drew back. The lady was, to all appearance, a great Bhakta, but Yâmuna stayed outside for a time and then asked the bystanders—"Is the selfish one, the hypocrite departed ? " "Why should you mind it ? " said one. "In the presence of the Lord there is no rich and poor, high and low, sinner and saint." "Nay, nay," replied the Teacher, "even in the all-purifying presence of the Lord, one should keep away from hypocrites ; for nothing can stand against the soul-killing emanations of such natures. They corrupt the purest, and inevitably lower him to their own level."—(*Vârt.*)

His Previous Incarnations.

Meanwhile, the revolving cycles had brought about the moment, when the Great Lord Ananta was to manifest himself in human form and limit his illimitable Essence.[1] His first incarnation was in the Trêta Yuga as Lakshmaṇa, the brother of Râma; his second was in the Dvâpara Yuga, as Balarâma, the elder brother of Kṛishṇa, and once more he came down on earth in the Kali Yuga.[2] The Karmic affinities of Kêṣava[3] and his wife attracted him

---

1 The following passages presage his incarnation :—

(a) "Long, long afterwards, the Lord himself will come down on earth as a Tṛidaṇḍa Sanyâsin, to restore the Good Law. At that time heretics and men of perverted intellects will confuse the minds of the people. Âsuric Ṣâstras, based upon fallacious arguments and various schools of thought, very attractive and almost indistinguishable from the Vêdânta, will turn away men's hearts from Vishṇu and cause them to forget His glory. That glorious incarnation will, through the good fortune of the Lord's devotees, come down upon earth, to explain and amplify the teachings of the great Sage Bâdarâyaṇa and of the Divine Singer of the Gîta. The Holy One would compose a Bhâshya on the Vyâsa Sûtras, to save men from the confusion and despair caused by sophistical doctrines and lead them to the True Faith."—(*Vriddha Pâdma Purâna.*)

(b) "His primal manifestation was as Ananta; his second as Lakshmaṇa, the younger brother of Râma; his third, as Balabhadra, the elder brother of Kṛishṇa; and once again will he come down on earth in the Kali Yuga."—

Nâradîya Purâṇa (Yâdavâchala Mâhâtmya).—(*Pal.*)

2 In the Supreme Heaven, the Mighty One turned to the Angels that stood around his throne and singling out Ananta and Garuḍa, said to them—"My home in the land of the Aryas has been defiled by the Dark One. The Vêdas and the Ṣâstras are but a tradition, and the once mighty Brâhmaṇas are fast dying out. Go down unto the Bhârata Varsha and restore the Good Law." "To hear is to obey," replied they reverently, and waited for fit vehicles.—*R.D.C.*

"Yea" spake He, " now I go to help the world
" This last of many times; for birth and death,
" End hence for me and those who learn my Law."—(*Light of Asia.*)

3 Kêṣava was an Amṣa of Nârâyaṇa, as also, Kamala Nayana Bhaṭṭa."—(*Prap.*)

Kêṣava Sômayâjin wrote many works on the Ṣiksha and the Ṣrauta of the Yajur Vêda, generally known as Kêṣavîa.—(*V.C.*)

to take birth of them, and the purity of their life, a legacy handed down to them by seven generations of spotless ancestors, guaranteed a fit vehicle for the Great Being to do his work in this world.[4]

His Birth.

And thus it was he came to be born of Kêṣava Sômayâjin at Ṣrî Perumbûdûr[5] (Bhûtapuri) in the Year of Grace Pingaḷa, the 940th of the Ṣaka Era, on a Thursday, the 5th of the bright fortnight, in the month of Chaitra ; the constellation of Ârdra presided over the moment of his birth.[6]

---

[4] Once upon a time, Kêṣava went, during a lunar eclipse, to Kairaviṇi (Triplicane) to purify himself by a sea-bath ; he took advantage of the occasion to pray to the Lord Pârthasârathi of Triplicane for a son, and performed an Ishṭi (Sacrificial rite) before his Shrine. That very night the Lord appeared to him in his sleep and said— "Your prayer is granted ; you will have me for your son."—(*Prap.*)

[5] A village in the Chingleput District, Madras Presidency, about 26 miles west of Madras.

[6] Era—4118 of the Kali Yuga.
—939 of the Sâlivâhana Ṣaka.
Lagna—Karkaṭaka (noon).—(*Prap.*)
Era—A. C. 1017—(*V. C.*)
Fortnight—7th.
Amṣa—Nârâyaṇa, Lakshmi, Ananta, Sênêṣa, and the five weapons.—(*Pal.*)
Day of the month—13th.
Yôga—Âyushmân. Karaṇa—Bhadra.
Sect—Vaḍama. Family name—Âsûri.
Gôtra—Hârîta. Ṣâkha—Yajus.
Sûtra—Âpastamba.—(*Per.*)
At the time of our Lord's birth :—

"The strong hills shook ; the waves
Sank lulled, ...Down to the farthest hells
Passed the Mother's joy, as when warm sunshine thrills,
Wood-glooms into gold, and into all the deeps
A tender whisper pierced. 'Oh ye,' it said,
'The dead that are to live, the live who die
Uprise and hear and hope ! The Lord is come.'
Whereat in Limbos numberless much peace
Spread, and the world's heart throbbed and a wind blew
With unknown freshness over lands and seas."
—(*Light of Asia.*)

Srî Saila Pûrṇa was informed of this and joyfully hastened to Srî Perumbûdûr; he congratulated Kêsava Sômayâjin on his being blessed with such a gem of a boy.[7] "He has all the auspicious marks of a Perfect Man; and there is no knowledge, human or divine, that he will not master; so let him be aptly named Lakshmaṇa,[8] after his prototype Ananta, the Great Serpent, the mystic emblem of Boundless Wisdom and Eternity." It required but very little effort on the part of the boy to master all the lay sciences of his time,[9] and when he was sixteen years old, his father found a wife[10] for him.

Under Yâdava.

Meanwhile,[11] it reached the ears of Râmânuja that Yâdava Prakâsa,[12] an Advaiti Sanyâsin of Kânchi,[13] was ably lecturing to numerous pupils on the cardinal doctrines

7 "This is that blossom on our human tree
Which opens once in many myriads years,
But, opened, fills the World with Wisdom's scent
And Love's dropped honey; from thy holy root
A Heavenly Lotus springs! Ah, happy House!"
—*Light of Asia.*

8 Some of his well-known names are :—

Lakshmaṇa	given by	Saila Pûrṇa.
Râmânuja	.. ..	Srî Varadarâja.
Udayavar	.. ..	Srî Ranganâtha.
Emberumânâr	.. ..	Goshṭhî Pûrṇa.
Bhâshyakâra	.. ..	Sarasvati.—(*Pal.*)
Râmânuja	.. ..	Mahâ Pûrṇa.
Yatîndra	.. ..	Srî Varadarâja.—(*Per.*)

9 After his thread ceremony (Upanayana) he was educated in his own home until his fifteenth year, where his father taught him all the Vêdas and the Vêdângas.—(*V. C.*)

10 His wife's name is given as Tangam Ammâl or Rakshakâmba.—(*Prap.*)

11 On the death of his father, he left for Kânchi.

12 Yâdava Prakâsa was at first a follower of Srî Sankarâchârya, but afterwards became a reformed Advaitee. His opinions are not accepted by the followers of Sankara. He wrote a commentary of his own on the Vyâsa Sûtras.—(*V. C.*)

13 He resided at Tiruppuṭkuḷi, near Kânchîpuri.

of Vêdânta ; and he proceeded thither to form one of the ever increasing group of his disciples.

Gôvinda.

Meanwhile Kamalanayana Bhaṭṭa had a son[14] born to him. Srî Saila Pûrṇa proceeded thither too, and recognising in the child a great worker for humanity, congratulated the father on the glorious future that was in store for his son and advised him to call the boy Gôvinda. The boy more than outran the fond expectations of his parents and friends ; and when he came to know that his brother Râmânuja was studying under Yâdava Prakâṣa, he joyfully joined him.

First Quarrel with Yâdava.

One day, Yâdava, in explaining the famous passages[15] in the Taittiriya Upanishad (Brahmânanda Valli, II Anuvâka, i) " Satyam gñânam anantam Bramha laid" down that the attributes of Beness, Knowledge and Infinity, could be predicated of Brahma only when the same cow could be proved to be brokenhorned, hornless, and full-horned at one and the same time. Then Râmânuja rose up and humbly

---

14 (*a*) Year—Krôdhana ; Fortnight—Full-moon ;
Week — Monday ; Constellation — Punarvasu. (*T. G.* 1880).

(*b*) Month—Vaiṣâkha ; Nakshatra—Viṣâkha.—(*Prap*).

(*c*) Month—Makara—(*V. G* ; *Pal*).

(*d*) Year— Durmati.
Sect—Vaḍama.
Family—Vartamṇi.
Gôtra—Bhâradvâja.
Household Deity—Nṛisimha.
Disciples—Parâṣara and Vêda Vyâsa Bhaṭṭa.
Term of life—105 years.
Works—Vijñâna Stuti. —(*Per*).

(*e*) Year—Pingaḷa.—*R. D. C.*

15 (*a*) This took place after the Brahma Râkshasa episode, nay, after Yâmuna's visit to Kânchi. (*Prap*).

(*b*) Yâdava's arguments are reproduced in the Srîbhâshya pp. 27, 28, 29; and the criticism thereon, pp. 78-103 and 156-161

said—"I submit that the passage bears another interpretation, that seems to me to be a little more logical. The attribute of Beness precludes all idea of momentary change; the attribute of Knowledge removes all possibility of the presence of Achit in His nature; and the attribute of Infinity puts an end to all conceptions of limitation of his essence. So I take that these attributes are mutually exclusive of one another and are not incompatible in one and the same being. Brahman stands out Eternal and entirely distinct from the rational and non-rational Universe." Yâdava Prakâṣa thought for a moment and tried to find a reply, but he contented himself with a grunt of dissatisfaction and remained silent.

His Second Quarrel.

Another day Râmânuja was anointing Yâdava Prakâṣa, when the talk turned upon the interpretation of the passage "Kapyâsam puṇḍarîkam êvam akshiṇî"[16] Chândôgya Upanishad, Chap. I, Sec. vi. 6, 7). Yâdava gave a very blasphemous and obscene rendering of it; Râmânuja's heart boiled within him at this wanton sacrilege, and tears of hot indignation ran down his cheeks. These fell upon the thigh of Yâdava and scalded it severely. The Sanyâsin

---

Thibaut's Translation); *vide* also the Grantha Edition of the Taittirîya Upanishad, where the arguments of the two schools are exhaustively discussed.

[16] Dr. Râjêndra Lâla Mitra translates the passage thus:—"That resplendent male of golden hue and whiskers, whose *whole body* even unto the nails is of gold, whom we behold in the interior of the Sun, whose eyes are like unto lotuses, red as the orb of the rising God of day." And the extract from Ṣankara's commentary runs thus:—

"Of this male whose whole body is golden, there is some distinction in the eyes. They are red like unto lotuses, which are bright, as the parts around the postial callosities of the monkey; Kapyâsa from Kapi, monkey and Âsa, to sit. Here the comparison is not unworthy, being between the lotuses and the parts around the callosities."

(*From Tukârâm Tâtya's Edition.*)

But Râmânuja derives Kapyâsa otherwise. Kapyâsa is that which forms an abode "to the rays of the sun." [*Compiler.*]

jumped up and looked at the face of Râmânuja that was black with suppressed wrath. "What is the matter with you?" asked Yâdava in surprise. "Nothing," replied Râmânuja, "but that I happened this day to hear a passage of the holy Sruti, interpreted in a manner outrageous to all sense of decency and logic, and *that*, by one whose learning and status in life ought to have taught him better." "Then, pray, learned sir," said Yâdava with withering scorn, "deign to shed a ray of your supreme wisdom upon your benighted servants. I sit at your feet to learn your famous explanation of the text." Râmânuja cared not to notice the coarse witticisms of Yâdava, but said—"Thus it seems, it has been interpreted of yore: The eyes of the Golden Person within the Solar Orb are as bright and lovely as the petals of the lotus that opens its bosom to the welcome rays of the Lord of Day. No right-minded Ârya would even dream of any other interpretation." Thus did our Great Teacher cross swords with Yâdava a second time and brave him to his face. The pent-up rage and envy of Yâdava Prakâsa swept away all considerations of prudence and he roared out: "This to me! Dare you beard the lion in his own den? You are too learned for me, Pundit. Get away from my sight and never darken my doors again." Râmânuja considered for a while and decided that it was the best course to be followed under the circumstances.

Yâdava's Plot.

Meanwhile Yâdava was not idle. He realised, more than any other, the miserable future that was in store for himself and his following, if Râmânuja was allowed to live and grow learned and powerful. He called to him some of his pupils, who, he knew, would stick at nothing to please him and said—"Look here. This Râmânuja is dangerous more than you think. Don't you see that he alone among you dares criticise my teachings ? If he be not removed from amongst us, you may rest assured that the days of Advaitism are numbered. Now, find me out some means of doing it, sure and secret." Beautiful suggestions were offered, each one more fiendish than the other; but Yâdava discarded them all as sinful. "Let us entice him to join us in a pilgrimage to the holy Benares, and once there, he would easily find his way to the bottom of the Ganges. It will effectually secure our ends and avert any consequent sinful effects." The proposal was applauded to the echo; and kind friends were not wanting who offered to bring Râmânuja back to the school. "Really, it is very hard on us," said one to him, "that we should have to pay for the vagaries of our teacher. Believe me, when I tell you, that we miss you sadly, more than you would give us credit for. The old man had a very hot hour of it, when we pitched into him and made him see that he was wrong as wrong can be. He himself now feels that his lectures are insipid and fall upon dull ears. You were unconsciously the heart and soul of us all. Verily, we realise the value of a thing only after we lose it. Forget and forgive, like a good boy, and come back to us." Râmânuja, who was the soul of candour, was melted at their disinterested affection and came to feel that he was rather hasty and imprudent. So, he went back and was welcomed by Yâdava with covert kindness. "I never thought I would feel your absence so badly. You should make allowances, you know, for the hasty temper of an old man and put up with my little eccentricities."

Sometime after, Yâdava said to his disciples—"I am getting old and am drawing near my end. I should very much like to breathe my last on the banks of the sacred Ganges." So they all prepared for a grand yâtra; and on the way, the others took very good care that Râmânuja and his brother Gôvinda had not much access to each other. They overwhelmed him with attentions and would not leave him alone even for a second. Very soon they were in the midst of the grand scenery of the Vindhya forests. Gôvinda, less unsuspecting than his brother, had long ago divined the cruel purpose that lay beneath all this seeming affection, all these overdone attentions, and was anxiously looking out for some nice opportunity when he could warn the guileless victim of their hellish plots, of his certain danger.

Gôvinda's Warning.

One night, in the small hours of the morning, Râmânuja got up and went away into the forest, to answer the calls of nature. Gôvinda, from whose eyes the anxiety for his brother's safety had banished all sleep, quietly followed unperceived. When they were well within the gloom of the forest, Gôvinda advanced and touched Râmânuja on the shoulder. The latter startled in surprise and fear; but was reassured by the sight of Gôvinda whose bright smile illuminated the rapidly clearing gloom of the night. "We have not," said Gôvinda, "much time to be together and would very soon be missed. A nice hole you have got yourself into, my brother, and nothing but your innate purity and innocence can get you safely out of it. The old humbug and his gang of ruffians—"like master, like man" — have inveigled you into this yâtra business, intending to give you your quietus in the holy waters of the Ganges. Get out of this place as quickly as you can and cheat the devil of what he considers his due. I shall back to them and take care to cover your retreat." He spoke and vanished, leaving Râmânuja standing there in that strange forest, alone and bewildered. Recovering himself, he struck out on a footpath and very soon enjoyed the pleasure that comes to every traveller whom the fates favour. He lost his way and wandered long and weary through the trackless wilds. His feet were swollen and bleeding, his body was lacerated with thorns and briars, he was weak from hunger and fatigue, and insufferable thirst made his tongue dry and his mouth parched. In utter despair he fell down at the foot of a tree and cried out from his heart—"Oh, Thou that watched me when I was in the womb, I take refuge in Thy mercy. Do with me as Thou wilt."

The Divine Hunters.

He swooned right away, and when he came out of it, he was conscious of a hunter and his wife bending over him with looks of ineffable pity and tenderness, both marvellously beautiful. Too weak to stand, he raised himself on his elbows and said faintly—"Who are you ? Whence do you come ? Where do you go ?" An indefinable sensation of peace and security was gradually stealing over him ; he could not account for it ; but it was exquisitely delicious, and he did not like to break the charm of it. A soft masculine voice, clear and melodious as of "silver hammers falling on silver anvils" broke the stillness of the forest, and seemed to him a part of the vision. "We come from afar, from Siddhâşrama, on the snowy Range, and proceed to the sacred Satyavrata (Kânchî)." Râmânuja felt a thrill of joy run through his frame at these words ; all his weakness forsook him in a moment, and, jumping up eagerly, he clasped the hands of the hunter in unrestrained gratitude and said—"I too want to get there if I can, but I have lost my way in this dreadful forest, and but for your unexpected appearance, I would have resigned myself to my fate. May I so much intrude upon your kindness, as to request you to get me out of this forest and set me on my way." "With great pleasure," said they and walked on before. Very soon, they came upon a beaten path that Râmânuja had not noticed before, and proceeded till nightfall, when they broke their journey and rested for the night under a large and leafy tree. Of necessity, they had to fast; but about midnight the huntress complained of a burning thirst. "There ought to be," said the hunter, "somewhere here a splendid well of cool, limpid water, sweet as nectar. Wait a while, my dear, and the bright rays of the morning sun shall not kiss yon mountain tops before I lead you there." Râmânuja was pained to the heart. "Alas! helpless wretch that I am, the strangeness of the locality places beyond my reach the one chance of evincing my gratitude to my heaven-sent benefactors."[1] He brooded over this thought for a long time and fell asleep just before daybreak.

His Miraculous Journey.

The sun was above the horizon[2] when he awoke, ashamed of having slept so late, and missed his morning devotions. He looked about for his benefactors of the previous day, but found them not. He ran about, hallooing to them all the while; but the vast woods around him gave him no answer except by their silence. Soon he caught sight of a foot-path leading out of the forest and had not gone far when villages

---

1. He said to them, "I believe that you are no other than the Divine Couple come down to help me. At present I am unable to fetch you water, but you shall have it at day-break."

2. (*a*) Said the Divine Pair—"Now it is day and there you see a beautiful well, full of crystal water. Bring it to us in the hollow of your palms for want of any better vessel." "With great pleasure," replied Râmânuja, and thrice gave them water to drink, but when he came up from the well the fourth time he found them not. [*Prap; R. D. C; V. G.*]

(*b*) The Divine Pair pointed out to Râmânuja, the Puṇyakoṭi Vimâna of Varada's temple and disappeared. [*V. G.*]

and plains, groves and fields, presented themselves to his astonished view. The surroundings seemed strangely familiar; but, for the very life of him, he could not account to himself for the phenomenal transit from the far away Vyndhia forests to what was plain as the southern parts of the peninsula. He proceeded towards a beautiful grove that lay near and, observing some men around a large well, asked them—"May I request you to let me know, an unfortunate traveller that had lost his way in the woods, what country this is and the town yonder." They laughed in mild amusement, that very soon changed itself to a look of pained pity. They winked at one another and gently shook their heads as if to say, "Poor chap! he has it bad; and he, so young and innocent!" But one of them put an end to the awkward silence by exclaiming: "Well, this beats me. You seem to be a native of these parts, young sir, and yet you cannot make out what place this is, though the Puṇyakôṭi Vimâna stares you in the face, as it were." "Ha! the sacred Kânchî!" cried Râmânuja, "then I am unfortunate indeed;" and he swooned right away. It all flashed upon his mind; the hunter and the huntress, marvellously beautiful; the indefinable sensation of calm joy and serene peace that they irradiated; the miraculously short time that he took to travel from the far Vyndhian forests to the sacred Kânchî; the midnight thirst of the fair huntress; the significant reply of the hunter about the well and its water, cool and sweet as nectar—Ah! what a delicate hint it was! that miserable inability of his to do them that much in the way of return for all their kindnesses to him; all these and a thousand and one little things, that never struck him before, presented themselves vividly

(c) The D. C. makes no mention of the yâtra, but states that, after his quarrel with Yâdava during the oil-bath, Râmânuja went away from his teacher and devoted himself to the service of Varada, to whose shrine he took a vessel of water every day.

before his half-dazed consciousness ; and along with these that closing episode in the life of the Great Yôgi Nâthamuni, when Srî Râmachandra, Lakshmana and Sîta came for their devotee in the guise of hunters to remind him of his seat in Srî Vaikuntha that was for so long a time empty. Joy of joys! What had he done in lives hidden in the far mists of time, to be so blessed above all men? They guided him through the dark mazes of the trackless forest safely on to their seat in the sacred Kânchî. Shall they not guide him through the darker mazes of life's trackless forest safely on to their Divine Feet in the Paramapada? So ran his thoughts. He got back to his house, and, acting upon the delicate hint thrown out by the Lord, [1] he carried every day to the temple a vessel of water from the well to be utilised during the bath of the Lord. Henceforth, to him, the well was the only visible reminder of their gracious visit and to the Srî Vaishnavas all over the world, a sacred memory and an object of profound reverence for all time to come.

CHAPTER VII.

His Life at Kânchî.

Râmânuja is now supremely happy, inasmuch as he can devote his whole time to the service of the Lord ; and there we shall leave him for a time and cast a glance at our friends, the old hypocrite Yâdava and his gang of desperadoes. It was not long before they missed Gôvinda and his brother; their suspicions were immediately roused, and guesses were freely offered as to their whereabouts.

1 He informed his mother of the miraculous adventure, who advised him to seek out Kânchî Pûrna. He was an amsa of Sabari, she said, and very dear to Varada ; he would direct him aright as to his future. And it was Kânchîpurna that suggested to him the idea of taking a vessel of water to Varada Râja. (*Prap.*)

At this juncture Gôvinda came among them, and was overwhelmed with questions. "Where is Râmânuja?" eagerly asked Yâdava. The innocent look of surprise and painful anxiety that Gôvinda put on, would have made the best actor die of envy. "Ha! what has become of him?" "He was not here when we awoke and we naturally concluded you were out with him." "I have been all about the place and I saw him not. Alas! my dear brother, where art thou?" And his cries were so heart-rending, that they would have melted the heart out of a cast-iron statue. They had enough to do to console him somewhat. They concluded that Râmânuja strayed from them in the dark and was carried away by some wild beast or other; and after due lamentations, proceeded on their journey.

The Conversion of Gôvinda.

One day while Yâdava was bathing along with his disciples in the waters of the sacred Ganges, Gôvinda found a lingam of Ṣiva unaccountably sticking to his palm.[1] Much amazed, he showed it to Yâdava and asked him what it meant. The ascetic was no less surprised and said: "Very strange! it is only very rarely that one is blessed in this peculiar way. You have realised, before any of us, the merit of bathing in the waters of the Holy Ganges. The mighty Lord Gangâdhara has deigned to bless you with his presence and contact."[2] Thereafter Yâdava and his disciples looked upon him with unwonted reverence and affection.

---

[1] Yâdava, by his magical powers, caused it to stick there.

[2] He recited the Môhana Mantra over Gôvinda (an incantation that makes the subject see and feel what the operator wishes him to—very much like hypnotic suggestions, but produced by quite different agencies—*Comp.*) and converted him to Ṣaivaism. The Lord, too, did not interfere, as he wanted Gôvinda to learn from experience the insipidity of following strange gods. (*V. G.*)

In course of time, they finished their yâtra and returned to Kânchî by way of Jagannâtha and Ahôbila. On the way, Gôvinda obtained permission of Yâdava to lodge the lingam in a suitable spot, and remained behind, while his teacher proceeded to Kânchî. He duly installed the lingam in his own village and spent his time in unremitting devotion to it. Meanwhile, Mahâdêva, the Lord of Kâḷahasti, wanted to have Gôvinda near him for a time, and directed him in a dream to that effect. At the same moment, the chief officials of the temples at Kâḷahasti were ordered in a similar manner to proceed to Gôvinda's village and invite him with all due honours in the name of the Lord. Gôvinda was gladly entrusted by them with the entire management of the affairs of the temple, and remained there, ever devoted to the service of Mahâdêva.

Râmânuja goes back to Yâdava.

The surprise and confusion of Yâdava and his disciples could be better imagined than described, when, on coming back to Kânchî, they saw Râmânuja "alive and kicking." They embraced him warmly, and Yâdava welcomed him back amongst them. "We gave you up for lost, and concluded that you had strayed away from us and had fallen a prey to wild beasts. Thrice fortunate are we, that it has been given us to meet you again. Tell us how you came out of it safely." Râmânuja then related to them all the wonderful events that befell him in the forest. Yâdava listened to it in silent amazement throughout; he could not but admit to himself that silent and mysterious forces were working in Râmânuja's case to bring about some stupendous future result; and Râmânuja was now to him a darker mystery than ever. He would not play with edged tools; he would leave him quietly alone and go on with his exposition as usual. And so it came about that

Râmânuja was restored to his old place in the school[1] and smoothly went on with his studies.

Yâmuna goes over to Kânchî.

Meanwhile Âḻavandâr was informed of these particulars by two Vaishṉavas, who happened to pay a visit to Ṣrîrangam,[2] and was overwhelmed with joy and amazement. "My prayers have been granted and my long cherished hopes seem about to be fulfilled. Verily, this heaven-favoured one is the future Teacher and I will not allow a day to pass without seeing him and get my expectations confirmed." He took permission of Ṣrî Ranganâtha and started for Kânchî. Tirukkacchi Nambi (Kânchîpûrṉa) the favourite disciple of Âḻavandâr, having been informed of this, advanced to welcome his master, accompanied by all the principal men of Kânchî and the paraphernalia of honour from the temple of Ṣrî Varadarâja due to such a distinguished visitor. They met, and Nambi fell at his master's feet bathing them with tears of joy. Âḻavandâr raised him, and embracing him warmly said: "Favoured servant of the Lord! I hope that the Lord accepts with pleasure as usual the Service of the Fan at your hands." "Even so, my Lord, through your grace." He then proceeded to the temple to offer his worship to the Lord Varadarâja; and while going round the courts chanced to meet a crowd of persons coming towards him. "Who comes yonder?" asked Âḻavandâr of Nambi. "The ascetic Yâdava Prakâsa, my Lord, and his disciples." "Oh! then I believe the young man Râmânuja must be in the group."

---

[1] For want of any one better, Râmânuja went back to him.

[*Prap.*]

[2] Yâmuna, perceiving that spiritual darkness was lifting off the world and that men began to evince a desire to hear the Good Law, guessed that the Great Incarnation had taken place and sent his disciples far and wide, with instructions to seek out the future Teacher.

"Even so, my Lord. Here is he, a head taller than the rest; you may go far and not set your eyes upon a nobler specimen of humanity." Âḷavandâr fixed his eyes wistfully upon the Future Teacher of men. It is not given for us, mortals, to know what passed at that moment. May be that the Teacher who was so soon to pass away transfused into the Teacher that was to be, all his powers, all his energies, all his wisdom; may be that their higher selves were holding high communion on the refulgent planes of spirit, exchanging thoughts, giving and taking; may be that they were both at the feet of the Lord, the one laying down wearily the burden that was too great for him, and the other joyfully taking it up, with the strong consciousness born of power, of serving the Lord better. Again, I say, we can but guess, and guessing is too often a sacrilege—a foolish "rushing in where angels fear to tread." But this much is true, this much was visible to all present. Âḷavandar's eyes grew marvellously bright with ineffable joy, and love unutterable passed from them and permeated the Teacher to be, encompassing him as with a halo of celestial glory.[1] He then prayed aloud to the Lord: "Oh Lord of Light and Wisdom! I take my refuge in Thee. Unfathomable is Thy nature. Oh! Lord of Mysteries, unthinkable is Thy might. Oh! Lord of Boundless Duration, deign to grant the humble prayer of mine, the most unworthy of thy servants. Grant me that Râmânuja be the Future Teacher of men and serve You better than I. Grant me that the Doctrine live through him and after him and guide many a way-worn pilgrim through the Valley of Death on to the radiant realms of Thy Divine abode. I

1 (*a*) He did not speak to Râmânuja, as he was afraid it might affect his studies under Yâdava. (*V. G.*)

(*b*) He could not get a chance to speak to him. *T. G.* (1880).

(*c*) The Lord did not want them to meet each other. "Then there is no use of my being at the head of Evolution. Between them

take my refuge in Thy infinite Mercy."[1] He then offered his worship to Varadarâja, and having taken leave of Nambi and his other friends returned to Srîrangam.

Yâdava and the Evil Spirit.

Sometime after it so happened that the daughter of the ruler of the province was possessed by a malignant Brahmarâkshasa, and the king sent word far and near for the most expert exorcists.[2] They came, they saw—but here ends the parallel between them and the great Cæsar, for they conquered not, but went away sad, conquered by the evil spirit. One day, one of his attendants said to the king: "They say that the holy ascetic Yâdava Prakâsa has but to approach your palace and the Brahmarâkshasa that has defied the ablest exorcists of the land would be only too glad to escape with his life." "Is it even so?" replied the king, "we have been indeed unfortunate in that it was not brought to our ears till now. Let the Sanyâsi be invited to the palace with all the honours due to a person of his holiness and learning." Accordingly the minister waited upon Yâdava and invited him on behalf of the king to come over to the palace and relieve his daughter from her great misery. Yâdava smiled and said: "Powerful indeed must be the evil spirit when His Majesty thinks that my presence there is indispensable. But I think it is

---

they will depopulate the world and send every one to my abode." So Yâmuna thought to himself, "I shall not send for him, he may come or he may not, surrounded as he is by bad men." (*Prap.*)

[1] He said, "Dispenser of Good! I take my refuge in Thy mighty grace, that causes the deaf to hear, the blind to see, the lame and the halt to walk, the dumb to speak fluently and the barren to bring forth children!" Thereafter he composed the Stotra Ratna in praise of Varadarâja, praying him to make Râmânuja the Future Teacher of the Law. (*Prap.*)

[2] This episode occurred immediately after he began to study under Yâdava; in fact, it was what induced Gôvinda to seek out his brother at Kânchî.—*Prap.*

enough if you go and tell the Brahmarâkshasa, from me, to quit the princess and flee this country."

Discomfiture of Yâdava.

And it was done forthwith, but with far different results. "Said he so?" laughed the Râkshasa, "just tell him from me, as he values his life, to kindly flee this country and avoid my presence." Tears of rage ran down the cheeks of Yâdava; he flew to the palace, followed by his disciples, and in the midst of a vast crowd advanced to the princess reciting a powerful incantation, when, behold! the princess stretched out her legs at him and said: "Thou fool! Do I not know what Mantra you are directing against me? It is thus and thus; and you imagine you can disturb my peace with such a trifle as that! You are as vain as a peacock and as ignorant as a log of wood. What do you know of your past birth and mine? Come out with it if you can." Yâdava hung down his head in shame and mortification. Naturally suspicious of everybody, he thought: "He might be trying a game of bluff upon me. Let me see it out." Said he: "May be you are Omniscient, may be you are Omnipotent. Kindly enlighten my ignorant self on the dark past of both of us." Loud laughed the spirit. "And so, you wish to try me! Well, there is no accounting for tastes. All right, please yourself. In your last birth [1] you ensouled the body of an iguana and lived in a hole on the banks of the great Madurântakam lake. Some Vaishṇavâs from Kânchî were proceeding on a pilgrimage to Tirupati and halted there to bathe and dine. You happened to partake of the remnants of their meal, and, in consequence, you are now a

1 In your twelfth birth from this, you were a mungoose residing in a hole in the Lord's temple at Gangaikkarai Kaṇḍam. You met your death at the hands of a hunter, but had the good fortune to be touched by a holy saint that lived there. *R. D. C.*

high class Brâhmaṇa and for the matter of that a learned one. I was a high born Brâhmaṇa in my last birth and through some serious mistakes in conducting a Yagña (sacrifice) am now a Brahmarâkshasa, but with a recollection of my past. Are you now satisfied?" "Let that be. Is there any here that can persuade you to quit this princess, and trouble her no more?"

Râmânuja drives it out.

The princess (or rather the spirit) then approached Râmânuja who was standing modestly in the back ground, and, laying herself at his feet, exclaimed, "If this Great One, the highest of the angels around the Throne of the Lord, deigns to order me to do it, I will consider it a great boon."

"Would you do so Râmânuja?" "Yes, my Lord," said he, and turning to the spirit, "Depart and trouble her no more. Peace be unto you and a speedy release." "Lord, thy will be done. But won't you bless this miserable sinner by touching his head with your holy feet?" Râmânuja did so, and the spirit rose up with tears of joy streaming down his cheeks and prepared to depart. "But wouldst thou not give a sign?" "Yes, I lived in a fig tree, and you will see it shattered the moment I leave the spot."[1] The next moment a great crashing sound was heard and the huge tree lay uprooted with its branches strewn far and around as if a tornado had passed over it.[2] Yâdava was smitten with fear and wonder, and was obliged to speak in terms of great praise of Râmânuja. The princess awoke as if from a deep trance, and looking about her wonderingly, was

1 Then turning to Yâdava, it exclaimed, "And thou of little faith, take refuge, before it is too late, in the illimitable grace of this Mighty One and save thyself from utter perdition." *(Prap.)*

2 Then there arose aloft a radiant form, to meet which came down countless celestial presences in their refulgent Vimânas; and glorified by them it was lost to sight in a blaze of light. *(Prap.)*

surprised and ashamed to find herself amongst strangers. She cast an inquiring look at her father, who replied with a smile : " My dear, you have suffered long and fearfully ; and but for that holy man there (for aught I know, he may be a Great Being from on high, come down on Earth for some great end) you would have continued to be in misery, Heaven knows how long. Go and take refuge in his illimitable mercy. " The princess, with streaming eyes, took hold of the feet of Râmânuja and reverently placing them on her head, sobbed : " Lord, Thou hast, out of Thy infinite grace, deigned to relieve your slave from a life of horror and misery. The Lord of the day expects no return from the millions to whom He gives life and light. Master, I take my refuge in thee now and for ever. " She then departed to the inner apartments. The king wanted to overwhelm Râmânuja with honours and rewards,[1] but our Great Lord rose meekly and said to Yadava : " Master, I think it is time for us to go to our maṭha. " Yâdava acted upon the hint and took leave of the king.

Yâmuna's Prayer.

One day Yâmunâchârya was explaining to his disciples the meaning of the stanza "இலிக்கத்தெட்ட புராணத்திரும்", when, a passing thought struck him and he remained plunged in deep abstraction " Alas ! Is there no one to take up my work after me ? Is this glorious soul-saving doctrine to die with me for want of a fit successor ? Lord of Mercy ! it cannot be so. Thou wilt not leave helpless the millions of thy children, footsore with the long and weary journey through lives innumerable and thirsting after the divine waters of wisdom. O ! that I could find a way to separate Râmânuja from Yâdavaprakâṣa and rest my weary head upon his shoulder. Oh ! Thou Lord of

---

1 The king gave him vast wealth, which he at once handed over to Yâdava. (*Prap.*)

Compassion at Kânchî ! I have served Thee to the best of my ability and if I have found favour in Thy eyes, I humbly pray You to give me Râmânuja."

His last Quarrel with Yâdava.

And so it came about that Yâdava, while lecturing to his disciples upon the srutis,[1] सर्वं खल्विदं ब्रह्म "All this is verily Brahman" नेह नानास्ति किंचन "There is no diversity whatever"—(*Brihad*)—contended that the Advaitic explanation [2] was the sound one, as it incontestably established the perfect identity of the individual and the supreme soul. Râmânuja humbly begged to differ, and refuted his arguments one by one clearly and unanswerably.[3] Thereupon Yâdava, white with rage, cried out : "This is the third time you have braved me; and, by God, it shall be the last. Go hence to some other who could teach you better." Nothing could have pleased Râmânuja better. He went back to his residence and informed his mother of the whole affair. "Well, well, my dear, it seems that you have had enough of studying Vedânta under Yâdava Prakâsa. Kânchi Pûrna is, I hear, very dear to the Lord Varadarâja and will advise you what to do with yourself in future." Accordingly, Râmânuja went to Nambi, and humbly requested to be advised. "It seems to me," replied Nambi, with an enigmatic smile, "that the Lord has a partiality to the water from the well by the roadside, and it would not be amiss if you take to the temple a vessel of it every day to be used during divine worship." "Thy orders shall be obeyed," said Râmânuja, and from that day forward he resumed his old service interrupted by the arrival of Yâdava from Benares.

---

1 The Prap. brings in the Kapyâsa incident just after Yâmuna's departure from Kânchî ; and makes it the cause of Râmânuja's final rupture with Yâdava. It makes no mention of the other quarrels. (*Chand. Up.* IV. 5, 7.) *Brihad. Up.* IV. 4. 19.

2 Vide Srî Bhâshya pp. 20, 21, 22, 23.

3 Vide Srî Bhâshya pp. 39, 47.

Yâmuna sends for Râmânuja.

Meanwhile, Yâmunâchârya was growing old and every day saw him weaker and more dispirited. Two Vaishṇavâs who came from Kânchî went to pay him their respects and from them he learnt that Râmânuja had left Yâdava and was engaged in the service of the Lord Varadarâja. The news came to him like manna in the desert. Turning to Mahâ Pûrṇa by his side, he eagerly exclaimed : "My son, here is the song of praise I have laid as an humble offering at the feet of the Lord of Kânchî. He has at last deigned to listen to my humble prayers and has taken Râmânuja into his service. Go thou and bring him to me." "You do me too much honour," said Mahâ Pûrṇa, and set out for Kânchî.

CHAPTER VIII.

The Passing of Yâmuna.

Sometime before this, Yâmunâchârya fell seriously ill[1] and his life was despaired of, when his disciples, Goshṭḥî Pûrṇa and Mahâ Pûrṇa approached him and submitted through Vara Ranga Gâyaka the following prayer :— "Lord, deign to impart to us some truth wherein we might take our refuge."

1 For many long years, he was suffering from a great carbuncle; and knowing it was a Karmic disease and incurable, he bore it all patiently. Mâranêri Nambi, one of the most devoted of his disciples, time and oft besought Yâmuna to transfer it to him. Shortly before his death, the Teacher called Mâranêri Nambi unto him and said ; "My son, I have borne this long and patiently ; and now, I take advantage of the repeated requests you have made me to bear it for a while. Dear to me you were ever, by your saintliness of life and purity of heart ; and now you are doubly so, if that were possible. Mahâ Pûrṇa will take all care of you and see that you want for nothing."—(*Prap.*)

His Last Words.

"Be it so," replied Yâmuna, "your daily worship [1] is the life of your life. Take your refuge in him. Always have before you the ideal of the holy Tiruppâṇâlvâr [2] who stands ever at the foot of the Lord and gladdens his heart with the strains of the Vîṇa. Know you not how Kuranga Pûrṇa (குறும்பறுத்தநம்பி) [3] found his way to the

1 "Yâga (one of the five Samskâras) or the worship of certain idols of Vishṇu, which is taught at the time of the initiation by the Guru presenting one for the disciple to worship; and thence the disciple should worship no other."—(*V.C.*)

2 He was an amsa of Srîvatsa, the lovely mole on the Lord's body. He was born in the year 343 of the Kali Yuga, at Urayoor, near Trichinopoly. He was found in a field of corn by some Panchamâs, who, finding that he would not take any sustenance from their women's breasts, fed him upon cow's milk. He was a born devotee and spent his time in singing the praises of the Lord, to the accompaniment of the Vîṇa. He took his station on the southern banks of the Kavêry, considering himself, through his early associations, too impure in body to tread the Holy ground between the two rivers. One day, the Great Mother said to the Lord: "How is it that my son Pâṇa stands aloof and never comes near us?" "Only excessive modesty," replied the Lord, and turning to Lôka Sâranga Muni, that stood near, directed him to proceed forthwith and bring Pâṇa unto him, upon his shoulders if he could not be persuaded to walk over. Sâranga immediately sought him out and, with great pleasure, carried him on his shoulders before the Lord. "So you have come at last," said the Lord, in feigned anger; "know you that we have repeatedly sent for you?". "Yes," humbly replied Pâṇa, "but could I presume to take advantage of Thy infinite grace to set at nought the rules of society that Thyself had laid down?" "They are not for such as you," rejoined the Lord; "well, since you are here, ever be near us." Pâṇa gazed long and with rapt ecstasy at the Divine Beauty and was lost in it. Then, in the presence of the vast concourse, the Lord took him unto Himself and he was seen no more on earth. He has left behind him ten stanzas beginning with Amalanâdippirân—a record of what he saw on that famous occasion. He was then 20 years old.—(*V.G.*)

3 Otherwise called Bhîma, was a potter by profession and dwelt some way from Tirupati. He and his wife were ardent devotees of the Lord Venkaṭêsa, and as became poor people, laid before his clay image at their house, clay lotuses in all humility and devotion. Now there was a Toṇḍamân king, who was, or thought himself, very dear to the Lord and who failed not to worship him every day with lotuses made

heart of the Lord Venkaṭêṣa? Behold Kânchî Pûrṇa[1] who has wound himself round the heart-strings of Lord Varadarâja? I tell you that Tiruppâṇâlvâr has so completely bewitched the Lord Ranganâtha that He must always have him by His side. And last, but not the least, observe Ranga Gâyaka who stands so modestly there. Who would ever dream, by looking at him, that he is dearer to Tiruppâṇâlvâr than his very life, than his hopes of salvation?" And turning to Ranga Gâyaka, who hung down his head in great confusion, he said: "My dear, I have taken my refuge in that Divine Being in whom are centred your hopes of eternal

of pure gold. One day, he was struck dumb to behold all his golden lotuses thrown down and lotuses made of clay occupy their place before the Lord. And that too, day after day, and in spite of the strictest watch that the king set to find out the criminal that dared insult his Majesty thus. At the end of many days he was no wiser, and following the suggestion of some one, he sought far and near for any devout worshipper of Venkaṭêṣa. After a long and weary search he came upon the potter and his wife; watched them lay their clay lotuses at the feet of the clay image of Venkaṭêṣa, and stood in mute amazement at the sight of such perfect devotion amidst such uncongenial surroundings. He recognised in him the Lord's favourite and his own master and forthwith took refuge in him.—(*Compiler.*)

1 During his incarnations on Earth, the Lord has, more than once, played the part of a servant towards his devotees, faithful and humble. But nowhere had he exemplified the truth that his devotees are greater than himself, more plainly than in the case of Kânchî Pûrṇa. There was not one act of service that his devotees performed towards himself but he discharged it faithfully in the case of Kânchî Pûrṇa. He would converse with him far, far into the night. Now Nambi would suddenly come upon him in the guise of one of his disciples bringing him his sandals; now he would come upon him as a servant of the temple, lighting him on his way home. So much so, that Nambi was quite vexed and ashamed. So, one day, he said to himself: "My Lord will very soon make me forget myself and what I owe him. I shall go over to Tirupati, where, I believe, it will not be so bad as here." But, after a time, he was surprised to hear Venkaṭêṣa say: "You have stayed here long enough. Repair to Kânchî and fan us there, where we require it more, because of the fountain of Fire from which we sprang." Nambi sadly returned to Kânchî, and when he was a short way from it, he was met by the Lord, who said to him: "And so, you would fly from us, would you?" "Nay, my Lord,

life." Vara Ranga could no longer contain himself, but falling at the feet of his illustrious parent, sobbed out: "Hast thou, then, my Lord, resolved to resume your place among the Immortals near the throne of the Lord and revel in the delights of the Ineffable Presence?" "Nay, nay, my son, grieve not. It shall not be said of you that you envied another man's good fortune. And now mark my words, you all. If one, having taken refuge in the Lord, presumes to trouble himself about his hereafter, he is in the wrong; if he thinks that he is concerned, in any way, with the care of his body while here, he is in the wrong; his taking refuge in the Lord is but a sham, for he trusts Him not with his future. He is no better than an Atheist. So, he should in no way concern himself about his future in thought, in word or in deed. The Lord has this natural and inseparable trait about Him—His grace is so illimitable as to bless with eternal life in Srî Vaikuṉṯẖa even those that say not: 'I salute Thee, Lord'. Similarly it is the natural and inseparable trait of the Jîva to take refuge in the Divine Mercy and rest his weary burden on the Lord. But if he sets about to compass his salvation by his sole exertions, it goes against the law of his nature. Nor should he idle his time away, depending upon the Lord for everything. This absolutely disqualifies him for the unapproachable eminence the Lord means for him as his servant. There can, then, be no relation of master and servant between the Lord and himself."

"If he who liveth, learning whence woe springs,
Endureth patiently, striving to pay
His utmost debt for ancient evils done
In Love and Truth alway;

---

your kindness makes me ashamed of myself." "Well, you will get over it, in course of time." And so he did; for the Lord never changed His ways. In fact, He used to walk arm in arm with the Divine Mother in the halls of the temple, visible to the eyes of Nambi alone.—(*R. D. C.*)

"If making none to lack, he thoroughly purge
The lie and lust of self forth from his blood;
Suffering all meekly, rendering for offence
Nothing but grace and good;

"If he shall day by day dwell merciful,
Holy and just and kind and true, and rend
Desire from where it clings with bleeding roots
Till love of life have end;

"He—dying—leaveth as the sum of him
A life-count closed, whose ills are dead and closed,
Whose good is quick and mighty, far and near,
So that fruits follow it.

"No need has such to live as ye name life;
That which began in him when he began
Is finished, he hath wrought the purpose through
Of what did make him Man.

"Never shall yearnings torture him, nor sins
Stain him, nor ache of earthly joys and woes
Invade his safe eternal peace; nor deaths
And lives recur. He goes

"Unto (Vaikuṇṭha). He is one with Life,
Yet lives not. He is blest, ceasing to be."[1]

'Then, what shall be our stay and support here, Lord?" "If you take your refuge in my unworthy self and centre your hopes in me, as the means and the end, it will but prove ruinous to me, as it will be an unwarranted exaltation of my unworthy self; and you will be the last to bring it about. Have for ever, as your guiding light, the truth pointed out by Srî Saṭhakôpa in the passage—' Those to whom it is given to devote themselves to the service of the Lord are my God and are enshrined in my heart of hearts.' "[2] The disciples listened with streaming eyes, and hearts weighed down with grief unutterable. Yâmunâchârya noticed this and said: "Once again, I say, grieve not for my miserable self. Are you not thrice blessed in

---

1 *Light of Asia.*

2 The meaning of this paradoxical passage seems to be:—

He should perform to the fullest the duties enjoined upon him by his caste and status in life, without in any way concerning himself with their results; that rests with the Lord.

being the happy owners of the three mansions[1] in the city of the Lord ?—the Holy Mantra, the Last Word and the Two Truths ! Are not Tiruppâṇâlvâr and myriads of others that have trod the Path Eternal before us witnesses to the truth of what I say ?" Then it was that Ranga Gâyaka made bold to say : "When your Divine self has decided to bless this earth no longer, what matters it if such insignificant earth-worms like ourselves cannot bear to be away from you, but make bold to shuffle off this mortal coil and follow you ?" Yâmuna seemed not to listen to his words and was silent. The other two disciples construed it as an approval and resolving within themselves not to survive their beloved master, took leave of him and went away. But in a very short time the news got abroad and was much talked of in the precincts of the temple. Then the Divine Lord of Compassion directed his high priest to send for the three to his presence, and said in a way that could not be mistaken : "I charge you, if you have the least regard for me, to do no such foolish act as you have contemplated, in case Yâmuna should depart from this earth." He then entrusted them to Vara Ranga and said to him : "Mind, I hold you responsible for these." "To hear is to obey," replied Vara Ranga, and forthwith repaired to his father and informed him of what took place. Yâmuna sighed and muttered : "Verily, how envious these men are of my poor self. They almost seem to grudge me the rest that I so much long for. So they think it is nothing to be blessed in being able to stand in the sight of the Lord Ranganâtha, enshrined on his island

---

[1] The three mansions are :—

Bhôga Maṇṭapa—Ṣrîrangam where the Lord takes his rest.

Pushpa Maṇṭapa—Tirupati, on account of the flower gardens thereon.

Tyâga Maṇṭapa—Kânchî, where dwells Varada (the Granter of Boons.)

These are respectively related, in a mystical sense, to the Ashtâkshari Mantra, the Charama Ṣloka and the Dvaya.—(*Compiler.*)

throne between the two rivers." Then he said aloud : " Once again, and for the last time, I enjoin you to commit no act of folly when I should go away from this earth. If you still persist, you will stand charged with having sinned against Puṇḍarîkâksha, Râma Miṣra and the other servants of the Lord that have gone before me." They stood rebuked and awed into submission. Âḻavandâr continued: " Never make any difference between the Lord and his servants. When you wash the feet of the Lord you meditate upon the spiritual hierarchy ending in Him and purify yourself by the holy water, do you not ? Well, in the case of his servants, entirely eliminate the idea of self from your mind and with your heart radiant with the image of your spiritual teacher, purify yourself by the holy water that has washed their feet. When it comes to you to do the same to others that desire it, let no idea of any worldly benefit accruing therefrom soil your minds even for an instant. Meditate upon your master in your heart and the spiritual hierarchy ascending from him and recite the Two Truths all the time. It is good for him that gives and him that receives. Again, when you happen to be in company with others and those of various stages of spiritual progress, if you soil your minds with worldly advantages, have an eye only to the physical encasement that enshrines the immortal Jîva within and ignore the other servants of the Lord that might be with you; you might be ever so great a Teacher, having a numerous following, but your disciples would profit nothing by taking the water that has washed your feet. Another point, nay, the most important and the last of my teachings to you—forget not to lay at the feet of the Lord, all that you have, say but a single flower. Take refuge in your Guru and proceed from the initial stage as the final one.[1]

[1] The three stages are:—Devotion to the Lord; devotion to the servants of the Lord; and devotion to their servants to the remotest degree.—(*Compiler.*)

These are the never-failing means of Salvation." He then called Vara Ranga to him and entrusted to his care Gôshṭḥî Pûrṇa and Mahâ Pûrṇa. Vara Ranga accepted the trust and said to them : " If you still persist in your act of folly when our master leaves us, you will for ever be excluded from any chances of joining the immortal bands of the E er-Liberated. Lay this to your heart." Âḷavandar's heart was glad at these words, and he said : " Look here, let the image of this Vara Ranga be ever enshrined in your heart of hearts. Take refuge in him as your means of salvation." " We obey, O Lord" replied the two, and from that moment looked upon him as their God, as their Lord, as their Master.

The Last Moments of Yâmunâchârya.

Subsequently Yâmunâchârya recovered from his illness and repaired to the temple and stood with bent head and joined hands before Ranganâtha. The Lord knew what was passing in his mind and called out to Vara Ranga. He at once responded and recited the decade (99th) in the Sacred Collect beginning with சூழ்விசும்பு.........[1] in the place of the stanzas used on such occasions. All present looked at one another in wonder and surprise, when lo! the garland on the head of the Lord slipped down to the ground. The priest was about to restore it to its place, when Vara Ranga sprang forward and presented it[2] to Yâmunâchârya. He accepted it with a glad heart and Vara Ranga, turning to him, said : " Ah ! Thrice blessed art thou in that thy prayer has been granted." Âḷavandâr

---

[1] It describes the progress of a liberated Jîva through the various celestial regions up to the Throne of the Lord and his reception thereat. It is usually recited during the funeral obsequies of any holy person. Here it presaged the near passing away of Yâmuna.—(*Comp.*)

[2] Vara Ranga presented him with the Saṭḥakôpa of the Lord —a metal disc on which is stamped the impression of the Lord's feet, placed on the heads of worshippers.—(*R. D. S.*)

then took leave of all present and returning to his maṭha, caused every one there to dine before him, and when they were gathered together after dinner, he prostrated himself before them all and humbly prayed to be forgiven if he had offended any of them, consciously or otherwise. Vara Ranga affectionately raised him up, saying: "My Lord, my Lord, do you want to destroy us for ever, body and soul—*you* to humble yourself before us! *you* to speak of any offence to us! *you* that are perfection itself! *you* that are our ideal, our God, our Lord, our only hope here and hereafter!"[1]

Sometime after, Âḷavandâr again fell ill and his disciples observing his increasing weakness and his too evident desire to lay down the burden of this life, sorrowfully said to themselves: "We do not know whether the Lord would permit him. Perhaps he might."[2] On the day of Vaisâkha, Âḷavandâr repaired to the temple and stood before the Lord. He gazed long and lovingly on the divine beauty of the Lord from head to foot and back again and could never take his eyes off him. Then he turned his looks on the favourite of the Lord that stood at His feet, as if he envied him his place there and would have been only too glad to exchange Ṣrî Vaikuṇṭha for it. He went back to his maṭha and having caused his disciples to dine before him, he requested that all the inhabitants of the place might be invited there in his name. When

---

1 He soon got better and continued to teach as before. Then it was that news was brought to him of Râmânuja's final rupture with Yâdava; and then it was that he despatched Mahâ Pûrṇa, with the Stôtra Ratna—an epitome as it were of his eight great works.—(*R.D.C.*)

2 He himself had his doubts of meeting Râmânuja on earth. He entrusted his chief disciples with some special teachings, to be handed down to Râmânuja, in case he should not see him. "For," said he, "there is no doubt he is the future teacher, and you have to seek him out and perfect him for his great work."—(*Prap.*)

they were assembled, he once again, in all humility, begged their pardon if he had offended them in any way. "One might as well speak of the Lord Ranganâtha offending against us," cried every one with voices choked with tears. He entrusted his disciples to the care of the people present, and turning towards the temple authorities, said: "I pray you all to see that the various details of divine worship be punctually and duly observed. Ever welcome and entertain hospitably, as your brethren in the Lord, the Teachers, their disciples and the strangers. You have heard me for the last time."

He then seated himself in the Padmâsana posture and wrapped in yogic meditation, took refuge in the holy Âlvârs. The sacred image of his master, Râma Misra, filled his heart and his sandals were placed before his eyes. He reverently laid them on his head and on his eyes; and while the disciples assembled were reciting the Brahma Valli, the Purusha Sûkta and குழிசம்பணிமுதல் ....the Great One left his body by the Sushumnâ Nâdi, and, breaking through the Brahmarandhra, [1] went

[1] "There are a hundred and one Nâdis proceeding from the heart; one of them penetrates to the crown of the head; moving upwards by that, a man reaches immortality; the others serve for departing in other different directions."—(*Chând Up.* viii., 6, 5.)

"Of those (the Nâdis) one is situated above, and piercing through the disc of the sun passes beyond to the world of Brahman; by way of that the soul reaches the highest goal."—(*Yâgnavalkya Smriti*, iii. 167.)

"The soul of him who possesses true knowledge departs only by the way of the hundred and first artery in the crown of the head. Through the power of his supremely clear knowledge which has the effect of pleasing the Supreme Person, and through the application of remembrance of the way—which remembrance is a part of that knowledge—the soul of him who knows, wins the favour of the Supreme Person, who abides within the heart and is assisted by him. Owing to this, the heart, which is the abode of the soul, is illuminated, lit up at its tip, and thus through the grace of the Supreme Soul, the individual soul has the door (of egress from the body) lit up, and is able

back to his mansion in Srî Vaikuntha.[1]

---

to recognise that artery......The soul of him who knows....follows the rays of the sun and thus reaches the orb of the sun; when he departs from this body, he goes upwards by these rays only." (*Chând. Up.* viii 6. 5; *Srî Bhâshya pp.* 738, 739—*Thibaut's Trans.*)

As to the path taken by the liberated Jîva thereafter, vide *Ib.* pp. 744—755.

The path from this world to Paramapada or Vaikuntha Lôka is called Archirâdigati or Dêvayâna. When a person attaining Môksha leaves his body, the Jîva goes with the Sûkshma Sarîra from the heart to the Brahmarandhra in the crown of the head, passing through the Sushumnâ, a nerve connecting the heart with the head; breaking through which he proceeds to the region of the Sun (Sûrya Mandala) through the Solar rays; and lastly, through a dark spot in the sun, to Paramapada.

He is directed on his way to Paramapada by the supreme wisdom acquired by Yôga. The Jîva thus proceeds to Paramapada with the aid of the Âtivâhikâs (bearers in transit) known by the names of Archis, Ahas, Pûrvapaksha, Uttarâyana, Samvatsara, Âditya, Chandra, Vaidyuta, Varuna, Indra Prajâpati, and lastly of Amânava (an incarnation of Vishnu). The Archis and the others here mentioned are certain hierarchies of Dêvas, and not the ordinary day, night, month, year, etc.

1 (*a*) When the Lord came to know that Râmânuja and Mahâ Pûrna were starting to meet Yâmuna, he said to himself: "Verily, I will not allow them to meet, for, between them, they will send every one down here to my world." So he sent for Yâmuna and said to him: "I give you permission to go back to Paramapada. Depart thou this very day." But Yâmuna, desirous to meet Râmânuja, humbly replied: "I shall avail myself of your gracious permission eight days hence." But he waited and waited, and in the end departed from this world with a heavy heart.—(*Prap.*)

(*b*) When he was about to depart, the disciples observed, to their great surprise, tears coursing down his cheeks. "What lies heavy on our Lord's heart? Deign to let us know," entreated they. "Alas! I pass away without having met Râmânuja, the Future Teacher. I would have a commentary written on the Vyâsa Sûtras, meeting all objections, clearing all doubts and unassailable from every point. I would like to name two persons, one after Parâsara, who has, in his Vishnu Purâna, so clearly and irrefutably established the supremacy of the Divine Pair; and the other after Srî Sathakôpa, who in his stanzas, has revealed the secrets of the holy Ashtâkshari—the quintessence of Vêdânta." He counted these points on his fingers and they remained closed. "The Mighty One," exclaimed his disciples, "would not allow his best beloved to depart with his heart's desires

Mahâ Pûrṇa at Kânchî.

His disciples and friends knew that the blow was preparing; Âḻavandâr himself had given them plain warning; but it was too great, too sudden. Vara Ranga was the first to shake it off, and set about the arrangements for the obsequies of the holy ascetic, through his eldest son (Piḻḻaikkaraṣu Nambi). They conveyed the body to the banks of the Cauvery and were about to lower it into the grave prepared for it, when———but let us not anticipate.

Mahâ Pûrṇa forthwith proceeded to Kânchî and preferred his request to Kânchî Pûrṇa, who, seeing that a mighty future was opening before Râmânuja, took Pûrṇa to the presence of the Lord Varadarâja. Mahâ Pûrṇa recited before him the song of praise composed by Yâmunâchârya and laid at his feet the prayer of Yâmuna. Nambi then advised him to place himself on the way along which Râmânuja would advance to the temple from the

---

unfulfilled." "Well, I go back today to the Presence of the Lord, and shall purify myself by the Holy Water." "But, my Lord forgets that all here are his disciples and there is none here whose feet my Lord can wash." "Nay, not so; when my grandfather, of happy memory, placed his sacred feet on the head of his disciple Puṇḍarîkâksha, the latter reverently requested permission to worship thereafter his holy sandals. They have been handed down to me and form the highest object of my veneration. I shall take the holy water that has washed them."

His last teaching:—

Those whom their Guru had taught to take their refuge in the Doctrine of Surrender (Prapatti) should evince their gratitude to him and his descendants, by every means that lie in their power; should faithfully obey their behests; should ever serve the servants of the Lord; should avoid giving offence to any one whatsoever; and should cause as many as possible to walk in the path of Surrender.—(*V.G.*)

(*c*) The date of his death:—

Month—Vaiṣâkha.

Date—6th.

Nakshatra—Ṣravaṇa.—(*Vârt.*)

sacred well and recite the mighty song of praise. Pûrṇa followed his instructions and came to the verse स्वाभाविका &c.[1] when he saw Râmânuja approaching with his vessel of water on his shoulder. The future teacher stopped to listen and, at the end of it, asked: "Who sang this?" "One, Yâmunâchârya, a holy ascetic of Ṣrîrangam." "May I bless myself with a sight of that Personage?" "Nothing easier; I believe I can take you to him." "May I request you to wait for me here until I come back from the temple where I am taking this water." "With pleasure," replied Mahâ Pûrṇa. Râmânuja hastened to the temple, took leave of the Lord and sought out Kânchî Pûrṇa, who heard him out quietly and said: "My dear Râmânuja, you do not know what pleasure it gives me to hear that you are to proceed to Ṣrîrangam and stand before my Lord and Master. For, Yâmunâchârya is my Guru, my spiritual father, as also that of Mâhâ Pûrṇa who is to take you to him. Go, and may all good go with you." Râmânuja joined Mahâ Pûrṇa and they travelled on to Ṣrîrangam. They were entering it, when they saw a large crowd approaching them.

Râmânuja's Disappointment.

"What means this sad procession coming towards us?" asked Mahâ Pûrṇa of a passer-by. "Oh, holy Sir, know you not that our great Teacher has passed away from us? Where have you been the while—you, the best beloved of the Master? We are following his mortal remains to the grave." Both fell down senseless, pierced to the heart;

---

1 "Brahma the Creator, Siva the Destroyer, Indra the Mighty, and the other Liberated ones are but as the drops in the vast ocean of thy greatness and glory. Verily, no one would deny that your omnipotence is natural (unacquired by Karma) and unlimited by time, space and substance." This forms the eleventh verse of the Stôtra.—(*Compiler.*)

the blow was the severer in the case of Râmânuja, as his newly-awakened hopes and desires were nipped in the bud. "Alas! ill luck dogs my steps from the very cradle. I was very unhappy in my relations with my first teacher; more than once I had to incur his displeasure and was shown the door. My life was attempted against and it was by a miracle that I escaped. And this holy man, to whom I felt instinctively attracted and from whom I fondly expected much, has gone away even before I could see him. I believe I had better give up the struggle and resign myself to my fate." "Nay, not so, my dear Sir," rejoined Pûrṇa; "the Dispenser of all mercies has some mysterious end in view in thus avoiding a meeting between you two, and frustrating, as appears to us all, your heart-wishes. But, I am one that believes that nothing is sent by Him but for our good and that everything comes to him who knows how to wait. Come, let us not grieve, as if we know not that our master is nearer to us now than before, and could assist us better than when he was in that unmanageable vehicle. But let us take a last look on the instrument that served him so well and that was to the world the only visible representative of the Great Being that had come down to work for them."

The Three Vows.

They then approached the place of interment, and Pûrṇa was welcomed back by his friends and brother-disciples with a smile and a tear. He very soon gave them to understand that the young man beside him was Râmânuja, whom their teacher was so anxious to see. All eyes were turned on Râmânuja, who, entirely unconscious that he was the observed of all observers, advanced to the earthly tenement of Yâmunâchârya, gazed long and fondly at it, and said: "I have not been entirely unfortunate in that I am able to bless myself with a sight of the vehicle that the Great One used in his holy work. But what have we here? Three of his fingers closed! Was it ever so?" No one had noticed it before and now they were struck with wonder and surprise. "They were all right when he was alive. How has it come about?" "May be that he had something at heart, which he did not live to accomplish. Are there any here who have heard him express any such wishes when he was teaching you?" "Ah! now that we come to remember it, he was always full of expressions of unbounded gratitude towards Vyâsa and Parâsara; his devotion to Srî Sathakôpa was a thing by itself; and he used to regret that age and infirmities did not allow him to write a Visishtâdvaita Bhâshya on the Brahma Sûtras of Vyâsa." Then Râmânuja lifted his head proudly and raising his right hand, cried aloud: "If I am allowed to remain on the earth long enough, if it be true that my Lord here is pleased with his humble servant, and if the Divine One deigns to grant my prayers, I here, before all of you, give my word that I will, to the best of my ability, carry out his last wishes. If my service is accepted, I pray that the closed fingers open"—when, wonder of wonders! the closed fingers opened [1] and those among them that could see with other vision than we mortals, observed a smile of gladness and satisfaction overspread the face of Yâmuna. The vast multitude stood speechless, struck with fear and amazement. They dimly realised

---

1 "If I had but been allowed to meet him, I would lay a grand royal road from here to the feet of the Lord in Vaikuntha, along which Humanity can, with ease, travel right up to the Throne of the Eternal." No sooner were these words spoken than three fingers of Yâmuna's hand closed. "For, here is the man," thought he, "who will fulfil the dearest wishes of my heart and none else." Râmânuja very soon read the sign and exclaimed: "I here promise to enter the Vaishnava Faith; to devote myself, my time and my energies to the task of saving Humanity. I shall lead them to the true Faith, shall perfect them in the knowledge of the inner meanings of the Sacred Collect, and shall make them live out the Doctrine of Prapatti." One

that a Great Being was with them and that they were standing in the presence of some great mystery.

The Future Teacher.

Vara Ranga, from whose keen vision nothing was hidden, in the far past or in the distant future, approached Râmânuja and said : " Verily, you are the best beloved of our master ; to you have descended, by right of merit, his life-work and his divine powers," and then, turning to those that stood around, he raised his voice and said : " Behold our future Lord and Teacher. Him had our master yearned to meet, that he might with his own hands transfer the heavy burden to his shoulders. Upon him has fallen the mantle of our teacher and may he wear it right worthily. Behold, once again, our Lord and Master, the saviour of humanity and the hope of untold millions. Behold the great Torch-bearer of Truth and, may it bring light and life to the souls of those in darkness and guide them to the feet of the Divine Vâsudêva." " Amen," shouted the vast concourse, and nothing was heard for a long time but blessings and prayers. Râmânuja received them with bent head and joined hands, but replied : " Great is the work entrusted to me and poor my ability ; but I trust to the Lord on high and to the Teacher here to strengthen my hands and enable to me discharge it." He then gazed long and lovingly on the mortal remains of Yâmuna and sighed : " How is it that the Lord Ranganâtha was hard-hearted enough to deny us even this trifling consolation—a parting

---

of the fingers of Yâmuna opened. Râmânuja continued.—" I shall embody the teachings of the Vêdas, the Sâstras and of the Great Gurus in a commentary on the Vyâsa Sûtras, and place the means of salvation within the easy reach of all." Another of Yâmuna's fingers opened of itself. Râmânuja went on. "I shall select a holy Vaishṇava and name him after the sage Srî Parâsara, who, in thy Vishṇu Purâṇa, had unanswerably established the pre-eminence of the Supreme Self, his relation to the Jîva and the path to Liberation." The last finger of Yâmuna unclosed.—(*Prap.*)

look, a last word ? I am not calm enough now to go unto his Presence. I *do* feel it an injustice done to both of us, and it becomes not His Divine Mercy." He then respectfully took leave of Vara Ranga, Mahâ Pûrṇa and the rest, and returned to Kânchî. Yâmuna's body was interred with the highest honors ever paid to mortal man.[1]

CHAPTER IX.

The Initiation of Râmânuja.

On his return, Râmânuja went to Kânchî Pûrṇa and informed him of what transpired. Nambi's heart was filled with unutterable grief at the loss, but he found that his loss was insignificant beside that of Râmânuja and consoled him saying : " Trust in the omniscience and the omnipotence of the Lord of Kânchî. Grieve not. Everything will come out right in the end. Hope and wait."

Nambi Refuses to Initiate Him.

Râmânuja took heart at these words and resumed his service to the Lord. His devotion and reverence towards Nambi grew day by day and, in his turn, Nambi felt himself attracted more and more towards the future Teacher. This close contact opened the eyes of Râmânuja to the greatness of Nambi and to his spiritual eminence, and he concluded that he could not find a better master to serve. So, he sought him out and, with humble salutation, said : "Lord, if it be thy will, deign to accept me as one of your pupils and set my erring feet upon the path that leads to the Lord of all." "Nay, not so, my dear Sir. Far be it from me to assume a position I am not qualified to. You wanted to do this, induced, perhaps, by the favour the Lord Varadarâja extends towards my unworthly self." "But," interrupted Râmânuja, " the Sacred Books teach us that

1. *Vide- Ṣuka Praṣna Samhita*, Chap. 39.

Great Ones do take birth in all classes of society and that birth is but a minor consideration in the case of those that have been behind the Veil and have seen the Lord face to face." "Nay, nay; you do me too much honour. I am entirely unworthy of it. But, even granting it for argument's sake, should we not be the first to see that the regulations of the castes and the classes are preserved in their original purity? Have not the Great Ones based the constitution of Society on these? What says the Divine Teacher?—'Whatsoever a great man doeth, other men do; the standard he setteth up, the people go by. There is no duty in the three worlds, O Pârtha, that I should discharge, nor is there anything that I could desire to attain, yet, I go through my round of duties. For, if I discharge not my duties as assiduously as any one else, men would follow my example all round, O son of Pritha. These worlds would fall into ruin if I did not perform my duty. The four castes were instituted by me according to the varied distribution of energies and actions. And would it be well for me to be the author of the confusion of castes and destroy these creatures? Those men, whose steps are not guided by the family or the caste Dharma, stray, of a truth, into the darkness of hell and rarely get out of it. So, having an eye, too, to the solidarity of society, thou shouldst perform thy duty. As the ignorant act from attachment to action, so should the wise act, Oh Bhârata, without attachment, to preserve the solidarity of society. Let no wise man unsettle the minds of ignorant people attached to action. Better one's own Dharma, though destitute of merit, than the Dharma of another though well discharged. Better death in the discharge of one's own Dharma, for, the Dharma of another is full of danger.' The man of perfect knowledge should not unsettle the foolish, whose knowledge is imperfect." "My devotion to you shall be none the less for the social barriers that prevent the realisation of my dearest hopes," sadly replied Râmânuja, and took leave of Nambi.

Nambi Dines at Râmânuja's House.

All the live long night he lay thinking how to accomplish his object. The next morning he proceeded to the residence of Nambi and entreated him to partake of a meal in his house that noon. "Be it so," replied Nambi, with a smile. Râmânuja returned to his dwelling and directed his wife to prepare her best against the arrival of his friend. He quickly went through his daily duties and took the way to Nambi's house along the southern street. Meanwhile, Nambi, whose keen eye nothing could escape, divined the intention of his friend[1] and had already reached the house of his host, taking the north road. He requested the lady of the house to serve him *at once*, representing that he was very soon due at the temple for his daily service, and was served as became his caste and rank; the lady then threw out with a stick the

[1] Râmânuja wanted to partake of the remains of Nambi's meal hoping thus to establish an indirect spiritual connection with him. The holy aura of the Teacher is communicated to everything that comes into contact with him. Articles of food take the emanations sooner and retain them longer, more so as they are consecrated by powerful Vedic mantras that transform them into spiritual ingredients that go to build up the higher vehicles of consciousness. Even today, in orthodox families, the wife invariably takes her meal from the leaf used by her husband; and I have personal knowledge of cases where the disciples of a teacher (even of the lay arts) eat off his plate, the remains of the dinner consecrated by his touch. To the earnest disciple and the faithful wife, the teacher and the husband is the only God they know of and care about.

In the present case, Râmânuja (who was but Lakshmaṇa in another body) had, during a former incarnation, partaken of the fruits that Kânchî Pûrṇa (who was but the great devotee Ṣabari in another body) had tasted previously to see they were presentable to Râma and Lakshmaṇa. Hence, though he was morally justified in doing so, still Nambi looked further and took his stand on the argument that it would form a bad precedent to those that saw not with the eyes of the spirit, but who wanted some excuse to break loose from the strict but wholesome social regulations.—(*Compiler*).

leaf from which he ate, purified the place with a solution of cow-dung[1], and was taking her bath a second time, when Râmânuja, having waited in vain for Nambi at his house, came back, hoping that his guest might have gone before him. "Why are you bathing a second time," asked Râmânuja. "Has Nambi been here?" "Yes, he was here," replied his wife, "and wanted to be served his dinner at once, as he had to go to the temple to attend upon the Lord. As he was a non-Brâhmaṇa, I threw out with a stick the leaf he ate from, purified the place with cow-dung, and am bathing a second time for having touched impure things." "Impure things!" exclaimed Râmânuja, and a torrent of invectives was rushing from his lips. However, he checked himself with a mighty effort and only said to her—"Wife, wife, you little know what you have deprived me of. He whom *I* choose to invite to dine in my house is sacred enough for *you*, I should think. Don't take too much on yourself, my dear, and interfere in things that you cannot understand; or, one fine morning you will find yourself on your way to your parents' house."[2] He then took his way to seek out Nambi, saying to himself: "Twice disappointed! There seems to be some fatality about it. Well, I will not fail this time." He approached Nambi and said: "There are some desires that lie next my heart; may I trouble you to know from

1 Nambi threw out the leaf into the street and the lady gave the remains of the prepared meal to beggars.—(*Prap.*)

2 The *V. G.* gives quite a different version of the episode:—One day, while Nambi was walking along the street, Râmânuja chanced to meet him and took him to his house. When he was seated, Râmânuja proceeded to touch his feet, when Nambi sprang up and exclaimed: "Desist. By the Sacred Feet of my master Yâmuna, I swear I shall not allow such an outrage to all Dharma. How dare you? Know you not that Puṇḍarîkâksha rebuked the great Nâtha Yôgi himself, for walking after a Kshatriya in a moment of abstraction?" "I obey," said Râmânuja; "your single word is of more weight with me than arrays of precedents and hosts of authorities." He then preferred his unspoken questions to the Lord Varada. On his

the Lord Varadarâja whether they would ever be realised? I know He can refuse *you* nothing."

The Six Words.

That very night, when he was alone with the Lord, the latter asked him with a smile: "Nambi, it seems you would like to ask of me something." "Even so, my Lord. Râmânuja had been to me this evening and entreated me to know from you whether some desires that he has at heart would be realised. He seems very much broken-spirited too, and one would think, from the way he spoke, that his everything depended upon getting a reply to his unspoken questions." "Is it even so? Well, this is the situation. There is a young man, one of the best beloved of my servants. He knows no other will but mine. He may, in this birth, receive instruction from more than one person, but it is all, mind you, more for form's sake—just like my own discipleship under the sage Sândîpini. What he wants to know, he has not told you himself, and I shall imitate his example by giving you only the reply you are to take to him. (1) *I am the Supreme Reality.* (2) *Essential difference between the Individual and the Supreme Soul is the True Doctrine.* (3) *The easiest way to my feet and the most direct, is Self-Surrender and Prapatti (taking refuge in me.)* (4) *It is not even necessary that one should concentrate his mind upon Me when he quits the body.* (5) *Such a one shall, at the close of this life, stand before me for all eternity.* (6) *The questioner should sit at the feet of Mahâ Pûrṇa, his spiritual father.*" The next morning Nambi sent for Râmânuja and communicated to him the reply dictated by the Lord. "Were these what you wanted to know from the Lord? I hope the replies tally with your queries." "How could it be otherwise,

---

return home he found that his ultra-orthodox wife had washed the seat on which Nambi had sat and had bathed for having touched it.

my dear master? What have I done to deserve so much of the Divine One?" "Indeed, Râmânuja, you are blessed above all compare. And, through thee, the Lord's work will be done, as it was never done before."

Mahâ Pûrṇa sent to Kânchî.

The disciples of Yâmunâchârya gathered round Mahâ Pûrṇa and asked him if he could tell them who was to be the teacher of the Good Law thereafter. "Have you so soon forgotten," said he, "the wondrous events that took place when the last remains of our master were committed to the earth. His heart ever yearned towards Râmânuja, and I am sure that his choice would not be anything but the best." "Even then, we request you to go to Kânchî, prepare him for the great work that lies before him, and bring him among us." "Be it so," replied Mahâ Pûrṇa, and set out for Kânchî.

Meanwhile Râmânuja prepared to set out for Ṣrîrangam to join Mahâ Pûrṇa as afore directed. He took leave of the Lord Varadarâja and of his kind friend Kânchî Pûrṇa, and halted at Madurântakam[1] to offer his worship at the shrine of the Lord Taṭâka Pâlaka.

The Unexpected Meeting.

He had no sooner entered the temple than he saw Mahâ Pûrṇa, and could scarcely believe his eyes. "Really, I begin to think my bad days are over. What a fortunate coincidence! Here is the very Master come to meet me whom I meant to seek at Ṣrîrangam. I plainly see the finger of the Lord in this." He then advanced towards Nambi, threw himself at his feet, bathing them with tears of joy, and informed him of the reply of the Lord of Kânchî to his unspoken questions. On his part, Mahâ

---

[1] In the Chingleput District, and one of the stations on the South Indian Railway.

Pûrṇa was no less surprised at the rapidity with which things were coming to a head. "I would entreat you," said Râmânuja, "to receive me as your pupil and open my eyes to the light of Truth; and that, right here and as soon as possible." "Why such a hurry? Wait until you are at Kânchî and in the presence of Him who has brought us together. I shall enroll you as one of the humble labourers in the Lord's vineyard." "What! *you* speak of delay! *you*, who saw what took place when I went to seek instruction at the hands of your master! Is our stay in this body so certain that we can afford to wait till we arrive at Kânchî!" "What eagerness! What a thirst for spiritual knowledge!" exclaimed Mahâ Pûrṇa to himself, and taking him to a Vakuḷa tree[1] in the courtyard of the temple (thenceforward to become as sacred and as famous as the

1. "(Thenceforward in all years
Never to fade and ever to be kept
In homage of the World) beneath whose leaves
It was ordained the Truth should come to Him;
Which now the Master knew; wherefore he went
With measured pace, steadfast, majestical,
Unto the tree of wisdom. Oh, ye worlds!
Rejoice! Our Lord wended unto the Tree!
Whom—as he passed into its ample shade,
* * the conscious earth
Worshipped with waving grass and sudden flush
Of flowers about his feet. The forest boughs
Bent down to shade him; from the river sighed
Cool wafts of wind laden with lotus-scents,
Breathed by the water-gods. Large wondering eyes
Of woodland creatures—panther, boar and deer
At peace that eve, gazed on his face benign
From cane and thicket. From its cold cleft wound
The mottled deadly snake, dancing its hood
In honour of our Lord; bright butterflies
Fluttered their vans, azure and green and gold,
To be his fan-bearers; the fierce kite dropped
Its prey and screamed; the striped palm-squirrel raced
From stem to stem to see; the weaver bird
Chirped from her swinging nest; the lizard ran;
The koil sang her hymn; the doves flocked round;

Bodhi tree under which Lord Buddha received his initiation) marked him with the sacred signs that form the badge of His service.[1]

Even the creeping things were ware and glad.
Voices of earth and air joined in one song,
Which unto ears that hear said, "Lord and Friend!
Lover and Saviour! Thou who hast subdued
Angers and prides, desires and fears and doubts
Thou that for each and all hast given thyself,
Pass to the Tree! The sad world blesseth thee
Who art the Lord that shall assuage her woes.
Pass, Hailed and Honoured! strive thy last for us,
King and Conqueror! thine hour has come;
This is the day the ages waited for!"—*Light of Asia.*

1. The initiation of the Srî Vaishnavas is based upon five Sacraments, called Pancha Samskâras:—

(i) Tâpa or branding on the two shoulders with the marks of the Sankha (conch), and the Chakra (discus), the emblems of Vishnu.

(ii) Pundra or two white lines (of a sort of white clay) on the forehead, with a red line (of powdered saffron, etc.) in the middle. They should be marked in eleven other places of the body, three on the stomach, one on the chest, two on the shoulders, three on the neck and two on the back. These twelve marks should be borne every day and are called by the 12 names of Vishnu:—Kêsava, Nârâyana, Mâdhava, Gôvinda, Vishnu, Madhusûdana, Trivikrama, Vâmana, Srîdhara, Hrishîkêsa, Padmanâbha and Dâmôdara.

(iii) Nâma: to bear the names of Vishnu; and one should be called by those names only.

(iv) Mantras, which are taught by the Guru at the time of the Initiation. The mantras of Vishnu are various:—the most important of them are one of six syllables, called Vishnu Shadaksharî; one of eight, called Nârâyana Ashtâksharî, and one of twelve called Vâsudêva Dvâdasâksharî. Of these, the Nârâyana Ashtâksharî, the Dvaya or Saranâgati Mantra and Charamasloka (Gîta, XVIII-66,) are called Rahasya Traya, Mantra Traya—the three secrets, the three Mantras—and are taught to every one at the time of his initiation. This initiation can be obtained by one of any caste or creed—even a Mlêcha or a Chandâla—and he becomes a Vaishnava. Vaishnavas should recite these Mantras a certain number of times every day.

His Initiation.

He then seated Râmânujâ on his right hand, placed his right palm on the crown of his head and his left over his heart, and gazed steadfastly into the eyes of his pupil. He meditated upon his master, and reciting the names of the sacred spiritual hierarchy, whispered into the right ear of his disciple the sacred Two Truths in all its glory. He then said to him aloud—"Of old, Srî Râmachandra, being prevented by his promise to his father from reigning in person in Ayôdhya, left with Bhârata his sandals as his representative, and proceeded to the forest. Similarly, my master, being prevented from initiating you himself, has placed his sacred feet on my head and deputed to me the responsibility. So, it is *he* from whom you have received your initiation and not from *me*." "My Lord and Master, may I ask you to enlighten me on this point. What is the goal to be attained? What are the means? Who is the aspirant?" "The Lord Varadarâja on the Elephant-hill at Kânchî is the goal to be reached; the means are the Two Truths into which you have been initiated; the aspirant is yourself. And now realise for yourself the goal through the means pointed out to you." The next day they were on their way to Kânchî, and, Kânchî Pûrṇa, having heard of their approach, came out to welcome them and reverence his brother disciple. Mahâ Pûrṇa proceeded to the temple, and in the company of Nambi offered his worship to the Lord. Nâthamuṇi, the great Yôgi, deputed his disciple Puṇḍarîkâksha to initiate his grandson yet to be born; he again, on his death assigned the duty to his disciple Râma Migra, who waited upon Yâmunâcharyâ for six months, got access to him, initiated him, and set him

(v) **Yâga or worship of certain idols of Vishṇu, which is taught at the time of the initiation by the Guru's presenting one to the disciple for his worship; and thence the disciple should worship it and no other.—(*V. C.*)**

face to face with the great mystery at Srîrangam. Similarly, Mahâ Pûrna, being directed thereto by Âlavandâr, sought out Râmânuja, initiated him, and set him face to face with the Lord Varadarâja. Mahâ Pûrna was but the visible instrument of Âlavandâr the medium or the outward link; but Yâmunâcharyâ was the real and direct teacher of Râmânuja.

CHAPTER X.

The Great Renunciation.

Thereafter Râmânuja took Mahâ Pûrna to his lodgings, arranged that he should dwell with him, and provided him with the necessary comforts.[1] For six months, Mahâ Pûrna instructed him in the Sacred Collect and the inner teachings of the Doctrine, which Râmânuja received with a reverent heart.[2]

The Second Offence.

One day, a Srî Vaishnava who came to anoint Râmânuja was faint and weak with hunger; and Râmânuja, noticing it, said to his wife: "The Brâhmana is hungry; serve him with meals." "They are not yet ready, my Lord." "Then, let him have the remains of what was prepared yesterday." "Unfortunately, I have nothing to spare even of that." Râmânuja, who knew his wife better than to take her at her word, sent her out on an errand, went into the kitchen and found plenty of the remains of the

1 Subsequently his wife too was initiated and they partook of the holy water that had washed the feet of Mahâ Pûrna and the remains of his meal.—(*R.D.C.*)

2 Mahâ Pûrna taught him the first two thousand stanzas of the Collect.—(*R.D.C.*)

The Vyâsa Sûtras and the Sacred Collect, everything except the works of Sathakôpa.—(*V.G.*)

previous day's preparations. As soon as his wife came back, he turned to her in great anger and said : " This is the second time you have offended against the servants of the Lord. You see the Vaishṇava is ready to drop down with hunger, and yet you deliberately lied to me and refused him food. What a hard-hearted woman I have for my helpmate ! Take care it does not occur again. "

The Last Offence.

Some days after, the same lady happened to pick a quarrel with the wife of Mahâ Pûrṇa about a vessel of water, and hot words passed between them.[1] This came to the ears of Peria Nambi, who rebuked his wife, and, before Râmânuja could know of it, set out with his people to Ṣrîrangam.[2] Râmânuja came home and was informed of the hurried departure of his master, and the reason thereof. Tears of grief and rage coursed down his cheeks and, turning round upon his wife, exclaimed : "Your cup of iniquity is full to the brim and over-flowing. The first time you prevented me from attaining my dearest wish as regards Kânchî Pûrṇa ; on another occasion you refused to feed a hungry Vaishṇava ; and now you have brought upon me the sin of having driven out my master, who is dearer to me than wife, than life, than everything else, here and hereafter. Really, you make a splendid wife for a poor man like myself, who has difficulties innumerable to fight against, without adding to them a woman who is bent upon ruining me body and soul. I have given you fair

1. They were drawing water from the well at the same time, when drops of water fell from the vessel of Mahâ Pûrṇa's wife, into that of the other. The latter declared it polluted, and hot words passed between them, in the course of which Râmânuja's wife taunted the other with her poverty and her low birth (Mahâ Pûrṇa was a forelock Brâhmaṇa).—(*Prap.*)

2. He was gone to Ṣrîperumbûdûr on business.—(*V.G.*)

warning and now you shall go back to your parents and take with you whatever you have brought from them. [1]

[1] Tanjamâmbâl trembled with fear and Râmanuja, who had not in his nature to be angry with any one, quieted himself for the time; but he was firmly resolved to take the earliest opportunity of sending her home to her parents. One day, he was in attendance on the Lord Varadarâja during the Grand Festival, when a Sri Vaishṇava came up to him and said: "Holy Sir, may I make bold to request you to give me a meal, I am dying of hunger." "With the utmost pleasure," replied Râmânuja, "but you see I cannot leave the temple at present; so go to my wife and tell her from me to attend to your wants. And pardon me my inability to discharge the rites of hospitality to you myself." The Brâhmaṇa did as he was directed; when, lo! the lady turned to him with flashing looks and exclaimed: "A nice man is my husband to send home to me such starving beggars to plague the life out of me. We are as poor as rats and have not the wherewithal to keep body and soul together. Go away from here to your generous host, who, I am sure, would entertain your reverence better than my poor self. Ah me! I am mated to a careless and improvident husband." The Brâhmaṇa went back to Râmânuja and in accents of concentrated anger, exclaimed: "Has my poverty and hunger degraded me so low in your eyes that you should even make a jest of it and send me on a bootless errand to be insulted by a woman?" Horrified at these words, Râmânuja fell at his feet, prayed him to calm himself and relate what had taken place. "Reverend Sir," said he humbly, "there seems to be some terrible mistake here. How could you attribute such deliberate wickedness to me? Now that you have obliged me so far, I entreat you to accede to one other prayer of mine." He quickly wrote a letter to his wife, as from her father's house, inviting her and himself to her brother's marriage that was to come off at no distant date. He gave the letter to the Brâhmaṇa, with the necessary instructions, and despatched through him valuable presents as sent by her parents. The Brâhmaṇa, hungry as he was, entered into the spirit of the plot and went back to Râmânuja's wife. "You have come back, have you? What fresh orders has my Lord for me?" snarled out the lady. "Nay, nay," replied the Brâhmaṇa, now all smiles and affability, "pardon me for the innocent deception I practised upon you a few hours ago. I did but try you, my dear; I am come from your parents to invite you and your husband to the marriage of your brother that is to come off shortly. Here is their letter to you, and here are the presents they have sent you, as a token of their love." The lady read the letter through, cast her eyes over the rich cloths, ornaments, saffron, etc, and was overwhelmed with joy. She made numerous enquiries about her parents and her people, which the Brâhmaṇa, carefully instructed beforehand by Râmânuja, answered readily and in great detail. "What a selfish wretch I am," cried she, "to weary you with

He Takes Orders.

He then concluded that he had had enough with the life of a householder, for which he could not command the prime requisite—an obedient and intelligent wife; and resolved to renounce it and take orders as a Sanyâsin.[1]

---

my questions, and you dreadfully hungry and tired after your journey. Excuse me my seeming rudeness to you before; wait but for a while and you will see how I receive and entertain my father's friend." She was as good as her word and the Brâhmaṇa received such a hearty welcome, as was never accorded to Râmânuja on any day of his married life. Meanwhile Râmânuja came home from the temple and was greeted by his wife with the news from her parents. He seemed to be mightily pleased and surprised, read over the letter, approved of the rich presents, and said; "Of course we *must* go over to the marriage. Unfortunately I am not able to accompany you there, as I have some urgent business here which I should attend to in person. But you can rest assured I will be there in time." He then requested the Brâhmaṇa to take her to her parents and, with a glad heart, saw her depart from his house with her dresses, her ornaments, her servants and everything she had brought from her parents. Thereafter, he thought no more of her; and she was to him as one dead.—(*Prap.*)

1. "If one then, being great and fortunate,
Rich, dowered with health and ease,
If one, not tired with life's long day, but glad
In the freshness of its morning, one not cloyed
With love's delicious feasts, but hungry still;
If one not worn and wrinkled, sadly sage,
But joyous in the glory and the grace,
That mix with evils here and free to choose
Earth's loveliest at his will; one even as I,
Who ache not, lack not, grieve not, save with griefs
Which are not mine, except as I am man;
If such a one, having so much to give,
Gave all, laying it down for love of men;
And thenceforth spent himself to search for truth,
Wringing the secret of deliverance forth,
Whether it lurk in hells or hide in heavens.
Or hover unrevealed nigh unto all;
Surely at last, far off, sometime, somewhere,
The veil would lift for his deep searching eyes,
The road would open for his painful feet,
That should be won for which he lost the world,
And death might find him conqueror of death.

He purified himslef in the sacred waters of Anantasaras, and, betaking himself to the sanctuary of Varadarâja, exclaimed. "Lord, I have had enough of the householder's life. I wish to take holy orders that I might more effectively serve you and your servants. Take me to your feet, O Lord, grant me the sacred three-knotted staff and the orange robe."[1] The Lord, mightily pleased that Râmânuja

---

This will I do * * *
* * * because my heart,
Beats with each throb of all the hearts that ache,
Known and unknown, these that are mine and those
Which shall be mine, a thousand million more,
Saved by this sacrifice I offer now.
* * I come! Oh, mournful Earth!
For thee and thine I lay aside my youth,
* * My joys, my golden days, my nights,
* * * Unto this
Came I, and unto this all nights and days
Have led me; * * * * I choose
To tread its (Earth's) paths with patient stainless feet,
Making its dust my bed, its loneliest wastes
My dwelling, and its meanest things my mates.
Clad in no prouder garb than outcastes wear,
Fed with no meats save what the charitable
Give of their will, sheltered by no pomp,
Than the dim cave lends or the jungle bush.
This will I do, because the woful cry
Of life and all flesh living cometh up
Into my ears, and all my soul is full
Of pity for the sickness of this world;
Which I will heal, if healing may be found,
By utmost renouncing and strong strife."—*Light of Asia.*

[1] So holy was the influence of that moment when our Lord renounced the world to save the world—
"That far and near in homes of men there spread,
An unknown peace. The slayer hid his knife;
The robber laid his plunder back; the shroff
Counted full tale of coins; all evil hearts,
Grew gentle, kind hearts gentler, as the balm
Of that Divinest Daybreak lightened Earth.
Kings at fierce war called truce; the sickmen leaped
Laughing from beds of pain; the crying smiled.
* * * *

should choose Him as his initiator into the Âșrama, said to him through His high priest: "Take them and wear them well. Henceforth you shall be known among men as Râmânujamuni."[1] He then sent for Nambi and said to him: "Find out a suitable Maṯẖa for our Râmânuja and instal him therein with due honours." "Happy am I, in being entrusted with this pleasant duty," replied Nambi; and forthwith arranged comfortable lodgings for the holy ascetic.

He tries to get back Gôvinda.

And Râmânuja resided there for a few months, strictly observing the numerous and complicated details of an ascetic's daily life. One day, his thoughts happened to turn towards his master Yâmunâchâryâ. "Great is the favour shown to his unworthy servant by the Holy One. It has removed, one by one, all the obstacles from my path and has led me unto the life I had so yearned after. And now I shall set about carrying out the last wishes of my master. But alas! I am alone and unassisted. Would that I had with me here my old mate Gôvinda! He is a man after my own heart; wordly pleasures and honours tempthim not; there are very few things about our literature, secular and otherwise, that he does not know; he has a keen and comprehensive intellect, and is devoted to me, heart and soul. But now, through some bad Karma of his, he serves another God than my Lord of Kânchî;

So glad the world was—though it wist not why—
That over desolate wastes went swooning songs,
Of mirth, the voice of bodiless Prets and Bhuts,
Foreseeing Him; and Dêvas in the air,
Cried 'It is finished, finished;' and the priests,
Stood with the wondering people in the streets
Watching those golden splendours flood the sky
And saying, 'There has happened some mighty thing'."

—*Light of Asia.*

[1] Yatirâja (The king of Ascetics)—(*V.G.*, *Per.*, *Prap.*)

whom can I pitch upon to show him his error and bring him back to my side ?" He then thought for a while and exclaimed "Now I have it. How dull I am grown ! Who can help me in this but my uncle Srî Saila Pûrṇa ? He is the incarnation of all virtues, a well of wisdom, deep and undefiled, and is as dear to Srî Venkaṭêsa as Kânchî Pûrṇa is to the Lord Varadarâja. He is *the* man for it." He then sent to him a friend of his with this request.: "It is known to you that Gôvinda, your nephew and my fellow-disciple, is, through some untoward Karma of his, attracted to the service of strange Gods, and is at present at Kâlahasti. I pray you to go to him for my sake, rescue him from his life of darkness and take him once more unto your feet."

Âlvân and Âṇḍân.

Dâsarathi [1] of Vâthûla Gôtra and Srî Vatsânka [2] of Hârîta Gôtra, came to know of Râmânuja's taking holy orders, and were overjoyed ; proceeding to Kânchî, they laid

---

1 Râmânuja had two sisters, Bhûmi and Kamala. The first married Ananta Dikshita of Purushmangala and their son was Dâsarathi, more commonly known as Mudali Âṇḍân. The other sister was the mother of Varada Vishṇu Âchârya (வரதவிஷ்ணுவாசார்).

(*a*) Âṇḍân was born in
Year—Prabhava ; Month—Mîna ; Date—25th ;
Fortnight—10th (Dark) ; Nakshatra—Punarvasu ;
Lagna—Kumbha : Sect—Vaḍama ; Family—Kandâḍai ;
Gôtra—Vâthûla ; Sûtra—Âpastamba ;
Sâkha—Yajus ; Amsa—Bharata.

He was to Râmânuja, as his Tridanḍa ; and the Master's sacred sandals are called after Âṇḍân. His term of life was 105 years and he was the author of a work called Rahasya Traya.—(*Per.*)

(*b*) Month—Mêsha.
Amsa—Râma, Chakra and Supratishṭha.—(*Pal.*)

2 Year—Saumya ; month—Makara ; Fortnight—5th ; Week—Thursday ; Nakshatra—Hasta ;
Parents—Ananta and Perundêvi ; Family—Kooram ;
Gôtra—Hârîta ; Sûtra—Âpastamba ; Sâkha—Yajus ;
Amsa—Râma ; Wife—Âṇḍâl.
Parâsara and Vêda Vyâsa Bhaṭṭa were his sons ;
Putra Putrârya ([illegible]), Chaturgrâma Vâsi ([illegible]).

themselves at his feet and said : " Master, admit us into

Ranganâthârya (ரங்கநாதாசார்யர்) were his disciples. He lived 108 years and has left behind him the following works :—(1) Varada Râja Stava ; (2) Sundara Bâhu Stava ; (3) Atimânusha Stava ; (4) Srî Vaikuntha Stava ; (5) Srî Stava ; (6) Yamaka Ratnâkara ; and (7) Gadya Traya Vyâkhyâna.—(*Per.*)

(*b*) His father's name was Râmâ Sômâyaji. He was the amsa of Râma, Sankha and Sarvanâtra.—(*Pal.*)

(*c*) There lived in Kooram, a village near Kânchî, a Brâhmana named Srî Vatsânka, who from his great wealth and noble qualities was generally recognised as the Lord of Kooram (Kûranâtha). He was known far and wide for his open hospitality ; and from morn to the small hours of the night, he welcomed guests of every description and entertained them right royally. His heart was ever open to the appeals of charity and his hand was never closed against the poor and the needy. One night, the Divine Mother at Kânchî heard a great noise proceed from a distance ; and, curious to ascertain what it was that gave rise to such an unusual sound, so late in the night, when sleep and darkness reigned over the world, she said to her Lord " Whence is this strange disturbance ? "

" Nay, my dear, neither strange nor unusual. I hear it every day ; and it is pleasant to my ears ; it is but the closing for the night of the huge brazen gates of the dining-hall of a great food-giver in a village not far from here."

" Ah ! is it even so ? How is it you have not thought of bringing him to see me ? And you have all along kept him to yourself, selfishly as it would seem."

Varada turned to Kânchî Pûrna, who was in attendance upon them, and directed him to bring Kûranâtha unto them. Nambi waited upon the great man the next morning and communicated to him the will of the Lord. Srîvatsa meditated for a moment and said sadly : " What do the scriptures say ? ' Let not thy right hand know what thy left hand giveth. ' And I am known as a great food-giver, am I ? I have unconsciously but assiduously intensified the spirit of Egotism in me, so far as to attract the notice of the Giver of All. What am I, the worst of sinners, the self-conceited worm, that I should pollute the holy sanctuary of the Divine Pair ; what do I not owe them, for their kindly awakening me to a sense of my own unworthiness and evil ways ? Humbly submit to the Lord from me, that I am as yet unworthy to stand in His presence."

He then distributed his vast wealth among the poor, and set out for Kânchî. His wife, a model of devotion and fidelity, followed him at a distance, unperceived. They were passing through a large forest, dark and lonely, when the lady ventured to address her lord and said : " Lord, I am afraid."

thy fold and permit us to bear the badges of the servants of the Lord." [1]

"Be it as you desire," replied Râmânuja. From that moment they never left his side and ever waited upon his person, anticipating his least wishes.

The Conversion of Yâdava.

Now, the mother of Yâdavaprakâşa, more intelligent and keen of observation than many of her time, was an ardent devotee of the Lord of Kânchî; Nambi too regarded her with great respect; and she had, on more than one occasion, free and confidential talks with Râmânuja about the comparative merits of the various schools of thought. Very soon she felt herself drawn to the teachings of Râmânuja, and one day as she was ascending the steps of the temple, said to herself: "What a good thing it would be if my son's eyes were opened to the beauty and greatness of the True Doctrine." At once there

---

Şrîvatsa started at the sound and looked back; he observed his wife and asked in amazement: "And who advised you to abandon your house, people, friends and comforts, to follow me, a homeless wanderer?"

"My heart, lord of my life, and my world is centred in you, my hopes here and hereafter. When was it otherwise?"

"Let that be. Have you brought away anything valuable?"

"Yea, my Lord, even this gem-studded golden goblet I have reserved for my Lord to drink from."

Âlvân laughed long and loud. "Thou innocent and faithful heart! When was a beggar ever known to drink from a gem-encrusted golden goblet? Hand it over to me." He flung it far, far away from him, and said with a smile: "Now your fear is far, far away from you."

They then proceeded to Kânchî and lived a humble life—he, with his soul centred in the Lord, and she, drawing her life and spirit but from him. But the keen eyes of the Teacher found him out; and the Master invited him to his Maṭha, received him with open arms, and admitted him as his disciple. He was the holiest and the most learned of all that sought refuge with Râmânuja; the Master had the utmost regard and respect for him; and Âlvân lay next his heart.—(*Prap.*)

1 And along with them Varada Vishṇu Âchârya ([illegible]).—*V.G.*)

fell upon her ears the words "very good, good indeed" uttered by some one there. She took this an auspicious sign and said to her son: "My dear, it seems to me (and you know that I would not decide in a hurry) that you had better pay greater attention to the doctrine taught by your old pupil Râmânuja and join the holy group of the Three-knotted."

Now Yâdava was not loth to do this. He had to admit to himself that the faith that he preached and practised had many irremediable defects in it; the objections raised against it by Râmânuja were working themselves into his mind and were more unanswerable than ever; he had not forgotten the scene at the king's palace, when the Brahmarâkshasa proclaimed and proved incontestably the superior greatness of Râmânuja, if it did not hint at something more mysterious; his miraculous escape from the Vindhia forests, and the divine help rendered to him then was still fresh in his recollections; and more than all, he held his own mother in the greatest reverence and had extreme confidence in her keen intellect and impartial judgment. So he replied: "Thy word is law unto me. But I should, as a penance for my having taken off the tuft of hair and the sacred thread, go round the world, which, being old and infirm, I am unable to do. I see the Path open before me; but, ah me! it is not given me to tread it."

That very night, the Lord of Kânchî appeared to him in his sleep and said: "*Go round my Râmânuja once* and take the orange robe and the three-knotted bamboo from his hands, and you will have done enough." Yâdava mistrusted this information and desiring to assure himself of the truth of it, proceeded to Nambi and said: "Holy Sir, may I request to lay before the Lord a certain prayer of mine and get His reply to it?" That night, when

Nambi was about to take leave of the Lord, he said: "Lord, Yâdavaprakâṣa wants me to get your reply to an unspoken prayer of his."

"Is it so? His mother desired him to take his refuge in the Law and accept the three-knotted staff like Râmânuja; he said that he was too old to go through the consequent penance of circum-ambulating the Earth; I told him to go round Râmânuja once and take orders; he wants to know whether the information conveyed to him during his sleep is in reality from me, and has asked it through you."

The next morning, Nambi sent for Yâdava and communicated to him the details of the previous night's conversation.[1] Yâdava could doubt no longer; he went to Râmânuja and, falling at the feet of his former pupil, said: "Holy Sir, deign to invest me with the orange

---

[1] The *Prap.* and the *R. D. C.* differ in the order of the events connected with this episode:—

(*a*) (i) Yâdava's mother once observed Râmânuja teaching his disciples; and being filled with an inexplicable reverence towards him, saluted him.

(ii) She went home and told her son to take refuge in him, as he was no other than the Great Ananta, come down in human form to restore the Good Law; Kânchî Pûrṇa and other wise men also held the same views; she was firmly convinced that the teachings of Râmânuja were the soundest and the most soul-satisfying.

(iii) Yâdava accepted, and urged the question of penance. "Go round him once, instead," said his mother.

(iv) He was not convinced; went to Râmânuja and asked him to prove his position about the caste-marks, the sacred Badges and the Saguṇa Brahma. Râmânuja deputed his disciple Âlvân, who very soon convinced Yâdava.

(v) That night the Lord confirmed his mother's words. He was not convinced.

(vi) The Upaṣruti, 'It is good'—He informed his mother of the dream, but still doubted.

(vii) He applied to Kânchî Pûrṇa—The Lord's reply settled Yâdava. —(*Prap.*)

(*b*) (i) A great discussion between Râmânuja and Yâdava about the Sacred Badges and the vertical caste-marks—Yâdava was worsted.

robe and the three-knotted staff and admit me as your disciple."

"With the greatest pleasure possible," exclaimed Râmânuja, "but you would have to pass through a long and weary penance first."

"But the Lord Himself has willed it otherwise," replied Yâdava, and he reverently went round Râmânuja and stood before him with folded hands.

Dâṣarathi and Ṣrîvatsânka were amazed at the wonderful coincidence of the desires of Yâdava with the will of the Lord, and said: "Master, we have heard that Jaya and Vijaya, the keepers of the Divine Portals, regained the Lord's presence through ceaseless hatred of Him.[1] But now we see it exemplified in the case of Yâdavaprakâṣa. Grant it that he may be taken to your heart along with us."

"Be it so" replied Râmânuja. And since Yâdava had, by his having taken the single-knotted staff, outcasted himself, Râmânuja admitted him again into it and formally made him go through the Chauḷa[2] and Upanayana rites; he then invested him with the orange robe and the three-knotted staff and named him Gôvinda Jeer; and lastly marked him with the Sacred Badges,

---

(ii) On another occasion Yâdava met Râmânuja and asked him to speak upon the glorious attributes of the Lord. Âlvân was deputed to do so; and recited a stanza from the Sundarabâhu Stava, that convinced Yâdava.

(iii) His mother wanted him to enter the Faith—The Upaṣruti—The question of penance—His mother's suggestion.

(iv) His dream—Applied to Nambi—The Lord's reply.

[1] They refused admission to the Holy Kumâras, Sanaka, and the rest into the Lord's presence; and were cursed by him to go down upon Earth. "Yet I give you choice of taking seven births as my devotees or three births as my foes." "The shorter, the better," replied they "We cannot afford to be so long away from you; and, moreover, our enemies occupy our time, our energies and our thoughts more than our friends."—(*Comp.*)

[2] The tonsure ceremony.

initiating him into the mystery of the sacred Two Truths.

"I would very much like that your great learning should not be lost to the world. Compose a work on the duties of ascetics, reconciling the various conflicting passages in the Smritis."[1]

"To hear is to obey," replied Yâdava, and in a very short time, produced the "Yati Dharma Samucchaya" in eleven chapters. He laid it at the feet of his master, who critically went through it and declared himself satisfied. Yâdava ever after remained with Râmânuja, as warmly devoted to him as he was before indifferent and doubting; and, dying soon after, found a place near the throne of the Eternal.

Ranganâtha Refused.

By this time, Âlavandâr's pupils at Srîrangam had come to know of Râmânuja's having taken orders and the events that followed; they consulted among themselves, and proceeding in a body to the presence of the Lord, prayed to Him to send for Râmânuja to dwell amongst them thereafter. In compliance with their request, Ranganâtha sent a message to Varada, to which the latter characteristically replied: "When we are prepared to forego our very self, we shall think of parting with our Râmânuja."[2]

This reply came upon them like a shock and took away their breath. "What shall we do now? Official methods have proved fruitless; and now we should seek to obtain by prayer, by entreaty, what we could not do otherwise."

1 "You have, all your life, been engaged in decrying the Vaishnava ascetics and holding up to ridicule their life and observances. Purify yourself of the taint by composing this work.—(*Prap.*)

2 Generous souls there are, that never send away any one disappointed. But who has ever heard of any one giving away the idea of self or of any one who asked it as a gift?—(*Prap.*)

They then sought out Vara Ranga and said to him: "Holy Sir, you are our only hope now. It is well known that the Lord of Kânchî never disappoints any one, only if he knows how to draw Him into a promise. He has a great weakness for good music; and you, as the highest representative of that art, would not find it very difficult to make Him forget himself and promise Râmânuja to you."[1]

"I can but try," modestly replied Vara Ranga, and forthwith proceeded to Kânchî, having previously obtained the consent of the Lord for his project.

The Power of Music.

His clansman Varada Gâyaka of Kânchî, hearing of his arrival, went out to welcome him, and lodged him in his house, where he rested for that day. The next morning, he proceeded to the temple of Varada Râja on his delicate and difficult mission.

Kânchî Pûrṇa, who was in attendance upon the Lord, came out to meet him and saluted him reverently. Mutual inquiries followed, and Vara Ranga expressing his desire to offer his worship at the feet of the Lord, Nambi took him into the Presence, where Vara Ranga found Râmânuja standing near the Lord, reciting the Varadarâja Ashṭaka. Vara Ranga prostrated himself at the feet of the Lord and stood with folded hands before him, when Varadarâjâ directed that the honours of the temple be shown him. Vara Ranga accepted them with humble thanks and Varadarâja said to him: "Vara Ranga, they say you are a past master in the art of song and Nâṭya. Sing us something."

"Supremely blessed am I in that my Lord should deign to notice me thus," replied Vara Ranga, and forthwith

1 The Lord Ranganâtha deputes him to go to Varada and get Râmânuja from him any how.—(*Prap.*)

began to recite, in heart-ravishing strains of celestial music, the stanzas of the Sacred Collect beginning with "என்னெஞ்சமேயான்" accompanying them with appropriate gestures, expressive of the feelings and passions. Every one listened in rapt ecstasy and felt themselves transported to Ṣrî Vaikuṉṯha, to the presence of the Divine One, where the Ever-Liberated sing for ever the glory of the Lord. The Lord Varadarâja, in the excess of his joy, directed that Vara Ranga be presented with the garland of pearls about His neck, with the golden cloth about His head, with His white umbrella, with His pair of Châmaras and every other insignia about His Divine Person. When, behold ! Vara Ranga, who was honoured more than ever mortal was before then, had the temerity to refuse every one of them and said with a shake of his head : "You do your servant too much honour, my Lord ; but he wants none of these. You are known as the Unrivalled Giver of Boons. Let me have of you the one that I so much crave for," and he went on with his song, throwing more soul and more fervour into it.

Then the Lord cried out : "Stop, stop, Vara Ranga. You may have anything you want except myself and my Queens."

Vara Ranga pointed out Râmânuja and said : "I pray you, my Lord, permit him to go with me."

"I am nicely caught and you have verily taken me unawares. I should have thought of it before. Well, ask of me anything else."

"It shall never be said of the Lord that he went back upon his word. Was that not your motto when you came down on Earth as Ṣrî Râmachandra ?"

"There you have me ; and now that you have had your wish, why do you delay ?" exclaimed the Lord in tones of evident displeasure

Vara Ranga was too wise to throw away his only chance and turning to Râmânuja, said: "Then be pleased to go with me, Holy Sir."

Our Teacher prostrated himself before the Lord and took leave of him, saying: "Wherever I might be, I am always with Thee and do Thy work." And turning to Dâşarathi and Şrîvatsânka, he desired them to go to his maţha and bring to him the image of the Lord Varadarâja that formed the object of his daily worship. Kânchi Pûrṇa followed them a part of their way and affectionately took leave of them.

CHAPTER XI.

Râmânuja at Srîrangam.

They approached the holy city and halted at the banks of the northern branch of the Cauvery. Râmânuja bathed in its sacred waters, put on the twelve marks, and waited the pleasure of Vara Ranga. Meanwhile the whole city came to know of his arrival there,[1] and a vast crowd composed of the disciples of Âlavandâr, the Jeers, the Êkângis and the Şrî Vaishṇavas of the place, proceeded to the temple and waited the commands of the Lord. Sênânâtha, the Celestial Generalissimo and the Master of Ceremonies, was directed to receive Râmânuja and bring him to the Sacred Presence.[2] They accordingly proceeded to the banks of the Cauvery, accompanied by all the paraphernalia of the temple. It looked more like the procession of the Ever-Liberated advancing as far as the banks of the Holy Virajâ to welcome a brother that was to take his place among them. Râmânuja came forward to meet

[1] Vara Ranga preceded him to the temple and communicated to Ranganâtha the success of his mission. The Lord praised him highly and showered honours upon him. "You are ever my faithful servant and never fail me in anything I entrust you with. *You* have succeeded where *I* have failed."—(*Prap.*)

[2] Mahâ Pûrṇa was given that honour.—(*Prap.*)

them, fell at the feet of Sênânâtha, Peria Nambi and the other elders, and followed them to the temple. They made the round of the streets and Râmânuja stopped at the Great Altar to offer his worship. He visited the sanctuary of the Divine Consort Ranganâyaki; sipped water from the sacred Chandra Pushkariṉi; and paid his respects to the sacred guardians of the Gôpura, and to the holy Âlvârs Srî Saṯhakôpa and the others. Entering the inner rounds of the temple, he cast his eyes reverently on the Vimâna that is shaped after the sacred syllable and visited the sanctuary of Sênânâtha.

Ranganâtha and Râmânuja.

He then penetrated as far as the Hall of the Divine Bridegroom (அழகிய மணவாளன் திருமண்டபம்), when Ranganâtha himself came out from the Holy of the Holies as far as the Hall to welcome his servant and returned to the sanctuary; Râmânuja followed into the Sacred Bedchamber and at last gazed on the Divine Loveliness of the 'Ancient of the Ancients.' That prime favourite of the Lord, Tiruppâṉâlvâr has described it for us in the decade அமலனாதிப்பிரான் in words that live for all ages. Never can the eyes that have rested but for a second upon the Divine Form be attracted to any other sight, in this world or in the higher ones. He fell at the feet of the Lord and remained there in rapt ecstasy and lost in thought that it would be sacrilege for us to guess. At last he got up and stood with joined hands, reciting the திருப்பல்லாண்டு (the Song of Blessing) and the Song of Praise composed by his Master Âḻavandâr; the high priest was then directed to pay him the highest honours of the temple and to place the Sacred Sandals on his head. Râmânuja received them humbly and with tears of joy, [1]

[1] "Lord of the Universe," said the master, "is it meet for Thee to advance and welcome me, the meanest of your servants?"

when the Lord addressed him and said : "Be it known to all this day that we give you and your followers the Double Sovereignty—over the world of men and over the world of the celestials. Take charge of our House and manage it carefully."

Râmânuja's heart was too full for any expressions of thanks; he only said : "To hear is to obey," and then turning to Mahâ Pûrṇa, he touched his feet and exclaimed: "Do I not owe all this to my having taken refuge in your feet ?"

"Nay, not so," replied Peria Nambi, "it is but the fulfilment of the prophecy of Srî Saṭhakôpa in the stanza "கலியுகம்கெடுக்கண்டுகொண்மின்"; and, as if wishing to avoid any more compliments to himself, said : "But, don't you think that you had better set about the duties enjoined upon you by the Lord ?"

Râmânuja enters upon his Duties.

"Even so," replied Râmânuja, and proceeding to the Hall of Audience, sent for the servants of the temple, and acquainted himself with the details of their work and the complicated ceremonies of the Lord's House; he personally inspected the various departments and nothing escaped him. The refectory,[1] the sacred ornaments, the wardrobe, the garlands, the lamps, the daily worship, the claims and complaints of the various officials and servants, the repairs, the flower gardens, the groves, the pleasure grounds, the vehicles, verything came in for the minutest scrutiny and suggestions for simplification and improvement. He placed one of his disciples, Akaḷanka by name, in direct supervision

"Nay not so," replied the Lord, "you have come a greater distance to see me and what I have done is but a poor return. Long have I watched over Humanity and I am tired and would rest a while. Take thou the burden from off my shoulders and rule thou in my place. Men shall call you "Vibhûti Dvaya Nâyaka." (உடையவர்)—(*Prap*).

[1] Âṇḍân was placed in charge of it.—(*R. D. C.*)

over the servants and arranged that the festivals be celebrated punctually and in all their pomp and grandeur—the daily, the fortnightly, the monthly and the annual.[1]

Srî Saila Pûrna's First Visit.

Some time after, the Srî Vaishnava sent to Tirupati returned to Srîrangam, and touched the feet of Râmânuja. Râmânuja gathered from his looks that he had happy news to tell, and asked him to relate at length the details

---

1 (*a*) The master expressed a wish to Mahâ Pûrna that he disired to learn the Sacred Collect with the appropriate music and expression of feeling and was directed to Vara Ranga for instruction in the Tiruvâimoli and Peria Tiru Moli (composed by Srî Sathakôpa and Srî Parakâla.) The master remained with Vara Ranga as his disciple until he mastered them thoroughly. He trained many others in the art, opened a separate street in Srîrangam for them to reside in, and arranged they should sing and dance before the Lord on public occasions.

(*b*) There lived at Nichulâpuri (Urayoor, near Trichinopoly) a famous wrestler and athlete by name Dhanurdâsa. He was at the head of his profession and the members of it far and wide acknowledged his superiority and paid him annual tribute. He had a wife by name Hêmâmbâ (the golden hued), who was famed all over the land for her marvellous beauty. They loved each other passionately, and Dhanurdâsa passed his days and nights in a dream of bliss, ever gazing into the dark unfathomoble depths of her wonderful eyes. One day she expressed a desire to attend the Spring Festival at Srîrangam ; and her husband, to whom her slightest wish was law, joyfully accompanied her thither. But, for his life, he could not keep himself from gazing into her fair face and handsome eyes ; so he held a large umbrella over her and walked slowly and unsteadily by her side, never taking his eyes off her face and drinking in the sweet poison of her beauty. This novel sight attracted the attention of the numerous passers-by, who spared not their criticisms upon this ridiculous uxoriousness of the great athlete. The master and his disciples were returning to their matha from their morning bath when this strange spectacle met their eyes.

"Behold," exclaimed the master, "the might of love. It had laid its finger on that strong man there, the bravest of the brave, and he is, but a feeble reed in its ruthless hands. It has made him so far forget himself and the world that he is not ashamed to attend humbly on a woman who may be, for aught one knows, his wife or mistress. Well, this very day I shall make him the best beloved of my Lord and the envy of every one else." He proceeded to his Matha and sent for Dhanurdâsa.

of his mission. " I proceeded to Tirupati and communicated to Ṣrî Ṣaila Pûrṇa your message. ' I should have done this of myself,' said he, ' and I am really ashamed that I should have to be reminded of it. But better late than never. What a mighty intellect is Râmânuja and what a golden heart he has.'

The Master received him kindly, and gazing full into his face with those inscrutable eyes of his that seemed to reflect every passing phase of thought in his mind, said: " My good man, whence are you ? What has brought you hither ?

" Having heard him out, the Master said, " I hope you will not take it amiss if I give you a piece of advice which you seem to want so much. No one denies that Love is a terrible tyrant and neither strength nor valor nor learning nor power escapes his rod. But how could you so far forget yourself and what is due to Society as to perform the offices of love to a woman, be she ever so lovely, in open day, on the king's highroad, and in the presence of a vast concourse ? —and you the bravest of the brave, that has laughed in the face of Death and braved it only to find it flee away before you ? It was an unusual sight and has made me sad ; hence the great liberty I have taken in speaking to you about a subject extremely personal and delicate."

" I am neither love-sick, " humbly replied Dhanurdâsa, with folded palms, " nor a runner after strange women. The woman you saw is my wife. She is fair beyond all description ; and then her eyes !—they are so lovely, so dark, so bright, so unfathomable. When I look into their depths, I forget myself and the world, and am content to gaze my life away. It would break my heart if that dear face and those lovely eyes of hers were to be touched by the fierce rays of the Sun, and I could not avoid sheltering them from it. Lord, I have kept back nothing from you, and I await your orders."

" Suppose I were to introduce you to another person, whose eyes are lovelier, deeper, darker and more unfathomable by far than those of your love."

" What then ?" broke in Dhanurdâsa eagerly, " would I not consider myself the most blessed, if I can but be allowed to serve that person ever, if I can but look for ever into those dark depths."

" Well, come along," said the master, and forthwith took him to the presence of the Lord Ranganâtha. " There is he who is the Perfection of loveliness ; there is already another lover of his who has forestalled you and is graciously allowed to stand at his feet and discourse sweet music unto him. Look upon that Divine Beauty and compare it with that of the woman you love so well." Dhanurdâsa looked at those wonderful eyes and *lost himself*. The Lord too

We all set out for Kâlahasti and camped under a large tree that dipped its flowing branches in the crystal waters of a tank. Soon after, we saw Gôvinda come there to draw water for divine worship, and he was reciting stanzas in praise of Rudra. When he drew near, Ṣaila Pûrṇa said to him: 'What would it profit theẹ if thou serve ever so faithfully Him, whose matted locks are adorned with Konrai flowers?' Gôvinda smiled a reply and went away. 'The seed is sown,' exclaimed Ṣaila Pûrṇa, 'and the Lord will see to its growth. We shall come again to reap the harvest.' We then returned to Tirupati."

His Second Visit.

"Some time after we went back to Kâlahasti and halted under the same tree. Gôvinda came there as before, when Ṣaila Pûrṇa, acting upon a sudden idea, wrote on a palm-leaf a stanza from one of Yâmunâchârya's

---

regarded him with unusual favour as one in whom the Master took a personal interest, and the famous athlete and passionate lover found himself passing away from this world of space and time into the unfathomable depths of unconditioned existence. Purified of all earthly taints and entirely inaccessible to the calls of hunger and sleep, he spent his days in gazing into those Divine Eyes. The Master then sent for him and allowed him to partake of the holy water that had washed his feet and of the remains of his meal. Very soon, he was initiated into the True Faith and became one of the humblest and the best beloved of the Master's disciples. Hêmâmbâ was informed of what had taken place; and, casting off more quickly and easily the trammels of worldly life, she sought out the Master and prayed to be admitted into the fold. The Master of Compassion gladly took her in, and in a very short time she outstripped most of the other disciples in purity of devotion, holiness of life and acuteness of intellect. And Dhanurdâsa was the man whom the Master selected out of many for the responsible office of body-guard to the Lord Ranganâtha. He brought with him to the Master's feet, his nephews Vaṇḍa and Ṣuṇḍa, who requested and obtained permission to supply the Maṭha with the articles of daily consumption.—(*Prap.*)

(*c*) He abolished the Vaikhânasa mode of worship obtaining in the Temple and restored the Pâncharâtra mode, whose superior efficacy Yâmuna had so conclusively established in his "Âgama Prâmâṇya."

—(*Prap.*)

works[1] and threw it in his way. Gôvinda noticed it on his path, picked it up, and, casting his eyes over it, dropped it and went on his way. On his return he picked it up again and walked on, seemingly absorbed in thought. Approaching us, he said, 'Here is something that you have lost.'

Ṣaila Pûrṇa replied: "No; others may lose what they seem to possess so safely now; but what we have is something that we can never lose."

"Let be. How is it that all of you walk in the same path?"

"Do you not see that the road is good and plain?"

"It is strange. This is the first time that I ever hear of any paths for the liberated."

"This is the road that one should take if he has anything valuable about him."

"Well, you have come, it seems, to see some of your relations off?"

"No, no, we came to buy cattle."

"With the orthodox, the dust of the cow's feet is sacred and purifying, is it not?"

"True enough if the choice is well made."

"What difference does it make if the vertical becomes horizontal?"

"The same difference that exists between the natural and the artificial."

"These views seem to be very recent."

"No, no, they have the sanctity of age and the authority of the wise."

"Are there not some preliminaries to be settled?"

"Not so, there is no difficulty with the preliminaries. It is only about the ultimates that there is difference of opinion and room for discussion."[2]

---

1 The same that converted Râmânuja.—(*R. D. C.*)

2 Govinda: Is not the doctrine contained in this stanza, the one that you have abandoned?

Gôvinda replied not; but after gazing intently at Ṣaila Pûrṇa he went away shaking his head. 'I am sure of him. Our efforts have not been, after all, in vain,' said Ṣaila Pûrṇa, and we returned to the Holy Mount."

Here Râmânuja interrupted the narrator, and turning to Dâṣarathi and Srîvatsâṇka said: "Behold the might of my Master's word! They have sunk deep into Gôvinda's heart; but, to keep up appearances, he argued with Ṣaila Pûrṇa who maintained the wordy contest nobly. And being possessed of a keen logical acumen and wide learning, he saw the truth of the positions advanced by Ṣaila Pûrṇa and went away silent. The numerous passages in the

---

Ṣaila Pûrṇa: No. Some others hold certain opinions which, I know, they will very soon have to abandon. But my faith is unassailable, and once chosen, always holds good and true.

Gôvinda: Variety is the law of the Universe. You find no two things perfectly identical. And what raises us above the animal creation is but our reason and the faculty of independent thought. Why then, should you all follow one beaten path, like dumb cattle? Strike out a path for yourself, each one of you.

Ṣaila Pûrṇa:—When the road is good, safe, short and comfortable, he is a fool who would cut across, for the mere pleasure of taking a separate course.

Gôvinda: When one has merged himself into the All, what road is unsafe for him?

Ṣaila Pûrṇa: He that has something to lose, would, doubtless prefer this road; but a beggar is safe on all roads.

Gôvinda: You have come here, I believe, to bring some converts to my faith and stay here to see them off.

Ṣaila Pûrṇa: We came to take in converts to our religion.

[Gôvinda takes the expression Paṣu and plays upon it.] You have come to buy cattle, have you? Well the dust raised by the cattle's feet is considered as highly purifying, is it not? [Paṣu means cattle and in Ṣaivite terminology, the Jîvas, who are the Paṣu, the cattle of the Îṣvara, the Pati, the shepherd.] You have unconsciously acknowledged the superiority of our religion.

Ṣaila Pûrṇa: True, if the animals were well selected and of good breed. [He takes the expression literally and replies.] True it is that the dust of the feet of the Lord's servants is pure beyond all description; but it all depends upon whether they are the servants of the One Lord or of strange gods.

Srutis, Smritis and the Purâṇas that inculcate the dual relations of the individual and the supreme soul, the superior efficacy of the vertical caste-marks and the inferiority of Rudra to our Lord, would have rushed upon his mind like a flood and shaken his previous convictions. Else he is not a man to give in so easily. What a man is our Saila Pûrṇa ! Verily, no ordinary skill in argument or depth of learning would be of any use with our Gôvinda." But go on with your narration. I am curious to hear the result."

" How could it be otherwise than favourable ? Even inanimate objects rise high in the scale of progress when coming into contact with your sacred person or when favoured with a glance of your eyes. How could Gôvinda, doubly related to you and to Saila Pûrṇa, continue insensible to the greatness of the True Doctrine, and lead a life of spiritual darkness ? Now, Saila Pûrṇa once more set out to Kâlahasti and we encamped in a grove on the outskirts of the place.

The Reconversion of Gôvinda.

He was holding forth upon the inner meanings of the Sacred Collect, when Gôvinda, advancing into the grove,

---

Gôvinda : How are the vertical caste-marks of superior efficacy to the horizontal ?

Saila Pûrṇa : The same superiority of a good and straight road to a bad and tortuous one. The vertical caste-marks are enjoined on us by the Vêdas, the Sâstras and the Purâṇas ; whereas your authorities for the horizontal caste-marks are either made up, or far-fetched, twisted and unnatural.

Gôvinda : Yours seems to be a new-fangled doctrine.

Saila Pûrṇa : Nay, I can prove it the oldest and based upon those authorities recognised by you as sacred and orthodox.

Gôvinda : Well, that remains to be seen. We should discuss every point from the beginning to the end. One should not take up anything without having thoroughly acquainted himself with its antecedents.

Saila Pûrṇa : Nay, not so, we all go together a great part of the way ; it is only about the goal, the ultimates, that we differ and have to discuss.

got up a tree to gather flowers for divine worship. The decade beginning with திண்ணன்வீடு (II. 2) came in for explanation and comment. Gôvinda desisted from his gathering flowers and listened attentively to the first three stanzas; but when Ṣaila Pûrṇa came to explain the fourth stanza, at the words "Whose feet shall we lay flowers at? To whom shall we offer our worship? There is but one answer—To no other than the Lord Nârâyaṇa," Gôvinda jumped down from the tree, flung aside the flower-basket he had in his hands, cast away the garland of Rudrâksha beads he wore about his neck, and crying aloud, 'To no other,' fell at the feet of Ṣaila Pûrṇa.[1] 'Save me, O Lord, from perdition, even me who take refuge in Thy infinite mercy. I have long walked in darkness and conceived it to be the noon-day brilliance. You have opened my eyes to the Light and it behoves you to set my erring feet on the Path, and guide me to the footsteps of the throne of the Eternal. I have ignored the Lord of the Infinite worlds and followed the mendicant with the matted locks; I have ignored the lovely lotus-eyed One and run after him with eyes of fire. I have ignored Him of the open hand, who held the mountain aloft for his friends and followers to take shelter from the heavy rains, and laid myself at the feet of one who wanders about with the beggar's bowl of a human skull. I have ignored Him whose breast the Goddess of Prosperity adorns and humbled myself before a lonely have-nothing. I have ignored Him from whose feet springs the sacred Ganges and waited upon one who ever roams about the impure cremation ground.'

---

1 When Gôvinda was on the tree, Ṣaila Pûrṇa said to his disciples: "Vishṇu alone deserves to be worshipped."

"Why not others?" asked Gôvinda from the tree.

Ṣaila Pûrṇa gave the same reply. Thus was exchanged question and reply three times and then Gôvinda rushed down from the tree.—(*Prap*).

Ṣaila Pûrṇa turned to us and said: 'I have keenly examined his features and am sure that the time of his bondage has drawn to an end. Nothing stands between him and the grace of Âḷavandâr.' He then raised him up, warmly embraced him, and consoled him, to which we all listened with pleasure and amazement.

> 'And betwixt them blossomed up
> From out a common vein of memory
> Sweet household talk and phrases of the hearth,
> And far allusion, till the gracious dews
> Began to glisten and to fall.' *

By this time the news had reached the inhabitants of Kâlahasti, who had from the very first divined our intentions and were not very affectionately disposed towards us. They now advanced towards us in a large body and said to Ṣaila Pûrṇa: 'Does it become one of your age and position to entice away by foul means our best man and leader?'

'You would do better to put that question to your best man here, who thus allows himself to be enticed by his uncle. Our ways of life and our modes of thought have nothing in common with yours; and you will never find me trespassing upon your paths,' replied Ṣaila Pûrṇa.

They then took Gôvinda by the arm and said: 'Come, let us go away from here.'

Govinda shook them off roughly and cried out: 'How dare you touch me? Here is the key of your treasury and here the signet-ring. I have done with you now and for ever.'

'We knew all this yesterday,' said they, 'but we hoped that you could be persuaded to come back to us and were prepared to fight for it. But last night, the Lord of Kâlahasti appeared to us in our dreams and said: 'The Vedic Dharma is almost at its last gasp through the fierce

* Tennyson's 'Princess.'

attacks of the Bouddhas, the Chârvâkas and the Pâshaṇḍas, and as on a similar occasion, the Lord himself came down upon Earth to restore the Law as Dattâtrêya, the Holy Ascetic, so he has now sent down Ṣêsha, Garuḍa and his spirit of the Throne to incarnate as Râmânuja, Gôvinda and Yâmuna ; the Conch and the Discus are Dâṣarathi and Ṣrivatsânka and the other spirits about the Throne have likewise manifested themselves in human bodies. We approve of this ; and as Gôvinda was bent upon staying at Benares, we dissuaded him from it by appearing in his palm, and have kept him with us till now. Now the time is come for him to do his work ; keep him not from it. Therefore take him away with you. May all good go with him and may he serve you as well and as faithfully as he has served our Lord.'[1] They took affectionate leave of us and we joyfully returned to Tirupati.[2]

Ṣaila Pûrṇa had the necessary purificatory ceremonies performed over Gôvinda and duly initiated him into the Faith. Gôvinda now knows no other master but him, and has devoted himself heart and soul to his service.[3] I was in their delectable company till now, and Ṣaila Pûrṇa kindly ordered me to take to you news of the happy result of the mission you entrusted him with."

"You have accomplished your mission," replied the Master, "right well and faithfully, and you have our thanks for the same. Henceforth remain with me."

---

1 On the day that Gôvinda was converted, the Ṣaivites quarrelled with Ṣaila Pûrṇa and prevented him from going away. That night they had the dream ; and the next morning they came to Ṣaila Pûrṇa and told him of it.

2 Govinda's wife followed him into the Faith and was taken to Tirupati.—(*R.D.C.*)

3 Sometime after, he sent word to his brother, Bâla Gôvinda, to come to him and share with him his newly found Light—which he did. Bâla Govinda was born in the month of Tula, under the constellation Aṣvini.—(*Per.*)

CHAPTER XII.

Râmânuja and his Teachers: With Mahâ Pûrṇa.

Soon after, Râmânuja waited upon Mahâ Pûrṇa and touching his feet, said: "I was not allowed to sit at the feet of our great master; but you have amply made up for it, by allowing me to call myself your disciple. I pray you to initiate me into the inner teachings of the Doctrine."

"With great pleasure," replied Peria Nambi, and forthwith made him acquainted with the deeper mysteries of the Two Truths.[1] "Beyond all words is the greatness of the mantra; its might is unthinkable; it is the essence of all Vedic knowledge; it burns away all undesirable karmic affinities; it raises its devotee immeasurably in the scale of spiritual progress; everything good accrues to him and nothing evil comes near him; it is the key to Eternal Life and Bliss; and the happy possessor comes not again among men but to lead them to the footstool of the Lord of Mysteries. But there are some other aspects of it which I should like you should learn of Gôshṭhî Pûrṇa, one of the best beloved disciples of my Master."

With Gôshṭhî Pûrṇa.

Râmânuja lost no time in proceeding to Gôshṭhî Pûrṇa, and throwing himself at his feet, said: "Lord, deign to instruct me in the sacred mysteries of the Doctrine." Gôshṭhî Pûrṇa, wishing to test him and ascertain if his

He gave him his son Puṇḍarîkâksha for his disciple. He was born in the month of Mithuna, under the constellation Uttarâshâḍha. (*Prap.*)

1 The Sacred Two Truths.

(*a*) 'It is as an inexhaustible treasure to a beggar.'—*Âḷavandâr.*

(*b*) 'The teacher is the knower; the visible image of the Deity is the object of knowledge; and the Two Truths the means.'—*Puṇḍarîkâksha.*

(*c*) 'It gives back life unto the Jîva, bitten by the deadly serpent of Material existence.—*Râma Misra.*

eagerness for knowledge was strong enough, replied carelessly: "I shall think of it when I find some one qualified to receive it," and sent him away disappointed.

Sometime after Gôshṭẖî Pûrṇa came to Ṣrîrangam to be present at the Holy Festival and was taking leave of the Lord, when Ranganâtha called him back and said: "Initiate Râmânuja into the sacred mysteries."

"But, Lord, Thyself has instructed us otherwise. Hast thou not said: 'Initiate a pupil after he has remained with you for a year. Let him be one who has his self under perfect control and offers himself entirely and unreservedly to the service of his Guru'."

"Nay, there are exceptions. Râmânuja is no ordinary disciple. He is an ideal one and something more. So you need not hold back."

On his departure, he said to Râmânuja: "Go over to me at my place."

And the Master did so, but was sent away with the reply, "Come to me some other time." Thus did he put him off eighteen times, and still no word of instruction. In great grief Râmânuja returned to Ṣrîrangam; but no word of complaint escaped him.

Sometime after, one of the disciples of Gôshṭẖî Pûrṇa came to Ṣrîrangam and paid his respects to Râmânuja, and to him confided Râmânuja all his sorrow and said:

(*d*) 'It is a draught of the waters of Immortality to the parched throat of the thirsty Jîva.'—*Mâlâdhara.*

(*e*) 'As the mother's milk to the babe.'—*Gôshṭẖî Pûrṇa.*

(*f*) 'It is as the marital necklet to a chaste wife.'—*Mahâ Pûrṇa.*

(*g*) 'As the crown and the sceptre to a king.'—*Râmânuja.*

(*h*) 'It takes a condemned one from the dungeons and sets him upon a throne?—*Embâr.*

(*i*) 'You take to the Lord an offering of a lime fruit and get an empire in return for it.—*Kurukêṣa.*

(*j*) The 'Chintâmaṇi' (the celestial jewel that brings to its owner anything he may wish for) sought the palm of a blind beggar.—*Dhanurdâsâ.*

"It becomes not one whose sacred breast the ever-green garland adorns, it becomes not him who holds the thousand-rayed Discus;" still he accused not Gôshṯẖî Pûrṉa, but the Lord—so high did he hold His servants, as more sacred than Himself.

The Vaishṉava put the matter strongly and feelingly before Gôshṯẖî Pûrṉa, who, impressed at last with his sincerity and earnestness, said: "If it be as you say, let him come to me alone with his staff and water-gourd."

Râmânuja hurried to Gôshṯẖî Pûrṉa on the receipt of this welcome intelligence, accompanied by his inseparable twin disciples. They fell at the feet of Gôshṯẖî Pûrṉa, who remarked to the Master: "I asked you to come alone with your staff and water-pot; but why have you brought these?"

"Nay, my Lord, I have come alone; this Dâṣarathi is my staff and the other Ṣrîvatsânka is my water-pot."

Gôshṯẖî smiled at his great love towards his disciples, and said: "Let not what you now receive go farther than you three;" and initiated them into the mysteries of the Eight-lettered Mantra.

They were given leave to depart; but Râmânuja remained there; and the very next day proceeded to the temple of the Lord Saumya Nârâyaṉa in that place, and gathering together all the Vaishṉavas he could find, gave out to them the teachings he had received the previous day. Gôshṯẖî Pûrṉa was astounded when he heard of this, and, having sent for Râmânuja, said to him: "I strictly enjoined you not to divulge my instructions to you. Do I hear aright that you have given them out in public to a promiscuous crowd?"

"Even so, my Lord," replied Râmânuja, "and I did it, taking my refuge in your mercy and with your feet enshrined in my heart of hearts."

Gôshṭhi Pûrṇa was unable to make anything of it; the reply was, if possible, more inexcusable than the act itself. "Have you any idea of the consequences of your having wilfully chosen to disobey me?"

"Eternal perdition."

"You knew it and yet you courted it."

"No one that has taken refuge in you, would ever bestow a thought on what becomes of his unworthy self. I placed your sacred feet before the eye of my soul and taught these Vaishṇavas, who will in turn hand it down to posterity; they are thus your disciples and are in consequence ever freed from the bonds of material existence; is that nothing?"

Gôshṭhi Pûrṇa was at a loss for words and remained plunged in thought. "What a golden heart!" said he to himself. "What an entire abnegation of self! What a whole-souled devotion to the service of Humanity! And *he* calls me his *Master*! Verily, the Lord was not wrong in calling him a perfect disciple and something more. Yea, I am not fit to untie the latchets of his shoes." He then exclaimed: "Of a certainty, thou art *our Lord*, Mannâtha (எம்பெருமானார்) and no other. Come to my arms, Life of my Life;" and, embracing him warmly, added: "Is it the Lord Himself? This doctrine was till now known as the Vedic Doctrine, but from this moment it has become 'The Doctrine of Mannâtha'! I intended to impart to you one more Truth, the most sacred and the last. But you seemed satisfied and I did not like to volunteer."

"Nay, my Lord, to think that there was something wanting in what you taught me, would be doubting your sincerity; to refrain from questioning you on that head, would leave you under the impression that I had not sufficiently grasped the tenor of your instructions. I was athirst for knowledge, but was at a loss how to ask for it ! My heart has been much troubled."

" What a curious nature is yours. Come to me some time hence and that *alone.*"

" I obey, " replied Râmânuja, and left for Srîrangam.

Sometime after, he went back to Gôshthî Purna and awaited his pleasure. The latter led him to a room above and took careful precautions that no one approached the place. He then made Râmânuja swear by his feet that he would not divulge it *to any one whatsoever* and out of his great love and compassion initiated him into the secrets of the Charama Slôka, the last and the most precious teaching of our Lord Srî Krishna. " Bear well in mind the injunctions of the Lord Himself—'Never is this to be spoken to any one who is not self-controlled nor without devotion, nor to one who desireth not to listen or yet to one who speaketh evil of me. He who shall declare this supreme secret among my devotees, having shown the highest devotion for me, doubtless he shall come unto me' —and take care it falls not upon the ears of the profane. "

" Never would I be guilty of such a heinous sin ; but my follower and friend Srîvatsânka is as faithful a servant of the Lord as one could desire and I cannot withhold it from him."

" He may, as you say, be qualified to receive it ; but even in his case let him wait upon you for a year ; test well his sincerity and earnestness ; and if you are thoroughly satisfied with him, instruct him."

" Thy commands shall be obeyed," replied Râmânuja and took leave of him.

Now was Râmânuja the happy possessor of the Word of God—yea, His Last Word. Now was the beauty and grandeur of the glorious Doctrine of Surrender unveiled to his dazzled eyes; he took refuge in the grace of the Lord and rested all his burdens upon him; and unlike Arjuna, the recipient of the teachings of the Lord, he forgot them not, nor did his acts belie them; perfect peace descended upon his heart like the silent dew of heaven; the idea of Self dropped away from him as the slough off a serpent, and he saw himself as one with all Humanity.

Initiation of Âlvân.

Immediately upon his return, Srîvatsânka waited upon him and to him said Râmânuja: "It is only now that Âlavandâr's grace towards me has borne fruit; it is only now that his prayers to the Lord of Kânchî have been answered; it is only now that the Holy Gôshthi Pûrna has made me the Heir to Immortality. He has strictly enjoined me, even in your case, to require of you to wait upon me for a year and to initiate you thereafter if I am satisfied with your earnestness of purpose and sincerity of devotion."

Srîvatsânka withdrew in sorrow and said to himself: "To wait for a year! and presume upon the certainty of my stay in this body till then! I *will* have it, or I die." A bright idea flashed across his mind and he cried: "Now I have it; the Smritis lay it down that a month's fasting at the gates of one's Guru is equal in merit to waiting upon him for a year. Any how I have minimised the evil," and for a month he waited at the gates of Râmânuja's Matha, fasting and sleepless, but calm and serene as ever. Râmânuja came to know of it and, touched to the heart with his devotion and earnestness, imparted to him the Last Word.

Ândân's Apprenticeship.

Then Dâsarathi touched his feet and said: "Deign O Lord, to instruct me, even me."

"I requested permission of the Teacher for Srîvatsânka alone. I would advise you to go to the teacher yourself and pray for instruction" was the reply of the Blessed One.

Âṉḏân did so, and waited upon the Nambi for six months; but the teacher noticed him not. One day he casually remarked to Âṉḏân: "I remember to have seen you with Râmânuja."

"Even so, my Lord, I am Dâṣarathi."

"What then?"

"I pray to be initiated into the inner meanings of the Last Word."

"Well, shake yourself free of your pride of learning, pride of wealth, and pride of birth, and Mannâtha himself would lead you to the Truth." He then touched Âṉḏân's head with his feet and sent him away with the words: "Despair not."

Âṉḏan returned to Ṣrîrangam a sadder and a wiser man. Divested of all his pride, he stood before his Master, the very soul of humility, and related to him what transpired. Râmânuja turned to his disciples and said, "Behold! is it the same man who went away from here? He is now, verily, a humble labourer in the Lord's vineyard. Now shall I initiate you, my Âṉḏân; and now am I entitled to call you and Ṣrîvatsânka my staff and water-pot." [1]

---

[1] Râmânuja gave out the Ashṯâkshari to the Vaishṉavas assembled at the festival of Ṣrî Narasimha Swâmi. Gôshṯhî Pûrṉa was overjoyed to hear of it and sending for the Master, said: "The Lord Ranganâtha once directed me to initiate some deserving disciples into the mysteries of the Charama Ṣlôka. On my submitting to him the dearth of such persons, he promised to look out and send some. I am sure you are he and will gladly instruct you." He then gave the Master his own son Saumya Nârâyaṉa for a disciple. [Saumya Nârâyaṉa or Nârâyaṉa Dâsa was born in the month of Karkâṯika, under the constellation Ṣravaṉa.—[*Per.*] The Master did not ask permission for Âlvân or for anybody else; but Âlvân begged to be instructed when the Master was at Ṣrîrangam. When Âṉḏân requested him likewise, he flatly refused, and directed him to Gôshṯhi Pûrṉa.

Subsequently Gôshṭhi Pûrṇa happened to visit Ṣrîrangam and went over to the Maṭha of Râmânuja,

---

"I shall instruct Âlvân and no one else." When Âṇḍân was serving as a hand-maiden at the house of Attulâi's husband, he corrected a passage read by some disciples there. They flared up at such an insult; but, coming to know who he was, fell at his feet and begged him to return to the Master. When the Master took him back, he was satisfied that his pride was humbled; he named him Vaishṇava Dâsa, 'The footstool of the Vaishṇavas,' and instructed him forthwith.—(*Prap.*)

Gôshṭhi Pûrṇa, wishing to test Râmânuja's devotion and to impress him with the greatness and glory of the Mantra, sent him away 14 times. Then, when he was on a visit to Ṣrîrangam, Some Ṣrî Vaishṇavas remonstrated with him on his procedure; and when he pleaded the Lord's prohibition as his authority, Rangânatha directed him to instruct the Master. On his return to his place, he sent for Râmânuja, who went up with Âlvân, Âṇḍân and Varada Vishṇu Âchârya. He approached Gôshṭhi Pûrṇa all alone, and was instructed in the Ashṭâkshari and the Charama Ṣlôka.

The name 'Emberumânâr' (Mannâtha) was suggested by the grateful Vaishṇavas, whom the Blessed One had so unselfishly benefited; and Gôshṭhi Pûrṇa but confirmed it.—(*V. G.*)

When Râmânuja informed Gôshṭhi Pûrṇa that Peria Nambi had sent him for instruction in the Ashṭâkshari, the latter gladly proceeded to do so. The Master requested to be initiated into the secrets of the Charama Slôka; but Gôshṭhi Pûrṇa put him off eighteen times.

When, at last, he was allowed to come, he approached his teacher's residence reciting the Tiruppâvai (a poem by Âṇḍâl, forming a part of the Divya Prabandha); and when he came to the passage சீரார் வளையொலிப்பவந்து திறவாய் மகிழ்ந்து (18), "Open the door to me gladly, to the sweet music of the golden bracelets," Dêvaki Piraṭṭi, the daughter of Gôshṭhi Pûrṇa, happened to open the door. The Master whose thoughts were far away, prostrated himself before her. [He saw in her only the Divine Bride, to whom the request is made in the stanza.] She was naturally agitated and ran in to her father in great fear and trembling. "What is it?" inquired her father with great solicitude.

"It is the holy Râmânuja and he has saluted me," replied the lady.

"What is there in it to cause you so much agitation?" rejoined her father, with a smile; and when the Master came in, asked him: "Well it seems you are engaged in meditating upon the stanza உந்து மதகளிற்றன். Is it not so?"

When he had instructed the Master in the Charama Ṣlôka, Gôshṭhi Pûrṇa of his own accord, said: "Well, let me place in your hands the Last Word of all knowledge, human and divine. Do not concern yourself about the means of Liberation, but fix your thoughts on the

accompanied by Mâlâdhara, another pupil of Âḷavandâr.

goal and direct all your energies to the attainment thereof. Serve the Lord with all thy heart, with all thy soul and with all thy means. The Lord is not the Goal as has been taught, and service the means; but service is the means and the end."

And the next day the Master made a universal gift of the Ashṭakshari and the Charama Ṣlôka to the assembled Vaishṇavas. It was also a Râmânuja (Krishṇa, the younger brother of Balarâma) who gave out the Charama Ṣlôka, on a former occasion. But it was to remove the doubts of a single person (Arjuna) and that to him alone. He chose a very unfit subject for instruction in as much as he forgot them soon after, and had to be taught again. But here Râmânuja gave out the Great Secret to all men and through them to all posterity; those whom he taught were freed from the bonds of material existence and stood before the Lord.—(*R. D. G*; *Vârt.*)

"Six things there are," said Gôshṭhi Pûrṇa to Râmânuja, "that a Prapanna (one who has taken refuge in the Lord,) should avoid—

(i) Âṣrayaṇa Virôdhi: The idea of I-ness and Mine-ness; a concern for the result of one's acts; a slighting of the intercessory grace of the Divine Mother; suspicions as to the goal to be attained.

(ii) Ṣravaṇa Virôdhi: Being attracted to the scriptures and the teachings that speak of strange gods.

(iii) Anubhava Virôdhi: The tendency to utilise for one's own enjoyment the objects that ought to be dedicated to the service of the Lord.

(iv) Swarûpa Virôdhi: Setting one's self up as independent of the Lord.

(v) Paratva Virôdhi: Recognising strange gods as the Supreme Ruler.

(vi) Prâpti Virôdhi: Embracing the views of those that take their refuge in the Lord alone, ignoring the Divine Mother. (—*Vârt.*)

Nâthaumni: 'The portions of the Ashṭâkshari inculcate respectively, knowledge, dispassion, and devotion.'

Embâr: 'It teaches the dependence of the Individual self upon the Lord.'

Âṇḍân: 'The knowledge of one's primal nature, the inability to save one self, the devotion to the Supreme One.'

Kurukêṣa: 'The nature of the Lord.'

Piḻḻai Tiru Narayûr Arayar: 'The Goal.'

Nanjîyar: 'The uselessness of taking refuge in any other than the Lord.

Nampiḻḻai: 'The five truths: The nature of Brahman, the object of attainment; of the Individual self, the attainer; of the means of attainment; of the results thereof; and of the obstacles thereto.'

(*Vârt.*)

Râmânuja welcomed them reverently and stood before Nambi with joined hands, awaiting his pleasure. Gôshṯhi Pûrṉa turned to Mâlâdhara and said : " Kindly instruct Râmânuja in the inner meanings of the Sacred Collect (Divya Prabandha)."

"With great pleasure," replied Mâlâdhara and they took their leave.

With Mâlâdhara.

Mâlâdhara began his course of instruction soon after and explained the stanzas as he had heard them from Âḻavandâr; but Râmânuja failed not to amend them with some new and original expositions. " I have not heard my Master explain them thus. Your views are new and have not the sanction of authority," retorted Mâlâdhara. When they came to the stanza அறியாக்காலத்து (II. iii. 3) Mâlâdhara understood it as a complaint of the devotee against the Lord.

" Nay, not so," put in Râmânuja, " the stanzas before and after, all speak of the Lord's illimitable grace, and why should this alone mean anything else? I believe that the following construction of the passage would bring out the meaning more clearly and forcibly."[1]

" Nay nay," said Mâlâdhara, whose pride as a Teacher was touched, " this is a Viṣvâmitra creation. I have not heard Âḻavandâr explain it thus." And from that day he stopped the course of instruction.

This came to the ears of Gôshṯhi Pûrṉa, who hastened to Mâlâdhara and asked him: " How goes on your course of instruction with Râmânuja ?"

---

1 Mâlâdhara construed the passage thus :—' When I was in the womb, untouched by material intelligence, you initiated me into the mystery of my relation to and dependence upon you ; and later on, cast me into this prison of flesh, that has completely effaced the recollection of all previous knowledge.' But Râmânuja construed it otherwise :—" I was plunged in the profound depths of ignorance ; you sought me out even there and turned my feet towards your Throne, and my heart towards your service."

"Not very satisfactorily. He has his own comments upon almost every stanza, such as I have never heard from our Master; it was too much for me and I gave it up as hopeless. Look here, he interprets அறியாக்காலத்து as conveying an expression of gratitude!"

"Is it so," replied Gôshṭhî Pûrṇa with a smile; "I have heard our Master explain it that way. But, have you not, by this time, come to understand that Râmânuja's discipleship under you (for the matter of that under any one) is like that of Srî Krishṇa's under the sage Sândîpini; a mere matter of form? He could never say anything that had not been sanctioned by our Master. Never imagine that you are teaching him anything new. It is a great mystery. Look at him with the eyes of the spirit, as I have done, and you will understand."

He then proceeded to Râmânuja's Maṭha along with Mâlâdhara and Mahâ Pûrṇa, where they were reverently welcomed by the ascetic.[1] Turning to Mâlâdhara, Gôshṭhî Pûrṇa said: "Continue the course of instruction, and finish it *even if you have to await his leisure.*" And so he did.

But, on another occasion, Râmânuja again begged to differ on the rendering of a certain stanza and said: "I submit that Âḻavandâr would never have understood it thus." Mâlâdhara took the opportunity to test the words of Gôshṭhi Pûrṇa and replied: "You have never even set your eyes upon Âḻavandâr and yet you speak of his heart thoughts very familiarly. Am I to take your words on trust?"

"Nay, not so," rejoined Râmânuja modestly "I thought you might have known it, that I occupied

---

[1] Mâlâdhara complimented Râmânuja on the superior aptness of his rendering of the passage and lost no time in informing Gôshṭhî Pûrṇa and Mahâ Pûrṇa of the wonderful intuition of the Master.

—(*V. G.*)

the same relation to him as Êkalavya held towards Drôṇa."[1]

Mâlâdhara remained silent, recalling the earnest advice given by Gôshṭhi Pûrṇa. "This, verily, must be a Great One come down upon Earth for some noble end. Happy am I in being allowed to hear all that Âḻavandâr had not taught me," and in the excess of his joy and gratitude, he rose and reverently saluted Râmânuja.[2]

With Vara Ranga Gâyaka.*

When the course of instruction was ended, Mahâ Pûrṇa directed Râmânuja to wait upon Vara Ranga and learn under him some of the inner secrets of the Sacred Collect.

Râmânuja waited upon him for six months, prepared his nightly draught of milk in a very attractive way and rubbed him down with saffron paste when he came home tired from his performances before the Lord during the great Festivals. On one of these days he was attending upon him at his bath, when his quick eye noticed that the saffron paste was not to Vara Ranga's taste, and in a moment he took it off and, with fresh paste nicely prepared, he rubbed him again and led him to the bath. Vara Ranga's feeling overcame him at this unequalled devotion.

---

1 Êkalavya, the son of Hiraṇya Dhanus, the king of the Nishâdhas, came to Drôṇa for instruction in the science of archery. But Drôṇa accepted him not, as he was a Nishâdha (hunter) and as he (Drôṇa) was bound by a promise to the Pâṇḍava and the Kaurava princes not to take in any other pupil. Êkalavya reverently took leave of Drôṇa, and proceeding to his forest home, made a clay image of Drôṇa, worshipped it as if it were his master, and practised in its presence the use of the bow, day and night. In consequence of his exceptional reverence for his precepetor and of his devotion to his purpose, he mastered, in no time, the science of archery and became unrivalled in the use of arms.—(*Bhârata, Âdi Parva*, Chap. 134).

2 At the end of the course, Mâlâdhara gave the Master, his son Sundara Bâhu for a disciple.—(*Prap*).

Sundara Bâhu was born in the month of Mêsha, under the constellation Chitrâ.—(*Per*).

He could not find words for some time; and, even then, could but say: "My son, my son, you have stolen my heart away, and with it the inmost secrets thereof. What can I do for you in return for all this kindness and attention to a poor old man? I give my all, the bed-rock on which I rest my hope of salvation, when I initiate you into the last and the greatest mystery of our Faith. To the earnest disciple, the Teacher is the supreme Brahman; he is the most priceless treasure; desiring him, the disciple has nothing more to desire; he is the supreme goal on the Path; he is the highest Mystery and the last word of knowledge. He is the *summum bonum* of all well guided efforts; he is higher than the highest, dearer than the dearest, in that he confers on us the life eternal and leads us from the Darkness into the Light that irradiates the footsteps of the Throne of the Lord. He raised me from the depths of iniquity; he led my feet away from the paths of the wicked; he taught me to love the Lord, to take delight in his service, to dance before His Presence; he took me by the hand and led me into the realms of the unknown and the unknowable, the Great One. He who ensouls the tiniest atom as well as the mightiest universe walks upon the Earth as the Guru, the dispenser of Life and Light. He is the Way and he is the Life. Take thou thy refuge in him. Now no veil hides from your sight the Throne of the Almighty. It is right before you; reach it."[1]

---

1 Vara Ranga instructed the Master in the Stôtra Ratna and the Chatusslôki of Âlavandâr and conferred upon him the title "Lakshmaṇa Muni."—(*R.D.C.*)

The *V. G.* makes Râmânuja receive instruction from Vara Ranga and from Mâlâdhara afterwards. Vara Ranga instructed him in the inner meanings of the Tiruvâimoli (திருவாய்மொழி) and Kuṇṇinuṇchiru thâmbu கண்ணிநுண்சிறுத்தாம்பு of Madhurakavi.—(*V. G.*)

Having no son of his own, he gave the Master his brother Choṭṭa Nambi as a disciple.—(*Prap.*)

His son (எண்ணாச்சான்) Ennâchchân and his grandson (பிள்ளையப்பன்) Piḷḷaiyappan became, later on, the disciples of the Master.—(*Per*).

A Doubt.

Was it not enough for Râmânuja to have sought Mahâ Pûrṇa as his Guru? Why should he sit at the feet of so many? Why should they, on the other hand, seek him out and teach him? Nothing is more simple. Âḷavandâr, being prevented from teaching him directly, entrusted the various truths of the Doctrine to different pupils, according to their stage of progress and degree of receptivity; and Râmânuja had to wait upon them all and gather the scattered threads of the teachings. Yâmunâchârya had specially pointed out Râmânuja to his disciples as the future Teacher—in fact, the most glorious of the whole hierarchy, and had enjoined them to impart to him the secrets he had entrusted them with. So they sought him out and offered to teach him; it was necessary that they should be related to him anyhow, either as teacher or disciple. Those that went before him became dear to the Lord, as his teachers; those that came after him were dear to the Lord as his disciples. Râmânuja was the brightest gem-pendant in the rosary of the Pearls of Faith.

CHAPTER XIII.

Râmânuja: the Teacher.

It was about this time that Râmânuja composed the Gadya Traya[1] and Nitya Grantha,[2] clearly and irrefutably establishing the Lord Nârâyaṇa as the supreme Brahman; and disciples came to sit at his feet from far and near.

---

[1] Gadya Traya, Ṣaranâgati Gadya, Ṣri Ranga Gadya and Vaikuṇṭha Gadya, in prose; a treatise in praise of Nârâyaṇa, written for the use of his disciples.

[2] Nitya Grantha: ordinances relating to the daily worship of Nârâyaṇa.—(*V. C.*)

[3] It was about this time that the Master initiated Chêlânchalâmbâl (கொங்குப்பிராட்டி).

His Life Aimed At.

Meanwhile, the reforms he introduced into the temple worship, the strictness of discipline that he enforced and his perfect unassailability by any temptations, roused the temple officials against him, who had waxed fat and led an easy life under a more lenient regime. They very soon understood that they were never safe as long as Râmânuja was at the head of affairs, and there seemed no chance of his being otherwise. Death alone could remove him from his place, and death alone would make him powerless against them; and his death they set themselves to compass. His habits were very regular; he lived upon the food that he begged from the householders, and limited his visits to seven houses. So his enemies bribed one of the seven to poison his food; and the wretch ordered his wife to take it to Râmânuja when he should come to their house on his rounds. She stoutly refused, but, being horribly tortured to do it, she placed it before him and went away with a heavy heart.[1] He noticed it, whose keen eye

Ṣaila Pûrṇa had a son named Kurukêṣa ([Tamil]) born at Kurukai or Tiru Nagari, in the month of Tulâ under the constellation Pûrvâshâḍha. His disciple was ([Tamil]) Vishṇu Chitta (*Per.*) who, from his very boyhood lived, as it were, a life apart from the world; his greatest pleasure was to hear the Sacred Collect recited and explained. Later on, he drank in with eager ears the accounts of the Master, of his divine virtues, of his ever-growing fame, and looked forward to the day when he would stand in his holy presence. Praṇatârti Hara ([Tamil]) whose father's sister was the wife of Ṣaila Pûrṇa, failed not to remark the same during his visits to Ṣaila Pûrṇa, and obtained permission for Piḷḷân to seek insruction, along with him, at the hands of the Master. They were gladly accepted by the Holy One, and, after his departure, became the founders of famous schools. The celebrated Vêdânta Dêṣikar was a descendant of Praṇatârti Hara.—(*V. G.*)

[1] Placing the poisoned food before the Mâster, she prostrated herself before him and took the opportunity to slightly scratch with her finger-nails the feet of the Blessed One. Râmanuja took the hint and threw it to a dog that died in horrible agony. Thereafter, he fasted for a month.—(*Prap.*)

nothing could escape, and a little thought over it revealed to him the state of things; he threw away the poisoned food into the waters of the Cauvery and from that time he discontinued his rounds, preferring to fast rather than expose his life uselessly.

Somehow Gôshṭhî Pûrṇa came to know of this, and hurried to Ṣrîrangam with the utmost speed. Râmânuja advanced with his disciples to meet him, and came upon him at noon-day in the burning sands of the Cauvery. He fell at the feet of his Master and lay there until he should be ordered to rise, but Gôshṭhî Pûrṇa looked on in silent indifference. This was too much for his disciples, who, already indignant that their beloved Master was obliged to fast, were now all the more enraged to see his bare body roasting on the scorching sands, and what was worse still, their Master moved not, nor gave the least sign of discomfort. But who would dare to speak out or complain, when their Master set them the example?

Praṇatârti Hara: The Daring One.

There was one among them, however, whose devotion to his Master was stronger than the fear of his displeasure or the possible anger of his Master's Master. And Praṇatârti Hara (for that was the name of this beloved disciple) burst out in angry tones: "What an affectionate Master you are! You are a nice pair, you and your disciple here. What shall I call a man who throws a delicate garland of sweet-scented jasmine flowers into the blazing sun? You have had enough of respect shown you and even more;" and he raised his Master from the ground.[1]

On another occasion, they tried to poison the Master through the Holy water offered to him in the Sanctuary. The Holy One knew of it and drank it with a smile and was none the worse. After repeated attempts, they gave it up as hopeless, were forgiven by the Master, and behaved better.—(*Prap.*)

1 "You heart of flint! you Forelock. Do you seek to kill my

The others trembled with fear at the consequences of these bold words, and Râmânuja the most: but Gôshṭhî Pûrṇa looked at the bold one with a smile and said: "Really, my friend, you think me an unfeeling wretch and curse me out of the great love you bear for your Master, do you not? But he himself will tell you that you may travel far and not find any one that loves him so well and dearly as I do. I did but try you all. I wanted to see whether there was any one in this group that loved him better than his life here and his hopes of salvation hereafter, and you are he. You cast these to the winds when you spoke thus; and I honour you all the more for it. I entrust you with the care of his health, and his life, and I shall seek it at your hands, yea to the seventh generation. From this day you will prepare his meals yourself and trust no other to come near it. On your life be it."

"As my Lord wills," replied the favoured one; while the others looked on in shame and amazement.

Yajñamûrty the Great.

About this time, there lived at Benares a famous ascetic, by name Yajñamûrty, who, having worsted, in disputations, all the Pandits of those parts, lorded it over them in the pride of his learning and numerous following. Happening, on one occasion, to hear of Râmânuja and his marvellous learning, he resolved to measure himself against the Teacher; and very soon he presented himself at Srîrangam with his numerous disciples and the cart-loads of books that he had written. He then sought out Râmânuja and said: "Allow me the pleasure of arguing with you on the respective superiority of our faiths."

"Please yourself," replied the Teacher, "but what is to become of you in case you have the worst of it?"

---

beloved Master?" and he forthwith placed Râmânuja upon his back and lay in his place.—(*Prap*).

"I shall renounce my faith and adopt yours.[1]"

"And I, in my turn, shall give up writing anything thereafter, and humbly confess myself defeated."

The Famous Contest.

The contest was to be carried on for eighteen days. On the sixteenth, neither had gained any advantage over the other. The seventeenth day went against RÂmÂnuja; his arguments could make no way against the pitiless logic of his foe; and Yajñamûrty went away with visible signs of joy while RÂmÂnuja returned to his Maṯẖa with a heavy heart. He offered his usual worship to the image of the Lord VaradarÂja, and, falling at his feet, exclaimed in deep sorrow: "Lord of my life! My only hope now and for ever! This doctrine has been handed down to me by the great S̱rî Ṣaṯẖakôpa; his successors have proved themselves worthy of the trust by carefully preserving it and spreading it far and wide. And is this glorious Doctrine to die through *me*? Am *I* the black sheep, the tainted wether of the flock? What have I done, Lord, to deserve such a disgrace, to be handed down to posterity as the ill-starred destroyer of the Faith? Till now you allowed us to rejoice in the conviction, supported by facts, that you were the only Reality, and that your Divine Attributes were not a mere figment of the train; but now it has pleased Thee to choose *my* time to bring in a foe who blows up my position and scatters to the four winds all my arguments. And what pleases *you*, pleases *me* too; for *I* have no will but *thine*." He felt himself too sick at heart to relish any meals, and fell asleep thinking.

The Divine Interference.

When lo! the God of his heart appeared to him in his sleep and said to him with an affectionate smile:

---

[1] And place your Sandals on my head.—(*Prap.*)

" And so you have decided that I had played you false and given you over, bound hand and foot, into the hands of your enemies. Really, my dear, I thought you knew me too well to suspect me of deserting a friend in his need, and much more yourself. Well, well, 'live and learn' says the adage. Arise and grieve not. See you not that I have given you a disciple, and one of marvellous powers ? As to his arguments, recall to your memory Yâmunâ's criticisms of the Theory of Illusion.'

Râmânuja awoke in wonder and fear; and no sooner the red morn had kissed the cheeks of the mighty mountain-tops than he was up and busy offering the daily worship at the feet of the Lord that loved him so well. Then, recalling to his mind the main points of attack, he set out for the Hall of Disputation in triumphant anticipation of certain victory.

The eagle-eyes of his opponent failed not to remark the air of confidence and success in the features of Râmânuja, and he said to himself; " This man went home last evening dejected and crest-fallen ; but this morning he comes back with the air of a conqueror. There should have occurred something in the interval to have produced such a wonderful change ; verily, something supernatural has intervened, and it is useless to contend against it. Better give in with a good grace and be spared the shame of defeat ? "

The Victory.

He hastened to meet Râmânuja, fell at his astonished feet, and saying, " I acknowledge myself defeated, " reverently placed his sandals on his head.

" But why do you not continue your debate with me ? " asked the amazed Râmânuja.

" When the Lord himself," replied the other, in great humility, " deigns to interest himself on your behalf, I make no difference between you both. I am silenced, and I only pray to be taken as your disciple and have my eyes opened to the Light of Truth."

"You have guessed aright," rejoined the Master, "but still allow me to point out the following seven defects in the position you advanced yesterday[1] :—

1. *Âsrayânupapatti.*—The difficulty of finding something for this Avidyâ to reside in. Inasmuch as the selfhood of the individual self is itself projected by Avidyâ, it cannot reside in the individual self and thus give rise to the illusion for which it is held responsible. And, inasmuch as Brahman has the essential nature of self-luminous intelligence, it cannot be the seat of Avidyâ. This supposed Avidyâ therefore can have no abode to reside in.

2. *Tirodhâna Anupapatti.*—Avidyâ cannot conceal Brahman whose essential nature consists entirely of luminosity; for that would mean nothing other than the destruction of the essential nature of Brahman.

3. *Swarûpa Anupapatti.*—As long as it is a thing at all, it must either have the nature of a reality or the nature of an unreality. But it is not admitted to be a reality; and it cannot be an unreality, for as long as a real misguiding error, different from the Brahman himself, is not admitted, so long is it not possible to explain this theory of illusion.

4. *Anirvachanîyatva Anupapatti.*—It is not possible for the illusion-producing Avidyâ to be incapable of definition either as an entity or non-entity. All cognitions relate to entities or non-entities; and if it be held that the object of a cognition has neither the positive characteristics of an entity nor the negative characteristics of a

---

[1] For fuller information see Srî Bhâshya: Thibaut's Translation, pp. 102—147.—(*Comp.*)

Srî Bhâshya. Trans. Prof. M. Rangâchârya, Vol. 1, pp. xxxi-xxii.

non-entity, then all things may become the objects of all cognitions.

5. *Pramâṇa Anupapatti.*—There is no means of proof by which such an Avidyâ can be brought within the range of our cognition, neither by direct perception, nor inference, nor scriptural authority.

6. *Nivartaka Anupapatti.*—The cessation of ignorance cannot take place by means of the knowledge that has the attributeless Brahman for its object; for, such a knowledge is impossible, and cannot be the complete knowledge of truth.

7. *Nivritti Anupapatti*—The Avidyâ of the Advaitins is irremovable.

Yajñamûrthy's Conversion.

Yajñamûrthy was silenced; he broke to pieces his one-knotted staff, threw himself at the feet of Râmânuja, and begged him to invest him with the orange robe and the three-knotted staff.

Râmânuja gladly consented, and, having the necessary purificatory ceremonies performed over him, took him into the order and named him Dêvarâja Muni,[1] in remembrance of the favour shown him by the Lord Dêvarâja in connection with his conversion. They proceeded to the Sanctuary of the Lord Ranganâtha, where Dêvarâja Muni offered his worship to the Lord.

He then took him to his own Maṭha and, showing him the image of the Lord Varadârâja, said with a smile: "There is he that has brought you to my side." Dêvarâja Muni fell at the feet of Him from whom he derived his name, and poured forth his thanks for this unlooked for grace of the Lord. Râmânuja arranged

---

[1] **He was also named Dêvarâṭ Dêva Mannâtha (அருளாளப்பெருமாள் எம்பெருமானார்) a combination of the names of Varada (Dêvarâṭ Dêva) and the Master (Mannâtha).—(*R. D. C.*)**

suitable quarters for his friend[1] (for so he regarded him, more than as a disciple); sweet companionship grew between them through similarities of tastes and pursuits. In course of time, Râmânuja perfected him in all the essentials and details of the Doctrine, and had so much faith in his abilities and devotion to the Faith that he came to be his most confidential friend and adviser.

The Master's fame spread farther than before, and teachers of men came to him from all parts of the land for instruction. Among them were three—Yajñêṣa (எசசான்) the son of Choṭṭai Nambi, Toṉḏanoor Nambi, and Marudoor Nambi, who desired to become his pupils; but he made them over to Dêvarâja Muni. Dêvarâja was afraid of the responsibility, and said: "I am entirely unworthy of the trust, but accept it since he wills it so. Take your refuge in him and centre all your hopes of salvation in him alone."[2]

ANANTÂḺVÂN.

One day, the Teacher was commenting upon the decade in the Sacred Collect beginning with ஒழிவில்காலமெல்லாம்—and when he came to the line[3] சிந்துபூமகிழுந் திருவேங்கடம் (III. iii, 2.) remarked by the way: "Is there any one who is prepared to proceed to the Valley of Flowers, lay out a beautiful garden, and wait upon the Lord Venkaṭêṣa with a garland of flowers every day?" Anantârya rose up in the assembly, and, touching the Master's feet, said: "Be it mine the service. Grant it unto me, O Lord."

---

1 "He is my superior," said Râmânuja to himself, "in intellect, learning and wealth. He has not his equal in argument; and it is only by the grace of Varadarâja that his heart has been turned to the Good Law."—(*Prap.*)

2 The episode about the confusion of the two Lords comes in here later on.—(*Prap*). (*T. G*).

3 Tiruvâimoḻi, III, iii. 2.

The teacher took affectionate leave of him; and he forthwith repaired to Tirupati, laid out a splendid flower-garden, and named it 'Râmânuja,' and very soon grew as dear to Lord Venkaṭêsa as Kânchî Pûrṇa was to the Lord of Kânchî.

The Master's First Pilgrimage.

Meanwhile Râmânuja had finished the course of instruction on the Sacred Collect, and requested permission of the Lord Ranganâtha to pay his respects to Varadarâja and Venkaṭêsa. "Come back unto me quickly," said the Lord, and gave him reluctant permission.[1] He then set out on his tour of pilgrimage[2] and reached Kânchî.

---

[1] When he was about to start, a Ṣri Vaishṇava came up to him and said: "I would like that you direct your agent to supply me during your absence with the grain usually allowed me till now, by you, for conducting my household worship."

The Master gave him his signet-ring to take to Dhanurdâsa, who would see to it. The faithful body-guard fainted away on hearing that he was to be separated so long from his beloved Master. The messenger took the news to the Master, who gently rebuked him saying, "And so you had not the presence of mind to recite, in his hearing, the stanza [illegible]?—Thiruvritham: Stanza 9. Try it now at least." The effect was magical, for Dhanurdâsa thought over the message left him by the Master, so skilfully recited in the words of the stanza and was consoled.—(*R. D. C.*)

[2] He visited on his way the shrines of Tiru Veḷḷarai and Tirukkôilûr.—(*R. D. C.*)

From the latter place he sent word to his disciple Yajñêsa of the Eight Thousand, to make arrangements for himself and his company. This was delightful news to the wealthy Yajñêsa, and he set about preparing a grand reception for his Master; but as misfortune would have it, entirely forgot the messenger sent him by the Master. The latter waited and waited, hungry and footsore; and went back to the Holy One, who listened to him and made a note of it for future use.

The next day they started from the place and soon came upon branching roads. "Where do these lead to," asked they of some cowboys that stood near.

"This" said they pointing to one of the paths, "leads to the grand dwelling of Yajñêsa to whom the Great Ones of the world

At Kânchî.

He at once sought out Kânchî Pûrṇa, his "guide, philosopher and friend," and saluting him reverently,

---

resort. And this, "pointing to another, "takes one to the humble cottage of Varadârya, whom the meek and the holy seek."

"Well," said the Blessed One, "we are neither great men nor wealthy; we are mendicants and humble; and as such, like to like, let us seek out Varadârya."

Now the host was out on his daily round for alms, and his wife kept house for him. The Master and his group approached the house and knocked. Varada's wife made out, as if by intuition, that it was their Master, who had thus blessed their humble abode; but she had not a decent piece of cloth to cover herself, and was sitting behind closed doors, in consequence. She was in a terrible fix; on the one hand the sense of womanly modesty forbade her to go out as she was and welcome the Master; on the other hand, if she gave no sign of any one being in the house, the Master will go away unwelcomed and disappointed. So she solved the difficulty by clapping her hands; and the Master, guessing the situation, threw his head-cloth inside. Very soon, she came out dressed in it and reverently welcomed the Master, as far as her poor means would allow.

She would not send him away without entertaining him and his disciples, but she had not a pie to bless herself with, nor could her husband assist her in any way. She said to herself: "My Master has given me Light and Eternal Life. My parents gave me this body and the life that ensouls it; but the Holy One has made me the happy owner of immortality. He is my Lord, my God, my Law of Right and Wrong; and shall I stop at any sacrifice to discharge to him, as best I can, the deep obligation I am under to him? The Holy Parakâla had himself set me the example when he robbed and waylaid travellers to entertain Ṣri Vaishṇavâs. Nothing I have is too valuable to be offered up in his service—body, life, wealth, name, fame, virtue, children, friends. Now that I recollect it, there is a Vaiṣya of this place that has long cast looks of desire at me whenever he met me. Poor man! to be caught by this painted sepulchre containing nothing but filth and bones; well, well, I shall even go to him at once and consent to make over this body to him, if he would but give me the wherewithal to entertain my beloved Master and his followers. Lord! I take my refuge in Thee."

She requested the guests to rest a while; and proceeded straight to the Vaiṣya's dwelling, who was taken aback to see her there, and much more to hear of his good fortune. He could scarcely believe it —it was so sudden, so unlooked for. Very soon, his servants were conveying to Varadârya's house articles of every description, enough to

exclaimed, "Happy am I in that it has been given me to pay my respects to you again. What do I not owe

---

last the Master and his company for a year, for he knew that she would be as good as her word and would make him the happiest of men.

The Master directed Lashmi (for so was she named) to prepare meals for them, which she did in no time. They made themselves perfectly at home; and after dinner, the Blessed One began to discourse to his disciples. By this time, Varadârya came in, and was overjoyed to see his beloved Master and his disciples in his lowly cottage, and equally surprised to observe thay had been right royally entertained. Having welcomed his guests and paid them his respects, he sought out his wife, who solved what seemed to him an inexplicable mystery. His joy knew no bounds. "You are too good for me, wife of mine; your ready tact, your keenness of perception and unparalleled devotion has saved me my life, my honour; you have made an unheard of sacrifice to enable me to discharge my duty to my Master. May the Searcher of Hearts reward you as you deserve and keep evil away from you. To all the world you are my wife; but in my heart of hearts I bow to you and acknowledge my gratitude to you for having taught me, by example, how to discharge one's duty by her husband and by her master. And now I shall wait upon our guests."

The Master directed the happy pair to take holy water from him and partake of the remains of the meal, which they did with thankful hearts. She then took what remained of both to the Vaiṣya, whose wealth was used to such excellent purpose. He partook of the holy water and remains of the meal and became a changed man. His eyes were opened, his intuition was roused, and the latent germ of spirituality and devotion in his nature was developed and active. He fell at her feet and with tears and heart-rending sobs, begged to be pardoned for his heinous sin towards her, who was now to him holy as her namesake, the Divine Mother. She consoled him as best she could, and yielded to his humble prayers to be allowed to approach the Master and beseech instruction. So she had to inform the Holy One of the whole affair; and the Master was speechless with amazement—for he knew not which to admire more, the utter devotion of Lakshmi or the stranger selflessness of Varada. He kindly admitted the Vaiṣya into the Faith, who, rightly attributing his base nature to the pride of wealth, placed all his worldly goods at the feet of the Holy One, and would not hear of any refusal.

All the while the other disciple Yajñêṣa waited and waited, but no Master, nor any other message from him to explain the delay. In despair, he set out the next morning, making the most minute

you, my Lord? It was you that guided my erring steps to the feet of the Lord, and I only pray that I continue to deserve that kindness at your hands to the very end."

---

inquiries about the party, and was rewarded by locating them at Varadârya's humble residence. He fell at his feet, with tears of joy, and said: "Lord, I was expecting you every moment, and concluded that you had been unavoidably delayed or missed the way. But I am glad to find you here with my brother Varadârya; he could ill-afford to be so troubled; may I beg you to come to your own house over there?"

The Master calmly heard him out, and, fixing upon him those wondrous eyes of his that read into the very heart of men and Nature, said, in tones of reproof and sorrow: "Nay, we know you not; nor have we any other house here but the one we are now in. We remember to have had a disciple of ours somewhere here, by name Yajnêşa. We knew him as a good man and a meek one, ever intent upon serving the servants of the Lord, and sent word to him of our approach. But our messenger found him not; there was another of the same name, a wealthy man and a proud one—a vain dispenser of charity. The humble servants of the Lord are as dust in his eyes, and we are less than they. If you happen to be he, we say we know you not. We hold that a man may possess every other virtue under the sun, but none the less, take the shortest cut to perdition when he slights the servants of the Lord. With us, the servants of the Lord come in first, and then alone the Lord. Good Sir, my messenger has mistaken the man and has put the wrong one to much trouble and vexation. For which we beg to be excused."

"Oh Lord!" cried Yajñêşa, "I am lost," and fell down in a heap, as if struck by lightning. The prospective spiritual death seemed to be heralded by a present real physical dissolution. The Holy One raised him up kindly, and directed his disciples to sprinkle him with Holy Water; whereupon he revived and rose up—a sadder and wiser man. He stood before the Master in fear and shame; but the Blessed One looked upon him sweetly and said: "Nay, my friend, now that we look at you more closely, you seem to be our old disciple Yajnêşa, but a little changed. You would do well to bleach yourself white of some few stains that have fallen upon your garments, to be more presentable."

Yajñêşa took the hint, and from that day schooled himself in lowliness of heart and humility of life by washing the clothes of the Srî Vaishṇavas of the place—Brâhmaṇas and others—as a constant reminder of what he should do in the case of his own inner nature. On his return from Tirupati, the Master stayed with him and was magnificently entertained.—(*R. D. C.*; *Prap.*)

"Nay, nay, my friend, you honour me too much. I nave but obeyed the Lord's will in this, as in all things else. Really, I would be glad to see any one who would not help you and serve you to his utmost. Well, do you not wish to offer your worship at our Lord's feet?"

Râmânuja smiled at this delicate hint to avoid any further allusion to himself and replied: "I only waited for your permission, my Lord." They then proceeded to the Sanctuary and Nambi introduced him into the Lord's presence.

Before Varadarâja.

Râmânuja and his disciples fell at the feet of the Lord, and stood with bowed heads and joined hands, awaiting the pleasure of the Mighty One. "You have been a long time away from us," said the Lord to Râmânuja, "and we missed you ever so much."

"That can never be," replied our Teacher, "You were with me, enshrined in my heart of hearts. At the rosy morn and at the dewy eve, I stood in Thy Presence and laid my offerings at the feet of your image," and then, turning to Dêvarâja Muni who stood by his side, he said: "Behold Him who has brought us together. He took you from the realms of Darkness and led you into the regions of Light. You are the living proof that my Lord has not forgotten his humble servant, but thinks of him now and then. Grant me leave, O Lord, to proceed to the Holy Mount."

"Be it so. Ever remember that I am with those that are devoted to Me and My service. How do you find your new disciple, he who bears My name so worthily?"

"Nay, nay, my Lord, no disciple of mine is he. Indeed you promised me such a one, but you have, as usual, performed more than you promised. He is the friend of my heart, my right hand, my colleague."

"Glad am I that you are satisfied with my choice. May he serve Me as well as you do."

Dêvarâja Muni burst into tears at this supreme condescension and exclaimed: "Life of my Life, you are my stay here and my only hope hereafter. Who am I to be spoken of in the same breath with my Master there? I am but the humble instrument that obeys the Master's hand. Lord, I take my refuge in Thee and Thy servants." They then left the sacred Presence, and having taken an affectionate leave of Kânchî Pûrṇa were soon on their way to the sacred hill.

The Mysterious Guide.

Once they happened to lose their way, and sought information of a solitary labourer who was watering the fields. He set them on the right path and was taking leave of them, when Râmânuja suddenly fell at his feet with great reverence, and poured forth humble expressions of thanks and gratitude. His followers were taken aback at this, but instinctively did likewise; and when they were out of sight, he turned towards them and said: "I saw you were surprised at my saluting a common Ṣûdra, but you would have thought otherwise had you but known who that Great One was that disguised himself under that unassuming form." They clasped his feet and exclaimed in accents of deep repentance: "Pardon us, O Lord, for even so much as harbouring a glimmering suspicion of your acts."[1]

At Tirupati.

They soon reached Tirupati, and the Teacher duly offered his worship at the shrines of the ten Âlvârs that ever wait at the foot of the Mount. He stayed there for some days, continuing his course of instructions to his

---

[1] This took place on their way from Ghaṭikâchala.

disciples. Viṭṭhala Râya, the ruler of the place, was so much impressed by the grand and noble personality of our Teacher that he very soon became a convert to the Faith and one of the most zealous of his pupils, and Râmânuja permanently settled thirty of his pupils in that place.

Anantârya and the others on the Mount came to know of this and hastened down to the presence of the Teacher, to pray him to come up to offer his worship at the shrine of Ṣrî Venkaṭêṣa. " Nay, it is not meet that I should so defile the sacred precincts when the Holy Âlvârs themselves have remained at the foot of it, deeming it a desecration to set their feet on the Mount.[1] I shall worship the Lord from here and rest content with the presence of the Great Âlvârs."

" If such be your pleasure, O Lord," said Anantârya "no one of us shall ever dare to do so and it shall be strictly seen to that no other does it hereafter. " There he had our Teacher nicely; for he knew well that the Master would be the first to sacrifice himself if it would gain another any advantage, be it the slightest.

" Be it so," reluctantly replied Râmânuja, " I shall go up," and having purified himself suitably, he set out to ascend the hill.[2]

---

1 The Holy Mount was Ṣêsha himself, and, as such, the Âlvârs would not do it. But Râmânuja reconciled himself to it, as he was no other than the Divine Ananta.—(*Comp.*)

2 On the way he was met by a Ṣrî Vaishṇava who professed to have been sent by the Lord Venkaṭêṣa to welcome him and offered him the food placed before the Lord and a mango fruit. "Whose disciple may you be, " asked Râmânuja.

"Anantârya's."

"Kindly recite his distinctive verse." (தனியன்.) Each teacher has his own distinctive verse composed by his disciples or admirers, commemorating his virtues.—(*Comp.*)

" With great pleasure. I take my refuge in the Holy Anantârya, blessed with every spiritual perfection, whose glance dispels darkness

Srî Sailá Pûrna.

Srî Saila Pûrna met him half way with the holy water and the other honours; and Râmânuja embraced his uncle's feet, and exclaimed,[1] "Lord, Lord, is it meet that you should trouble yourself so much on account of my unworthy self? Could you not have sent these by one of your servants?"

"I might have done it and I sought high and low all over the Mount for any one whom I could call my servant; but I found no one whose master I am fit to be."

Our Teacher was abashed at this supreme humility and lowliness of heart and replied: "How long is it since I have forfeited the privilege to be called your footstool? Of a truth, it is not without reason that you are called the Keeper of the Lord's Heart."

Upper Tirupati.

They proceeded on their way, and when they were near the precincts of the temple, the temple officials, the Jeers, the Êkângis, and the Srî Vaishnavâs of the place came to meet him, accompanied by the paraphernalia of the temple. He bathed in the waters of the sacred tank, adorned himself with the Sacred Badges, and, going the round of the four streets, paid his worship at the shrines of the Holy Ones that dotted them. On his way he stopped to visit the flower-garden named after him and turning to Anantârya said: "You have proved yourself a true son and a worthy disciple; and amply have you rewarded

---

of heart and in whom the afflicted find a sure and safe refuge." The next moment he vanished from sight, in a streak of lightning.

"It is the Mighty One himself, that has thus blessed the meanest of his servants," said the Master in awe.—(*R.D.C.*)

[1] "It was thy kindly face that beamed upon me in the cradle; and thy grace has made me what I am. Grant me that I deserve it to the very end, and pardon me for having delayed so long to pay my respects to your holy feet."—(*V.G.*)

me for having brought you up." He then entered the temple and was very soon conducted to the Holy of the Holies.

Before Venkatêsa.

He stood before the Sacred Presence and bathed the feet of the Lord with his tears of joy, exclaiming :" Lord, long have I sought for peace and rest, through births innumerable, through joys worldly and divine, and found it at last in the shadow of Thy Sacred feet." Srî Venkatêsa then directed that the highest honours of the temple be shown him. He accepted them humbly and was given permission to depart. He prepared to descend at once saying, " This is the Mount of the Celestials; Holy Sages, Great Beings, and the Angels of the Sacred Presence reside on it, and it is not meet that we should presume to be in their company."

" Nay, not so," replied Saila Pûrna, " the sacred books enjoin us to abide at Holy places for three days at the least."

" True, it is even so," assented Râmânuja, and stayed there on the Mount for three days, observing a strict fast and lost in deep Samâdhi. At the end of that time, he proceeded to the Sanctuary of the Lord, and stood with joined hands before him; the Lord spoke unto him and said, " Have we not, at our mansion in the south, made over to you and your followers the sovereignty of this world and the next ? "

' Even so, my Lord," humbly replied Râmânuja; " Blessed am I and my biethern here to hear it once again from your divine lips."

The Master receives instructions in the Râmâyana.

They then descended the Mount and our Teacher broke his fast at the house of Saila Pûrna. He remained there for a year, receiving instructions in the inner meanings of the Sacred Epic, the Râmâyaṇa.[1]

GÔVINDA.

He failed not to remark that Gôvinda, his brother and friend, was extremely devoted to Ṣaila Pûrṇa, so much so that it became a passion with him. His hand assisted in every detail of the household work, and his keen eyes were ever on his Master, ready to anticipate his least wishes. Râmânuja's heart was glad at the sight of such whole-souled devotion, and he mentally decided to ask him of Ṣaila Pûrṇa.

How to make a Bed.

One day Râmânuja remarked that Gôvinda, after making his Master's bed, laid himself on it for a while and then went away. He was shocked beyond measure and mentioned the incident to Ṣaila Pûrṇa. The latter sent for Gôvinda and said to him. "Well, my son, I hear that you laid yourself on the bed you have made for me; is it so?"

"It is even so, my Lord; I do it every day."

"What? Every day? Do you know the consequences of such a disrespect towards your guru?"

"Sure enough; the deepest and the darkest hell."

"You know it and yet chose to act so."

"Yes, my Lord; and I believe my election is not wrong; for, if I could but secure you a sound sleep of nights, undisturbed by any roughness of bed, or any worrying of insects, I would deem myself happy and fortunate in being allowed to suffer in hell for ever."

---

1 He requested the Master to accept as disciples his two sons—Ṣaila Pûrṇa the younger, born in the month of Vrishâbha, under the star Viṣâkha (*Per.*) and Piḷḷân; he laid special stress on the peculiar nature of Piḷḷân and recommended him to his care.—(*V.G.*)

Ṣaila Pûrṇa and Râmânuja felt the tears starting from their eyes at the sight of such unheard-of self-sacrifice and could not find words to praise the devotion of Gôvinda.

The Friend of All.

Another day, Râmânuja was walking through the gardens adjoining the house of Ṣaila Pûrṇa, when he observed from a distance Gôvinda insert his hands into the jaws of a serpent, bathe and go about his service. He called out to his brother and asked him what it was. "I saw," replied Govinda, "a serpent in great pain, hanging out its tongue; it had run a thorn into it. I extracted it and was glad to see that it gave him much relief." Râmânuja was mightily pleased at heart and warmly applauded his compassion to his dumb brethren, even to the most deadly.

An Odd Gift.

The year drew to an end all too soon, and our Teacher said to Ṣaila Pûrṇa: "Master, allow me to depart for Ṣrîrangam from which I have been too long away."

"Be it so," sorrowfully replied his uncle: "I shall not keep you from the service of the Lord. You have come far and stayed long with me and have gladdened my heart. I am very sorry I cannot do anything for you in return."

"If my Lord is pleased to grant a boon to his servant, he would even make bold to ask for Gôvinda, whom, at my request, you have rescued from darkness and admitted into the bands of the Faithful. He would be of invaluable assistance to me and serve the Lord better than many." "Really, I am fortunate in possessing something you can ask for. You but remind me of what I ought to have done long ago, and I forget I simply held him in trust for you."

He then sent for Gôvinda and, in all formality, made a gift of him to the Master, saying : "Gôvinda, this day I have given you to Râmânuja to serve him as faithfully as you have done me. See that you deserve his friendship and grace." Râmânuja joyfully accepted the gift, and, rendering thanks to his Master, took Gôvinda with him and left for Kânchî.

He visited the sacred shrines on the way and offered his worship to the Lord therein; in course of time, he reached Kânchî and stayed for some time with Kânchî Pûrṇa.

A Deserter.

Meanwhile, he came to notice that Gôvinda pined after Ṣaila Pûrṇa and was wasting away. So he called him to his side and said affectionately: "Gôvinda, I think it would do your heart good to pay a visit to Ṣrî Ṣaila Pûrṇa." Gôvinda was ashamed to think that Râmânuja had discovered his weakness and shyly said : "Even so, my Lord, but I dared not ask it."

He flew back on the wings of speed and presented himself before the gates of Ṣaila Pûrṇa. His uncle was informed of this and sent back this reply: "What does the madman here ? Tell him I do not know him." Here his wife interfered and said: "He has come far and is tired and footsore. It would not be amiss if you allow him to see you and give him a meal. It will so gladden his heart."

"Wife," exclaimed Ṣaila Pûrṇa in angry tones, "You know not. Shall I go back upon my gift and encourage deserters ? No one is bound to feed cattle that have been sold to others. Send the idiot about his business and that quickly."

Gôvinda heard this in blank despair, and returned to Râmânuja a sadder and a wiser man. Our Teacher praised the uprightness and purity of intention of Ṣaila Pûrṇa; and, keeping Gôvinda ever with him, very soon won his love and devotion by his affection, greatness of heart and nobility of soul; so much so that Gôvinda never for once in his after life had reason to regret having been made over to his brother; on the other hand, he thanked the Lord every moment of his existence for having sent to him this blessing in disguise.

Back at Srîrangam.

The Master then took leave of Kânchî Pûrṇa and went back to Srîrangam, where the whole place came out to meet and welcome their Master after his long stay away from them. He presented himself before the Lord and was welcomed back by these words: "So you have come at last. Really, you have been a long time at it."

"Lord," replied Râmânuja, "was I ever really away from you? Nay, I was closer to your heart, in that I had nothing else to divert my attention. Grant me that I deserve the same gracious remembrance throughout." He then returned to his Maṭha and took up his old round of duties.[1]

CHAPTER XIV.

Râmânuja and his Disciples: Gôvinda.

Gôvinda was ever in attendance upon his Master.[2] Lectures, expositions, disputations, conversations, he never

---

1 After he became a Sanyâsin, he remained for some time at Kânchî teaching many disciples. From this place he went to Tirupati and delivered many discourses on Vêdânta in the temple of Srî Venkaṭêsa in Upper Tirupati. He there reorganised the worship of Srî Venkaṭêsa. He visited the sacred places of Southern India and the Vishṇu Temples therein, preaching to multitudes and initiating many persons, and finally settled himself for some time at Srîrangam. —(*V.C.*)

2 His brother Bâla Gôvinda and his mother came to live with him at Srîrangam where the Master arranged lodgings for them. Bâla Gôvinda discharged the duties of a householder; whereas Gôvinda, though his wife lived with him, was a Brahmachârin.—(*Comp.*)

missed them; he passed his nights in holding forth to his admiring co-disciples on the divine virtues of the Master or in blissful contemplation of them. He knew no fatigue and almost did without sleep. One day they were assembled together and the talk happened to turn upon Gôvinda. The other disciples warmly praised his wide learning, his deep intuition, his supreme devotion to the Lord and to his Master, and his unparalleled indifference to the world and its fleeting joys.

When to Praise Oneself.

To the surprise of all, Gôvinda joined them and lauded himself louder than any, Râmânuja, no less astonished at this, turned to him and said: "What is this, Gôvinda? True it is that you deserve what is said of you, and much more, but it would speak better of you if the expressions of approval came from others, and if you modestly declared yourself entirely unworthy of them. I scarcely expected it of you that you would blow your own trumpet."

But Gôvinda, nothing abashed, replied with a smile: "Lord, when these my brethren praised me they really praised the man who was in Kâlahasty, worshipping strange gods and delighting in darkness; for the qualities they ascribe to me I had even then. But, Lord, you came down upon Earth to lead me, as I believe, to the very footsteps of the Eternal. *Then*, I was the lowest among the low, and *now* you have seated me higher than the highest. Can I not then boldly affirm it and challenge anybody in this world below and in the worlds above to dispute with me the crown of bliss and glory you have placed on my brows? These my friends knew but imperfectly the extent of your kindness towards me and your disinterested efforts on my behalf. And who but I have a right to applaud it? If I praised myself, I but glorified the Divine Master in whose presence I stand, and through whose illimitable grace I and these souls have shaken off the dust of material existence from our feet and revel in the delights of supreme wisdom and Eternal service to Him and to those that are dear to Him. If I have erred, I beg to be corrected."

What could the Master say to such perfect devotion? Tears of joy coursed down his cheeks, and taking Gôvinda to his arms, he cried: "Well hast thou done, my friend and brother, and richly hast thou deserved it. Pray for me to the Lord that I too should become as simple and as pure-hearted as thyself. Alas! How far I am from it!"

Before a House of Ill-Fame.

Another day, a Srî Vaishnava came upon Gôvinda standing speechless and oblivious to all his surroundings before the house of a nautch-girl of the temple (one of the Master's disciples)—a house of ill-fame. He even forgot that it was time for him to perform his daily prayers—a duty no Brâhmana would neglect, however worldly he might be, and however low he might have sunk. He reported it to the Master, who at once questioned Gôvinda about it. "Most true my Lord; the sweet strains of the song of praise of my Master ravished my heart and I forgot myself in the contemplation of His divine graces, suggested to me by the association of ideas?"

"True it is that they were singing the song of praise," put in the Vaishnava Brâhmana. Râmânuja stood speechless, wondering at the grand nature of the Personality that was too deep even for him.

Gôvinda and his Wife.

As said before, Gôvinda did not sleep of nights; nor was he at any time alone. The Golden-hued Person in the Solar Orb and in the Ether of the Heart was to him a living reality, ever illuminating every thing around with his refulgent rays and dispelling all darkness, spiritual and physical. He was ever in his presence and merged in the contemplation of the divine glory, while his personality was absorbed in the service of his beloved Master.

One day his mother came to him and said : "My dear, you are sadly neglecting your duty by your wife. Know you not that it is the prime obligation laid upon every Brâhmaṇa, to perpetuate his line, and see he leaves behind him a successor to take up his work ? "

" Be it so, " replied he. " Let her come to me when it is dark and when I am alone. "

She waited and waited, but could not come upon him as he desired her to do. She then took this to the Master, who sent for Gôvinda, and said to him :

" Gôvinda, you neglect your duty by your wife ; see that you are not wanting in it. "

" As my Lord wills it, " replied he ; and one auspicious night, he sent for his wife :

A Strange Bridal-Night.

but, strange to say, instead of spending it with her in the delights of Love, he caused to unfold before her wondering eyes the Divine Glory of the Lord in the Heart and talked the night away in sweet discourse on the greatness and compassion of the Lord of Love and Life. His mother came to know of this and mildly remonstrated with her son about his strange behaviour.

" What ! Dare I pollute the Holy Sanctuary of the Lord in the Heart, with thoughts carnal and impure? Dare I draw into the Light of the Supreme the foul things of darkness? Alas! I sought for darkness and solitude. But the Lord is ever with me and never can there be darkness where he is, nor solitude."

The by-standers took this information to the Master who said to Gôvinda, smiling: "How did you pass the night?"

"In the search-light of the Inner Ruler, I could not find the darkness and solitude necessary for the purpose."

"If it be that your dispassion towards the world and its doings is so marked, why do you not take orders and follow the natural bent of your heart? You would then be freer to work for Humanity."

"It has been my heart's wish for a long time, but I dare not ask it of my Master, lest he should be displeased with me, and think me as yet unfit to take up the heavy responsibility."

EMBÂR.

"None would doubt it, least myself," replied the Master; forthwith he invested Gôvinda with the staff and the orange robes, and joyfully welcomed him as a fellow-labourer in the Lord's vineyard. "I shall give you my own name," said he, "and shall think myself honoured by your accepting it."

"No, no, my Lord," cried Gôvinda in great consternation. "Can there be a greater sacrilege than that I, who am less than the dust under thy Holy Feet, should have the audacity to wear the same name as thyself? Yours is but a cruel kindness. I am all too weak and unworthy to bear it. Let me have something safer."

"Be it as you desire," replied the Master, "I shall only shorten it for your sake, and you shall henceforth be known among the Elect as Embâr."

Which Lord?

Some time after, two Vaishṉavâs travelled from the west to sit at the feet of the Master. They entered the town and asked a passer-by to direct them to the Maṯha of our Lord.

"Which?" replied the person addressed to.

"What!" asked they in amazement: "Are there two of them, then? How does it come that the Doctrine has two teachers? A secession! and that, so soon!"

"No, no," rejoined he. "The Lord save us from such a mishap. Know you not that there is the Lord Dêvarâjamuni too?"

"Now, we have never heard of him, nor do we much care. We would be guided to the Maṯẖa of our Lord Râmânujamuni."

"Ah! I thought you knew," rejoined he, and directed them forthwith.

This came to the ears of him who was the unconscious cause of all this confusion, and disturbed him greatly. "Alas! I owe it all to myself; I have sinned against my Master in that I have lived away from him and gave room for men to speak of me on the same footing with the Holy One."

He caused his Maṯẖa to be levelled to the ground, and, falling at the Master's feet sobbed out: "Lord, Lord, is it not enough that this child had gone astray from the light of thy grace and wandered far in the darkness, ever so long? And how long, O Lord, how long dost thou mean to keep me aloof?"

"What is this,?" asked the Master in utter bewilderment; whereupon Dêvarâja then related the incident in all its details. Râmânuja heard him out in silence and said: "What then do you want me to do?"

"From this moment let me remain with you for ever and devote myself wholly to your service."

"Be it as you desire," assented the Master, and from that moment they were inseparable.

Dêvarâjamuni.

Râmânuja knew nothing that he did not impart to his friend; so that in a very short time, Dêvarâja had very little to learn from any. His name lives down to all ages in the splendid service he did to humanity—his monumental works, 'Gñâna Sâra and Pramêya Sâra.' In these works he has placed within the easy reach of all, nay, even the women and the non-initiated, the precious treasures of the Doctrine, that lie imbedded in the sacred Scriptures of our land. And he has left on record that famous dictum of his, the sum and substance of all knowledge, human and divine, and the sweet balm of comfort to many a tortured heart—"*To the true disciple the Master is the supreme Brahman; service to him is the end and aim of his existence.*"

THE SRÎ BHÂSHYA.

Now the Master thought the time had come for him to carry out his Master's last wishes—wishes unspoken, but all the more sacred in the eyes of Râmânuja. He called his friends and disciples together and said to them: "Now I shall set myself to redeem the *first* promise I made to my Master. The world has long enough been led by false lights and torn by conflicting sects, each claiming that its broken piece of glass reflected the Light Eternal. The adherents of the Illusion Theory contend that the knowledge arising from the meditation of the Great Sentences is the surest means to liberation; others, that knowledge and works should go hand in hand; but the Great Teachers have always understood that work is an inevitable element of knowledge, that it really connotes the acts of knowing, meditation, and active realisation, and that the Path to the throne of the Eternal lies through knowledge purified by Bhakti and intensified by Upâsana; and I shall, to the best of my humble abilities, re-embody these ancient truths in a commentary on the Brahma Sûtras of Srî Vêda Vyâsa, the incarnation of the Lord Himself."[1]

"Who," cried all of them with joy, "more capable than thou, O Lord, of Wisdom! It will be a grateful offering at the feet of the Holy Âḷavandâr and prove a perennial fountain whose cool waters of immortality will slake the burning thirst of many a parched throat and blackened lip."[2] The Master turned to Srîvatsânka who stood by—when was he not?—and said: "Take it down as I dictate; but write not a word that you do not approve."

---

1 There were many teachers of the Visishṭâdwaita philosophy before the time of Râmânuja:—

(*a*) Bôdhâyana—a Rishi and the disciple of Vyâsa. He left behind him a great commentary on the Brahma Sûtras, in 100,000 grandhas. He is referred to both by Sankara and Râmânuja.

(*b*) Dramidâchârya—the author of a 'Dramida Bhâshya' on the Brahma Sûtras (also of a Tîka on the above.—(*Pal.*)

(*c*) Tanka or Brahmânandi—also called Vâkyakâra—was the author of a Vârtika on the Brahma Sûtras.

(*d*) Guhadêvâchârya.

(*e*) Âchârya Bhâruchi (referred to by Vijñaêsvara in his Mitâkshara) the author of a commentary on the Brahma Sûtras.

(*f*) Bhagavat Srîvatsânka Misra, a very old, if not the oldest, Bhâshyakâra on the Brahma Sûtras.—(*Pal.*)

(*g*) Nâthamuni—the author of Nyâya Tatva, a philosophical treatise on the Visishṭâdwaita system and of Yôga Rahasya, on the secret doctrine contained in the Yôga system. He lived in the 8th century A. D.

(*h*) Yâmunâchârya—the author of Samvit Siddhi, Îsvara Siddhi and Âtma Siddhi, Âgama Prâmânya, etc. He lived about the beginning of the 11th century A. D.—(*V.C.*)

2 He was informed that there was preserved in the famous Sarasvatî Bhâṇḍâra at Srînagar, Kashmir, a copy of the abridgement of Bôdhâyana Vritti in 25,000 grandhas (the original was a voluminous work of 2,000,000 grandhas) and proceeded thither with Âîvâñ, (Âṇḍân, Varada Vishṇu Âchârya, Embâr and the others—*R.D.C.*) to have a look at it. He requested the ruler of that country to allow him to have it for some time; but the Pandits of the place, whom he had worsted in argument, induced the king to refuse him. Whereupon the Blessed One asked and obtained permission to read through

And so it went on day after day. On one occasion, it so happened that the Master came to a Sûtra that dealt with the question: "Is the individual Ego a knower?" and, commenting upon it, his words gave room for others to misunderstand it that the Jîva was a knower but not dependent upon the Lord. Such a status was in no way different from an identification of the Individuality with the Personality and was plainly heterodox.

---

it once, as his enemies were sure he could in no way profit by a single reading of such a voluminous work. But they reckoned without their host; the Master had Âlvân to read to him the Vṛitti at nights and within a month they were ready to start for Ṣrîrangam. The ruler of the place was greatly impressed with the deep erudition, the holy life, and the sincere earnestness of the Master, and permitted him to take the book along with him. But this got to the ears of the Pandits who followed the party and stole away the precious work. It was brought to the notice of the Master, who regretted the loss of such a useful aid in the composition of his Bhâshya.

"I believe," humbly submitted Âlvân, "I can remedy that misfortune a little way. Where would my Lord have me recite the Vṛitti from the beginning to the end, here or between the Two Rivers?"

The Master gave him one of his rare smiles and said: "I knew as much all along; but I desired to have it confirmed by your own lips, for the benefit of our friends that know you not as well."—(*Prap*: *V.G.*, *Pal.*)

But the *R.D.C.* differs from the above account in the following respects:—

(1) The Master composed his Bhâshya, after his return from his grand tour throughout India, and not before.

(2) During his tour, he visits Ṣrînagar and defeats the Pandits therein, the Ruler of the place presiding over the disputations as Umpire. He is asked to verify his authorities and refers to the works of the later teachers based upon Bôdhâyana's Vṛitti. The King sends for the works and is surprised to find them correct in every point.

(3) He then allows the Master to read through the work *once*.

(4) He requests him to put his views in writing, to see whether the image of Sarasvati in the Library would accept it. The Master composes the Vêdânta Sâra in one night and has it placed in the hands of Sarasvati. The King and the Pandits are struck with awe to find it on her head, when they opened the doors again.

(5) She asks him to explain the Kapyâsa Ṣruti and accepts his explanation in preference to Ṣankara's.

The Master at fault.

So Srîvatsâ kept quiet and wrote not.

The Master, whose mind was otherwise engaged, chanced to remark it, and said: "Write on."

But Âlvân seemed not to listen.

The Master, considerably put out at this unusual obstinacy, struck him with his foot and cried: "Get out;" and Âlvân lay where he fell.

The Master left the place, muttering to himself: "Then you had better write the commentary yourself."

The others remained awe-struck at this unwonted display of temper and, when the Master had gone away from among them, went up to Âlvân where he lay and said: "The Master is displeased with you and has spurned you away. What do you now mean to do?"

"*Mean*!" cried Âlvân with a laugh, "What have I to do with *meaning*? I am the property of the Master and shall lie where I am thrown. It concerns me not."

Meanwhile the Master thought over the passage and came to understand why Âlvân objected to write it down. The ambiguity was plain enough. His heart was greatly troubled and he blamed himself heavily for having lost his temper over it. He sent for Âlvân and asked his pardon in humble tones.

"My dear friend, I have thought over it and confess myself mistaken; you were in the right and I was wrong

---

(6) He is allowed to take away the Vritti, but is soon robbed of it. But the *D.C.* has it that Râmânuja, after settling at Srîrangam, began his tour throughout India; in the course of which he visits Srînagar, and is presented with the Bôdhâyana Vritti by Sarasvâti. He goes to Tirupati where Saila Pûrna welcomes him and presents him with Gôvinda (no mention of him either before or after). He returns to Srîrangam and composes his great works.

to treat you so. Can you ever forgive me? I am almost ashamed to ask it of you; so little claim have I upon your forbearance."

"Lord, Lord," cried out Âlvân in despair, "Do you want to drive me mad? What have I done to deserve such a misfortune? Alas! that my Master should be so estranged from me as to consider me as something not his own and ask my pardon; Woe is me!"

"Nay, not so, my dear," rejoined the Master: "at the foot-steps of the Throne of the Lord, there is no rank, no master and no servant; all are equal in the eyes of the Great Father;" and he dictated the passage anew, plainly and without any ambiguity, emphasising the absolute dependency of the Jîva on the grace of the Lord; and Âlvân wrote on.[1]

Thus were composed the Srî Bhâshya, the Vêdânta Sâra, the Vêdânta Dîpa, the Gîta Bhâshya, and the Vêdârtha Sangraha[2]—the corner-stones of our Faith and the Gospel of Humanity.[3]

---

1 On another occasion he sent Âlvân to Gôshthî Pûrna, with the question—"What is the chief characteristic of the Individual Self?" Âlvân waited upon the Great One for six months and returned with the reply—"Let him write that dependence upon the Lord precedes consciousness (knowership) and every other characteristic of his." (*R.D.C.*)

2 Srî Bhâshya—a large commentary on the Brahma Sûtras of Bâdaarâyana, according to the Visishtâdwaita philosophy. In this work he criticises the other philosophical systems, especially that of Srî Sankarâchârya.

Vêdânta Dîpa—a smaller commentary on the Brahma Sûtras.

Vêdânta Sâra—a gloss on the Brahma Sûtras.

Vêdârtha Sangraha—a discourse on the Upanishads.

Gîtâ Bhâshya—a commentary on the Bhagavad Gîtâ.—(*V.C.*)

3 Later on he formally took refuge in the Lord Ranganâtha, who accepted the act and promised him Liberation. And the Gadya Traya is a record of that experience of the Master. He pointed out the means in his Bhâshya, the practical realization of those means

ÂNDÂN.

When the Master took the vows of the Order, he was asked : " Do you renounce everything ? "

" What ? everything ! You do not mean the inseparable concomitants of my body too ? "

" No, no. "

" Say my three-knotted staff. "

" No, of course not. "

" Very good. Then I need not renounce my Dâṣarathi and right glad am I of that. "

" How could it be ? That is a worldly tie and you cannot retain it. "

" Oh, no. Know you not that Dâṣarathi is my staff, and I cannot throw *it* off. "

One day, when the Master was about to retire for the night, he casually recited a stanza of the Sacred Collect, as only *he* could. Dâṣarathi, who was attending upon him at the time, became entranced with the melody of it and stood motionless, his thoughts far away.[1]

The Master, noticing this, said gently, as if to himself : " Verily, the Vêdâs have come down to us in the form of the Sacred Collect and we should thank Srî Ṣaṭhakôpa for his inestimable boon to humanity. "

On another occasion, during the Great Festival, the Lord was taken in procession to the Cauvery and the Master followed, taking the arm of Dâṣarathi. But, on his return from the bath he exchanged it for that of Dhanurdâsa. The disciples were surprised at this open and

in the Gadya Traya; and in the Nitya Grandha he lays down the life of Service that such a one should lead, as long as he is associated with his material vestures.—(*V.C.*)

[1] Râmânuja was teaching him the Collect and Dâṣarathi stopped repeating it after him.—(*G.L.R.*)

deliberate defiance of all caste etiquette, and said "Lord, how is this?"

"Do you not see," replied he, with some asperity, "that Âṇḍân is a Brâhmaṇa of Brâhmaṇas and as such my equal by birth and by family connections? He might feel it in his heart that he is made to occupy an inferior position by my taking his arm. But the other, Dhanurdâsa, it is impossible for me to offend; he has not the pride of a high class Brâhmaṇa and will only feel himself honoured by my taking his arm."[1]

---

[1] The Master took his arm to protect himself from any impure magnetic emanations from others.—(*R.D.C.*)

Then the World-honoured spake,
"There is no caste in blood
Which runneth of one hue, nor caste in tears
Which trickle salt with all; neither comes man
To birth with tilka-mark stamped on the brow,
Nor sacred thread on neck. Who doth right deed
Is twice-born, and who doeth ill deeds vile."—*Light of Asia.*

His disciples were obliged to accept the logic of it, but were not able to reconcile themselves to the practical application of it. From that day, they treated Dhanurdâsa with scant courtesy, almost with contempt ill-concealed. The Master failed not to notice this; and wishing to teach them a salutary lesson and bring out the excellent qualities of Dhanurdâsa, he directed one of his confidential attendants to enter, at night, the hall where the disciples hung their clothes to dry, and tear away a hand-breadth from the garment of each.

Next morning the disciples went to dress themselves and were indignant at the mischief played upon them. Each accused the other of being the author of that silly practical joke, and very soon there were heard murmurs, that deepened into angry complaints. The holy hall, for some time, echoed to the vilest recrimination and the foulest abuse, that ever fell from the lips of a Ṣrî Vaishṇava. What a mockery!

The Master, who had arranged the scene, sent for them and rebuked them sternly for their ungentlemanly behaviour that would disgrace a Pariah.

Some days after, the Master sent for Dhanurdâsa one night, and remained talking with him far into the small hours of the morning; he had previously instructed the proud disciples to repair to the house of Dhanurdâsa and take advantage of his absence therefrom and of the sleep of his wife to cunningly steal away the ornaments from her body.

The Strange Hand-Maiden.

One day Attuḻâi, the daughter of Mahâ Pûrṇa, requested her mother-in-law to accompany her to the river side, where she went to have a bath. "Is it so?" sneered the enraged lady; "Where are the hand-maidens

---

The holy Vaishṇavâs did their work admirably; they had divested her of most of the ornaments on one side of her body, when she happened to awake. Seeing that some Srî Vaishṇavâs were engaged in removing the ornaments from her person, she lay still, fearing to disturb them. When they proceeded to the other side of her body, she gently rolled over to give them greater facility for their work. They got frightened and ran away.

The Master was duly informed of it; and he dismissed Dhanurdâsa to his home, having previously directed the *holy thieves* to follow him and report.

Dhanurdâsa found his wife awake at that late hour of the night. He was surprised at it, and much more so when he remarked that she had her ornaments only on one side of her body.

"What means this whim of thine?" said he.

"No whim of mine," replied she with a smile; and proceeded to relate to him the incident of the Srî Vaishṇavas. The athlete listened to her recital with pleasure and approval until she came to that portion of it, where the frightened disciples took to their heels, when he broke forth in anger. "How dare you behave so insultingly towards the holy disciples of the Master? What business is it of yours, what they did? We are less than the dust beneath their feet, and we are honoured and blessed by their taking back their own; for do we not owe everything we have to their grace and to any merit we might have acquired by serving them? You have irrevocably offended them, and the best thing you can do is to take back the other ornaments to the holy disciples and entreat them to forgive us." She stood abashed and was proceeding to the Maṭha; but the disciples had before that informed the Master of what they had seen at the house of the famous athlete.

"A nice group of Brâhmaṇas, you are!" said the Master to them with withering scorn, "and honour me greatly by your being disciples of mine. Verily, you are the salt of the Earth; you are the descendants of the Holy Rishis of yore, and well do you sustain their reputation. The kingdom of God is composed of such men as you; and each one of you has his place by the Throne of the Almighty; and Dhanurdâsa is beneath your contempt. You flew at each other's throats for the loss of a hand-breadth of cloth and used such language as a fish-wife would be ashamed of; and Dhanurdâsa is angry with his wife for having frightened you away from taking all her ornaments. You

that you have brought from your parents' house gone to, that you should want *me* to fill their place?" The girl was deeply wounded at this hit at her poverty, and took it to her father. "What is it to me?" cried Mahâ Pûrṇa, indifferently enough. "It is your Jeer's affair."

The Mâster heard her patiently and pointing to Âṇḍâṇ, who stood near, said to her: "Here is your servant and hand-maiden from your father's house. He will attend upon you." So Dâṣarathi became a servant of her husband's household and went about his work calmly and cheerfully. The elder members of the house were horrified at this sacrilege, and said to him in fear and awe: "Holy Sir, what have we done that you should be so offended with us? Why should *you* perform menial work?"

"*I* know nothing of it. My Master sent me here and here I remain. Disturb me not."

They proceeded to Mahâ Pûrṇa and entreated him to order back Âṇḍân. "Are you bent upon destroying us root and branch? Who are we that the holy Âṇḍân should serve us?"

---

thought I had polluted myself by taking his arm the other day. But, wise men that you are, I declare I feel myself stifled with your impure emanations and restore myself to spiritual health by being in his company for a while."—(*Prap.*)

a. Peria Vâcchân Pillay in his commentery on v. 99, Nammâlvar's Tiruviruttam, relates the following incident of the athlete-devotee. One day he happened to listen to Kurêşa when he was reciting the Sacred Collect and was so carried away with it that he burst into tears. "What a golden heart!" cried out Kurêşa, "I would gladly exchange with thee, all my vaunted erudition and intellectual gymastics."

b. This again from The 36000 (a Commentary on the Tiruvaimoḷi vii. 4. 1.) is characterstic. Dhanurdâsa used to walk before the Lord Ranganâtha with a drawn sword, ready to cut down any that dare insult Him when he was taken out in procession. Hence his name Mahâmati, that belonged, of right, to Vidura, for his careful examination of the seat which Şrî Krishṇa used, when in his humble abode.—(*G. L. R.*)

"What knew *I* of it? Ask Râmânuja." They did so and were rewarded for their trouble by getting this cutting reply: "It seems your daughter-in-law was directed to avail herself of the servant from her father's household. *I* am his humble servant, as also Âṉḏân and other disciples of mine. If *he* is not to your taste, *I* will gladly take his place But if you don't relish his serving her in your house, he will do it from here." They hung their heads in shame, glad to be let off so easily.

MÂRANÊRI NAMBI.

Mahâ Pûrṉa performed the last rites of Mâranêri Nambi, and that as in the case of a holy Brâhmaṉa. The Master came to hear of this and said to Mahâ Pûrṉa: "Revered Sir, I have enough to do and more to bring men to strictly observe their duties. Is it kind of you to undo my work and set up another rule of conduct?"

"Is it so?," replied the teacher, "I think you are wrong. The Lord took birth in the line of Ikshvâku to live out the life of an ideal householder, is it not? Well, you don't think that *I* am greater than Ṣrî Râmachandra. Yet *he* cremated with his own hands the remains of the great Jaṯâyu, *a bird*!! Nor do you suppose that Mâranêri Nambi deserved it less.[1] Take another instance. I don't claim to be greater than Yudhishṯhira; nor is Mâranêri less deserving than Vidura; yet Yudhishṯhira cremated the remains of Vidura with his own hands; and Vidura only a Ṣûdra!! Are we to take the words of Ṣaṯhakôpa as the ravings of a maniac?"[3]

"True, very true," rejoined the Master, lost in thought.

"But I would like to know," asked Mahâ Pûrṉa, in his turn, "why Mâranêri Nambi took his departure·

---

1 *Vide* Râmâyaṉa, Âraṉyakâṉḏa, Chapter 68, Verses 30, 31.

2 *Vide* Mahâbhârata; Âgrama Vâsa Parva, Ch. 26.

3 Tiruvâimoḻi iii. 7 ([illegible]) and viii. 10 ([illegible]), describing the glory of the servants of the Lord.

from the body without even once saying, 'I take my refuge in the feet of the Lord. I take my refuge in the holy Yâmuna.'"

"May be he was engaged in meditation upon the two verses."[1]

"What! the incoherent words of love-sick men!"[2]

"And it is *the object of their love*, *the Great Mother*, whose grace speaks for us with her Lord." [3]

The Dumb Sishya.

One day, the Master took a certain dumb man into a room, and having closed the doors, directed him to touch his feet. The man readily grasped the Teacher's meaning and from that moment took his refuge in the Master and was saved.

Now Âlvân happened to pass by and witnessed the whole scene through a crack in the door. "Alas, that

---

1 The two verses inculcating the Doctrine of Refuge (Saraṇâgati). The first is from Râmâyaṇa, Yuddha Kâṇḍa, Chapter xviii, Verses 32½, 33½. "If any one seeks refuge of me, *be it only once*, and prays, 'I am thine : do with me as thou wilt', I swear him absolute safety from all beings. This is *a sacred vow* with me."

The other is from the Gîta, Chapter xviii., Verse 66. "Quit hold of *all Dharmas* and take refuge in *me and me alone*. I shall free you of all sins; grieve not."

2 The first was spoken to Vibhîshaṇa by Srî Râma, love-sick after Sîta; and the second by Srî Krishṇa, love-sick after the Gopîs. [What a world of mystery lies concealed in this paradoxical statement! —*Comp.*]

3 The Srî Vaishṇavâs of Srîrangam and his own relatives cried out upon Mahâ Pûrṇa for this act of sacrilege, and looked down upon him. But his daughter Attuḷâi could not bear to listen to the flippant criticisms passed upon his conduct, by men at her husband's house, who were utterly unable to comprehend her saintly father's inner life and spiritual eminence. One day, however, she felt she must speak out or die; and her pent-up rage burst out in hot words. "Then, by the feet of Srî Saṭhakôpa, I swear that none of you shall henceforth worship Ranganâtha, nor partake of any thing offered to him. He is polluted beyond all redemption, by the touch of the Pariah Tiruppâṇâlvâr, whom he has absorbed into himself." And thereafter she lived with her father.—(*Prap.*)

I should have wasted my days in the useless study of the Vêdas and Sâstras. Had I been a dumb man and an ignorant one, the Master would have taken pity on me too, and pointed out the path to me as plainly and easily as he did now."

What to Meditate Upon.

Another time, Gôshṭhî Pûrṇa was seated in profound meditation, when the Master approached him and said : "Lord, may I know what you are meditating upon? What is the mantra you recite then ?"

"With pleasure," replied Gôshṭhî Pûrṇa, "I meditate upon my Master as I have seen him during his bath in the sacred Cauvery, with his body half immersed in the waters thereof and reciting the purificatory mantras appropriate to the occasion. *I have no other mantra but his holy name. To the earnest disciple his master is the highest object of contemplation and his name is the most sacred of Mantras.*"

ANANTÂCHÂRYA.

He constructed a tank at Tirupati, and called it 'Râmânuja' after his Master. During the progress of the work, one of his disciples observed him, weak and tired as he was, staggering under a large basket of earth he was carrying away from the tank; and respectfully offering to relieve him, tried to take the basket from him. Anantâlvân blazed out into sudden wrath : "Impious one! If *I* lay down this basket, I would indeed grow weak ; but if *you* dare to touch it, by God, your hands shall fall by your side, shrunken and powerless." But the disciple was an old hand and would not be thus scared away. So he again proceeded to take the basket away from him. "What ! " cried Ananta, with a laugh of supreme scorn, "and so you would deprive me of my living, would you ? A nice servant the Lord would have in you. May be you are too great to take another basket yourself and serve the Lord likewise."

Another day, he was digging at the tank and made his wife, who was big with child at the time, carry away the earth on her head. The Lord Venkaṭêṣa was pained to the heart at this unfeeling act (as he thought); so he met her half-way disguised as one of her husband's disciples and relieved her of her load, as if by her husband's orders. It surprised Ananta to see her return so quickly every time; he watched her from a distance and pounced upon the same audacious boy. "You mischievous imp! How dare you come between me and the service of the Lord? I shall make your back smart nicely for this;" and he rushed at him with his spade uplifted. The offender dropped the basket, and ran away with all speed; and Ananta, who followed close upon his heels, saw with amazement and awe, that he disappeared within the temple.[1]

On another occasion, he was in the garden, gathering flowers for the garland he daily laid at the foot of the Lord, when a snake bit him severely in the hand. He quietly bathed in the sacred tank and went back to his work. A friend of his happened to notice it and said: "What carelessness! Allow me to get you medical assistance in time."

---

[1] Ananta knew him to be the Lord and saying: "Lord, art thou bent upon spoiling my work and depriving me of my only means of subsistence?" ran after him.—(*Prap.*)

a. G. L. R. hints that the Lord was the other party in the first incident; and gives a different ending to the second. Ananta ran after the offender and hit him under the chin. But every one was surprised to find that the image of Venkaṭêṣa was bleeding profusely at the same place, and the temple servitors had to stop it with a bit of camphor. In memory of it they keep it on to this day as a part of the daily service and the camphor is distributed to the eager devotees.

"Ho, ho," laughed Ananta, "here is a mighty uproar about a trifle. If the *biter* proved stronger, I would but bathe in the waters of the holy Viraja and stand before the Lord of Vaikuṇṭha; if the *bitten one* proved too tough, I would bathe in the sacred tank on the Holy Mount and stand before the Lord Venkaṭêṣa."

While on a journey to his native parts [1] he halted near a water-course to partake of the food he had brought with him from Tirupati and found to his utter amazement that it was covered with ants. He was seized with a great fear and turning to his disciples said: "These be those about whom the Holy Saint sang: 'May I be born on the Holy Mount as any insect, however insignificant?'[2] Convey them back carefully and reverently to where they were. It was not given me to be born within the sacred precincts of the Holy Mount. Why should I offend these who can claim that envied distinction?"

One day he was preparing the garland for the Lord, when Venkaṭêṣa ordered his attendance before him. Ananta pretended not to hear; and when the garland was ready, proceeded to the shrine. "Well, Ananta," said the Lord in tones of evident displeasure, "so you would not come when I called for you. Am I nothing in your eyes?"

"I know not that," replied Ananta, not a whit taken aback, "I only know that when engaged in the service of the Lord or of his servants I have no eyes nor ears for anything else."[3]

---

1 Kôsala country—(*Prap.*) Kosala country (the present Mysore). He was born at Kirangûr (Sirupputtur) near Seringapatam. (*G.L.R.*)

2 Kulaśêkhara Âlvar, vi. 10.

3 "I am here to carry out the orders of my Master, who has sent me here to prepare garlands for you; and while engaged in that holy work, what have I to do with you? What do I lose if I obey you not?"—(*Prap.*)

Verily, this was cool enough; but the Lord would not stop there; he would tempt Ananta further.

"What! Even for me?"

"Well, did I make any exception? I think not."

This was worse; and strange enough, the Lord was more mystified than offended at this evident snubbing administered to him; he had a vague presentment that Ananta would come out right in the end with some unanswerable reason. So he decided to see the matter out and said:

"Now, if I ask you to go away from here, what would become of the boasted service you lay so great a store by."

"Ah, my Lord," rejoined Ananta, in slow thoughtful accents, "there is the hitch. Since you would have me speak out, here goes. I pin my faith to the words[1] of the Holy Saint; and if they go for anything, it would seem *you are the late comer.* The hill and the shrine belong of right *to the servants* of the Lord. *You* but came here *a day* before myself; both of us are here by the kind permission of the spirit of the Holy Mount.[2] And when *he* asks me to quit (I have done nothing to deserve it), well, I shall think about it. Meanwhile let us talk of something else more probable and profitable."

Such was the fearless spirit of the disciples of the Master, that made them place service to Humanity even above the *Lord himself*, and such was their unparalleled devotion to it. Alas! that our age should be so degenerate that men of that stamp are become but a name and a dream.

CHAPTER XV.

His Tour Throughout India.

The disciples of the Master requested him to undertake a pilgrimage to the holy shrines all over the land, that

1 Nâmmâlvâr iii. 3. 8.

2 Âdiśesha, who manifests himself as the Holy Mount.

he might weed out the obnoxious heretical sects that struck their roots far and deep and establish the Good Law. And Râmânuja joyfully agreed to do so. He readily obtained permission from Ṣrî Ranganâtha and set out on his tour.

He began with the Choḷa Kingdom, visited Kumbhakônam and the other sacred shrines therein[1]; and passed through the land of the Pâṇḍyas to Râmêṣwaram.[2] On his return, he visited Ṣrî Nagari to offer his worship to Ṣrî Ṣaṭhakôpa[3]; and proceeded to Tirukkuruṅguḍi, (about 20 miles south of Tinnevelly.—(*G.L.R.*)

---

1 He visited Tiruvâli-Tirunagari, where Parakâla was born, and was making the round of the sacred shrines about it, when he saw a Pariah woman coming towards him. "Stand aside, good woman, until I pass on," called out the Master to her; but she, unheeding, moved not an inch and said "Aside! Which side? Towards you, the holiest of the Brahmaṇas? Towards the sacred shrine of Tirukkaṇṇapuram behind me? To the right, towards the Tirumaṇan Kollai where Parakâla waylaid the Lord; or towards the Pipal tree used by him as a watch tower? Towards my left, where rests the Lord of Tiruvâli? Which way, Soul of Purity, shall I turn?" Râmânuja had caught a Tartar and no soft one. "A thousand pardons, noble lady," exclaimed the Master with sad humility. "Length of years and shallow pedantry have but intensified that haughty pride of mine and cast a thicker veil over my eyes, which denies me even the sweet privilege of recognising the Lord's Elect. These Sacred Badges would become you better than this proud idiot of a Sanyâsin." And he prayed her to grace the Vaishṇava fold with her noble presence and take her legitimate place near the Lord in the temple, where you see her even unto this day.—(*G.L.R.*)

2 He visited Vrishabhâdri, (10 miles north of Madura.—*G.L.R.*) and offered his worship at the shrine of the Lord Sundarabâhu ([illegible]); then Madura, where he successfully disputed with the Tamil poets of the Sangam; then to Ṣrîvilliputtûr, sanctified by the presence of Periâḻvâr (Vishṇuchitta) and the divine couple Ranga Mannâr and Âṇḍâl. The latter looked upon the Master as her big brother and called him so. He next proceeded to Kurukoor. On his way he met a young girl of whom he asked: "How far is it to Kurukoor?" She quoted a stanza from the Sacred Collect to show that it was within calling distance. The Master was struck with her brightness and piety, and followed her to her house, which he honoured by staying there.—(*R.D.C.*)

3 At Kurukoor he prayed to Ṣaṭhakôpa that his sandals, that had till then been called 'Madhura Kavi' after the ideal disciple, might

The Divine Pupil.

He entered the house of the Lord, reverently clasped his feet and awaited his commands. Then spake the Lord to Râmânuja.[1] "Countless times did we come down on Earth to reinstate the Good Law; and many were the means adopted by us to wean men from their ways of ignorance; but, strong in their Âsuric nature, they turned a deaf ear to our teachings and would not come into the fold.[2] How did you boldly undertake and

---

thenceforth be known as 'Râmânuja'—a request that was readily granted. While there, the idea occurred to him that he should name some worthy disciple of his after the great Saint and he cast about for a proper person to receive the honour and bear the responsibility. Then Pi**ḷḷ**ân, the son of Ṣaila Pûrṇa, stood forth and respectfully offered himself a candidate for the same. The Master was more than satisfied; he rejoiced in having secured such a grateful offering to the Saint and adopted Piḷḷân (who was thenceforth known as Kurukêṣvara திருக்குருகைப்பிரான் பிள்ளான்) as his spiritual son. The name had been associated with such mighty personages as Ṣaṭhakôpa and Gôshṭhî Pûrṇa, and Piḷḷân was not the one to lower its prestige.—(*R.D.C.*)

a. Another version has it that he went from Tirunagari to Trivandram, where he wished to introduce the Pâncharâtra worship; but the Lord sided with his Nambûdri priests and would not have it. But finding that Râmânuja was obstinate, he had him transported when asleep to a rock on an islet in the Sindhu river, a mile from Kurungudi; Ramanuja awoke and finding himself in a strange place, called out for a favourite attendant of his, Nambi by name. When lo! Nambi appeared, waited upon him, and led him to the temple, where the Master found, to his dismay, that his humble servant and the Lord were one and the same. (*G.L.R.*) But the *Prap* relates the same incident as having happened at Jagannath, and with a different sequel. See later on.—(*Comp*).

1 While the Master was preparing to go to the shrine, the Lord Kurangêṣa appeared to him as a Ṣrî Vaishṇava Brâhmaṇa and said to him: "Instruct me in that Mantra through the power of which you have converted men whom the Divine Incarnations themselves had given up as hopeless." The Master did so and initiated him into the Two Truths; he caused the necessary Saṃskâras to be performed over him and gave him the name of Vaishṇava Nambi, whereupon the Brâhmaṇa vanished from view. Later on when he proceeded to the temple he was struck dumb with awe to see the caste-marks he had placed on the new disciple's forehead, adorning that of the Divine Image.—*V.G.*

2 They regarded me as nothing higher than Râma the king or Krishṇa the shepherd.—(*Prap.*)

successfully carry out the work that we had almost given up in despair? Wherein lies the secret of your success? What is the magic influence you exercise over the minds and hearts of untold millions? I would very much like to know the recipe of the panacea that you seem to possess for all the ills man is subject to."

A dubious smile played over the features of the Master and he said, half in jest: "Ask and it shall be given unto you. I keep back nothing from any that comes unto me, provided they ask it *in the right way*."

"True, we have forgotten it," replied the Lord, and caused a seat to be placed for the Master near himself.

Râmânuja, who heartily loved a joke, entered into the spirit of the fun, (as he thought); he mentally placed his teacher Mahâ Pûrṇa on it, saluted his feet and, standing by it, whispered into the ears of the Lord the Two Truths, the most sacred and mysterious of all the Mantras. The Lord received it reverentially as a disciple would, and, saluting the Master, exclaimed, "I take my refuge in Râmânuja"; and the Master gave him his baptismal name as 'Ṣrî Vaishṇava Nambi.'

By the Lord's command the Master was then taken round the town in procession, and on his return to the temple he fell at the feet of the Lord and said, "Lord of Mercy, pardon thy servant for his unheard of presumption and audacity; *it is the rule and the tradition* and he dared not depart from it even in jest."

"Nay, nay," replied the Lord, "you did right, *we* meant it not in jest; and right glad are we to see you bear your office so worthily. And now, a happy journey to you and success all the way."

The Master then travelled through the western parts, [1]

[1] He broke his journey at the shrines of Tiruvaṇparichâram: Tiruvâṭṭâr, &c; at Travancore he converted the king and founded a Maṭha.

visiting Travancore on the way. Thence he went north,[1] halting at Muttra, Sâligrâma, Vaikuṇṭha, Dwâraka, Ayôdhya, Badari, Naimiṣâraṇya, Pushkara, Gôkula, Brindâvana.[2]

Before Sarasvatî.

At Bhaṭṭi Maṇḍapa, a curious event took place that lifted the veil a little from the mystery of the Great Personality that was working among men. There he proceeded to the Sanctuary of Sarasvatî and was asked by the Goddess to explain the Kapyâsa Ṣruti.

"It simply means that the eyes of the Golden-hued Person in the Solar Orb are as lovely as the petals of the lotus, that welcomes with open lips the burning kisses of the Lord of Day," replied the Master.

---

1 Along the sea coast. On his way he paid a visit to the famous Dakshiṇâmoorty, one of the most learned men of his day. The Master stayed with him for a time and perused with great pleasure the many erudite works of the great man of letters. He showed him *his* works in return and requested him to express his candid opinion on them. "The works of Ṣankara," said the savant, "are like a jewel sunk deep in slime and mire, but your writings, thou holiest of men, are like a bright flashing gem seen through translucent limpid water." And this, coming as it did from one who was born of the amṣa of the Great Initiator (Dakshiṇâmoorty), was praise indeed, and sweet to the heart of the Master.—(*R.D.C.*)

2 The following is the clearest and best description of the places visited by the Master during this tour :—

'He went to Northern India, by way of Tirupati, Ahobilam and the Mahârâshtra country, preaching everywhere as he travelled. He visited Girnâr (Dattâtrêya Kshêtra) in Guzerat and Dwâraka. Thence he went to Prayâga (Allahabad), Benares, Madhura (Muttra) and Haridwâr. From there he went to Badarikâṣrama (Badrinâth) in the Himalayas; thence to Ṣrînagar in Kashmir; then through Kurukshêtra to Ayôdhya and Gaya. Thence he went into Bengal to visit Kapilâṣrama (Sundarbunds, south of Calcutta). Thereafter to Jagannâthapuri and other sacred places on the Coromandel coast, ending his journey at Ṣrîrangam.—(*V.C.*)

But the D.C's account varies :—

After settling at Ṣrîrangam, the Master began his long tour throughout India. He first went to Kashmir to the Ṣaradâpîṭha where

"Excellent," cried out Sarasvatî clapping her hands in delight. "You are my man and well you deserve the title of Srî Bhâshayakâra, '*The* Commentator.' I give you also the Lord Hayagrîva for you to worship."

"May I know," reverently asked Râmânuja, "why I am so peculiarly fortunate as to deserve all this honour and kindness. My interpretation of the passage was nothing remarkable for ingenuity or originality."

"Nay, therein lies the point; your explanation, though perfectly natural, sounds to me all the sweeter by contrast with the profane and obscene rendering of it given by Sankara in this very spot."[1]

The Kashmir Pandits.

It goes without saying, that wherever the Master went, he was invariably engaged in subtle dialectics with the representatives of other schools of thought and as invariably came out successful. They all became his

---

Sarasvatî gave him the Bodhâyana Vritti. He returned by way of Tirupati, where Saila Pûrna welcomed him. Thence to Kurukoor, Kurungudi, Trivandrum, Ramêsvaram, etc. Thereafter he composed his great works.

2a. Muttra, Nanda Vraja, Govardhana, Brindâvana, Sâlagrâma, Mukti-Nâthakshêtra, Vaikuntham, Dwâraka, Ayodhya, Badarikâsrama, Naimisâranya, Pushkara and Bhatti Mandapa (probably Bhanti Mandala near Lahore) and Kashmir. —(*G.L.R*).

1 She came out of her Sanctuary, took hold of his hand and saying, "I am glad that the true meaning is still among men", placed his Srî Bhâshya reverently on her head.—(*Prap.*)

Sarasvatî advanced to meet him, received him with all respect and carefully went through the Bhâshya. "Unlike Sankara you have given to the world the real interpretation of the Srutis; *your* commentary alone deserves to be distinguished as (The Srî Bhâshya) and *you* alone the proud name of "The Bhâshyakâra" (*The* Commentator).—(*V.G.*)

The Goddess Sarasvatî appeared to him and questioned him on many difficult points in the Vedanta. Being satisfied with his answers, she gave him the title of Srî Bhâshyakâra and an idol of Hayagrîva.—(*V.C.*)

pupils, as also many others who were attracted to him by the fame of his great knowledge and holiness. So it came to pass that the ruler of the place was filled with such a profound admiration of Râmânuja's depth of erudition, keenness of intellect and sanctity of life that he sought permission to become one of his disciples. Now, the local pandits, finding that their occupation was gone, had recourse to the black magic to make away with their enemy. The Master came to know of this and said with a smile: "Well, let us see this fun out," and stayed there some days longer. When, lo! a strange sight was seen in the streets of the town. Learned Pandits and hoary Ṣâstris ran naked along the streets, tearing their hair and uttering insane cries. They went at one another's throats, clawed one another's faces, howled and danced like maniacs and diversified their amusements by paying themselves the same attentions.

The king was sad at heart, and guessing where he had to seek for explanation, fell at the feet of the Master and said: "Lord, surely I thought that these vermin were beneath thy notice; but now I see they have somehow succeeded in raising themselves to that bad eminence."

"Nay, not so," replied the Master, laughing, "we moved not in the affair. It was only their lower nature reacting upon themselves. You know that these entities, when directed against any one whom they cannot approach by reason of his superior power or utter purity of heart and life, turn back upon the sender and rend him to pieces."

"But, I beg to submit that the fools have had enough and will not forget this lesson in a hurry. It is not a very pleasant sight, and if my Lord has no, strong objections, I would intercede for them."

"Be it so," replied the Master, and restored them to health and sanity by sprinkling them with water that had washed his feet.

The king was mightily pleased, and when the Master took leave of him he accompanied Râmânuja many miles on his way. [1]

The Blessed One next passed through the Holy Vâraṇâsi to the holy shrine of Purushôttama,[2] Ṣrî Kûrma

---

[1] He next proceeded to Badrinâth, associated with the Divine Incarnations Nara and Nârâyaṇa. It was the place where the Eight-Lettered Mantra was given out to Humanity; and naturally enough the Master spoke on it long and in detail to crowded audiences. It was while there that he took in a certain disciple named Nrisimha and conferred upon him the proud title of "Sênâpati" (Generallissimo). He became, later on, the disciple of Âṇḍân.—(*R.D.C.*)

His next visits were to Ayôdhya and Mithilâ, the birth-places of Ṣrî Râma and Sîta.—(*R.D.C.*)

Âṇḍân did not follow the Master during his tour.—(*R.D.C.*)

(*a*) He visited, on his way, Dêva-Prayâg, ([illegible]) between Haridvâr and Badrinâth.—(*G.L.R.*)

(*b*) *G.L.R.* relates the Episode of the Bodhâyana Vritti in connection with this visit, but makes no mention of Râmânuja's being allowed to take it away, with him; the king would only allow him to read it once and return it.

[2] Purushôttama, the Lord of Jagannâtha was first worshipped by the Holy Angels in Ṣrî Vaikuṇṭha under the name of 'Nîlâdrinâtha'; then by the king Indradyumna; then by Gâlava Mâdhava; and lastly by the Kings of Katak.—(*R.D.C.*)

The Master was extremely displeased with the lives of the priests at Jagannâtha and the mode of worship they had established in the temple. The Lord, too, seemed to take it all pleasantly and resigned himself in their hands. The Master called them together and spoke at great length upon the reproachable lives they were leading and upon the heterodox mode of worship they had introduced in the temple, unauthorised by the Ṣâstras, nay, emphatically condemned by it; he told them how he had reformed the ritual in the places he had visited and proposed to introduce the Pâncharâtra mode of worship, as being more pleasing to the Lord. They gave him no reply but left the place in evident displeasure. The Master was much annoyed at this insult and obstinacy, and forcibly displaced them, appointing his own men in their stead to conduct the worship accosding to the Pâncharâtra Âgama. That very night the priests proceeded in a body to the shrine, and, falling at the feet of the Lord, cried out:

"Lord of our Life! We have been your servants and devotees from time out of memory, father and son, and have served you to the best of our humble abilities. Thou seemed to be pleased with it; and we have found favour in Thine eyes. And now, here comes one of your servants who wants us to change our lives, our habits and our time-honoured worship. If we have been in the wrong all along and have displeased you, we would have known it first and best from you. But we have taken silence for consent: and surely you did not wait *for this man* all these ages to set us on the right path. He has insulted us and dismissed us with disgrace—*we* your devoted servants, *we*, to whom belongs this place by right and your worship. He is backed by the king, whom he has won over by his great learning and wonderful powers. *You* are our King; and we look up to *you* for support. If we have found favour in Thine Eyes, stand by us at this crisis and see us triumphantly through it. If not, we have been all along in the wrong and have resolved to expiate our mistake with our lives. We leave this shrine with your assurances of protection, or we will be carried out as corpses."

The Lord was in a nice fix; he liked the priests, their mode of worship, and carried out certain objects of his through them. Râmânuja was equally dear to him and was right from *his* own standpoint. He was resolved to please both, or at least to avoid any unpleasant consequences that might result from an open collision. So he gave the priests his strongest assurances of protection and support, and sent them away with glad hearts.

The next day the Master presented himself before the shrine and prostrating himself before the Lord, said with joined hands: "When you made over your work to me, you promised to resign yourself into my hands and abide by my acts. Was it not so, my Lord?"

"Yes. We do remember what we said to you, when we sent for you to our presence at Srîrangam. We gave you sole and complete sovereignty over the Universe and its inhabitants, here and elsewhere."

"I am glad that my Lord does not put me to the necessity of reminding him of his promise. I am also honoured beyond words, in that my Lord has kept his word and has allowed me to arrange things in my own way and according to my lights. I only pray that He would extend to me the same privilege here too and allow me to reform the mode of worship, as I have done at Srîrangam and in many other shrines."

"Nay, nay, my dear. I have granted you *the whole world*, and in return ask of you to leave me alone *here*. I like these men, and their mode of worship. They serve certain ends of mine, which no other can, *not even you*. I am sure you would not deny me this trifle."

The Master felt his prestige was at stake; and a defeat might affect his work with men badly. So he insisted again and again and the Lord was equally uncompromising. In the end he left the shrine in high disappointment, but fully resolved to carry out his idea at all costs. The well-being of a whole world, the success of the True Faith was of greater importance to him than the displeasure of the Lord. He could brave *that* and take the consequences; they would affect only *himself*; but he would not see his work undone nor give a handle for his enemies against him. But the Searcher of Hearts was beforehand with him; he would not refuse the prayer of his devoted priests; he would not wound the feelings of his Râmânuja by openly thwarting his measures; but all along there was a sense of uneasiness in his mind about the course he meant to take; for he could not deny to himself that Râmânuja had his promise and was within his rights. So he cut the Gordian knot by directing Sri Garuda to convey Râmânuja to Sri Kûrma, during his sleep.

The Master awoke and found himself in a strange place; before his eyes stood the image of Mahâdêva, and all around him the attendants of the Holder of the Trident; he could make nothing of it; he had not his pupils with him, nor even the necessary articles for his daily worship. So he fasted that day and remained plunged in unpleasant reveries as to the *rationale* of this most peculiar experience of his. That night, the Divine Voice spoke to him and said: "My dear, I am sorry that you had to fast all day, because you could not get the Sacred Earth and the other articles of worship. But had you been less centred in yourself and seen with the eyes of the spirit, you would have seen not the image of Mahâdêva that puzzled you so much, but the Great Tortoise. And a few yards from here you will come upon a water course, the waters of which are as holy as that of the Milky Ocean; and all around it lie thick layers of the Sacred Earth." The Master looked as he was directed and saw indeed before him the Mighty One, the Great Tortoise, with the marks of the Discus on its shell; the image of the Lord of the Burning Ground and of his fearful servitors were nowhere to be found; and a few yards away from him, there appeared to view a beautiful well, with crystal water bubbling out of it. "Are you now convinced, you great Sceptic? You have to thank yourself for this unwelcome journey of yours; for I could see no other method of diverting you from your obstinate resolve, whose consequences you took not the trouble to ascertain. Remain here and restore my worship among men. Your people will join you here in a few days."

The Master bent the forces of his powerful intellect to the task of reviving the worship of the Lord in Sri Kûrma.

Meanwhile his followers bewailed his sudden disappearance from among their midst and sought for him far and wide, until the Lord Purushôttama appeared to them as an aged Brâhmana and said: "I hear that your Master is at Sri Kûrma, where he is all in all with the king; and I see no reason why you should not join him there and help him on in his holy work of restoring the True Faith among men."

Ahobila[1] and returned to Tirupati.

Now, there is a strange peculiarity about the manifestation of the Lord on this Holy Mount. It combines in itself the dual aspects of Vishṉu and Ṣiva and the appearance of the image of the Lord seems to lend a curious support to this view. The Ṣaivaites about the place claimed that the Deity there was a distinct manifestation of Ṣiva and that the temple should be made over to them in consequence.

The Master at Tirupati, as an Umpire.

The matter was referred to Râmânuja as umpire, and he took the shortest and the least objectionable method of solving the difficulty. He caused to be placed before Ṣrî Venkaṭêṣa, the Trident and the Kettledrum of Ṣiva, as also the Conch and the Discus of Vishṉu and decided that the issue was to depend upon the choice made by the Lord. Strict precautions were taken against any unfair meddling on the part of either party, and the vast multitude awaited in awe and suspense the dawn of the day that was to decide once for all the fate of the temple and its future history. It was day-break, and Râmânuja was seen approaching the temple with the representatives of both the sects. The doors were opened and the Committee of Inquiry proceeded to the Holy Sanctuary. The priests drew back the heavy curtains of the cloth of gold,

The Master remained at Ṣrî Kûrma for some time, reorganising the worship there; he arranged that the future Krishṉamâ Châria should be born there and institute the Vaikhânasa method of worship.

He next proceeded to Warangal, rendered famous by its association with Pratâpa Rudra, the great man of letters; overcame the sceptics in disputation, and instituted the worship of the Lord in his manifestation of "Pânchâla Râya."

Thence he went to Chicacole (Ṣrîkâkulam) where he worshipped at the Shrine of Ṣrî Vallabha and named him anew—"Telugu Râya." —(*R.D.C.*)

[1] On the sacred hill, Simhagiri.—(*Prap.*)

and, Wonder of Wonders! the Conch and the Discus, the Symbols of Vishṇu, were on either hand of the Lord, and the Trident and the Kettledrum lay far away. The Vaishṇavas shouted themselves hoarse with joy, and the vast multitude outside taking up the cry, cheer after cheer rent the sky, startling the calm morning on the mountains. The Ṣaivaites slunk away abashed and mortified; and our Master was hailed as the Saviour of the Lord. What a title! Had he not really saved the Lord from a very unpleasant contingency? And did not his action decide the fate of the temple for all time to come, and, nay, what was more important, the fate of the millions whose spiritual destinies hung in the balance? [1]

---

[1] The Master placed on the breast of Ṣrî Venkaṭêṣa an image of Lakshmi; hence one of his titles. "The father-in-law of the Lord Venkaṭêṣa."—(*Prap.*)

Venkaṭêṣa had, on a former occasion, given away his Conch and Discus to his favourite devotee—the Toṇḍamân King—when he went to war against his foes. Hence the Ṣaivaites claimed him as their own. Since the Master gave him back his natural weapons, another of his titles is, "The Restorer of the Conch and Discus."—(*V.G.*)

(*a*) Pêyâlvâr has so described him in 63 of the 3rd Tiruvandâdi ([Tamil]). The *G.L.R.* gives some references to prove this point :—

(i) The Tiruchânoor temple might have been a combined Ṣiva-Vishṇu temple, as the one at Chidambaram and at many other places.

(ii) Many important Ṣiva temples have within their precincts a shrine of Vishṇu, generally facing the west; the inscriptions name them Mêlai Ṣrî Kôil.

(iii) The Tirupati temple was Vaishṇava during the time of Rajaraja, the Chola King (4th Century), who made extensive grants to it.

(iv) It must have been so during the times of the Triad who sang the Têvâram; for while they had sung the praises of the deities of Tiruppparankunram, Tiruvaṇmiyûr, Kâlahasti, they have curiously omitted all mention of Tirupati.

(v) Ṣilappadikâram, a Tamil classic, describes the Lord of Tirupati as Vishṇu ([Tamil], 41-51).

(*b*) One Tâlapâkam Chinnayya, a favorite devotee of the Lord of the Holy Mount, found no greater pleasure in life than in singing the praises of his Beloved, to which the complaisant Ṣrînivâsa would

From Tirupati, the Holy One journeyed south, visiting on his way Kânchî, Triplicane,[1] Madurântakam (a place holy in his eyes for all time, as the spot where his Teacher Mahâ Pûrṇa, opend his eyes to the Light), Tiru Ahîndrapura, (near Cuddalore) and the sacred places in the east and in Toṇḍamaṇḍala. He next took his way to Veeranârâyaṇapura, the birth-place of the great Saint Nâtha Muni, and visited the spot sanctified by the Samâdhi of the Great One. Having thus made the round of the Earth, he crowned it with another visit to the Sacred Bridge (Râmêṣwaram) and returned to Ṣrîrangam.

Back to Ṣrîrangam.

The whole place turned out to welcome their beloved Master, now rendered doubly so from his long absence from their midst and by his triumphant tour throughout the land. His feelings could better be imag ined than described as he stood before the Lord of his Heart.

---

dance in accompaniment. When the Master visited the Hill he prayed the Bhaṭṭa to know from his Lord whether he would find a place near Him, when his house of clay should crumble down.

"Verily," replied the Lord, "he shall sit with me in my high abode and right glad would I be to have him there."

"Surely, not nearer thee, Lord" exclaimed Chinnayya, in unconcealed disappointment and mortification, "than myself! My place is next to you, by right of service. Is it not?"

"You!!!" cried the Lord, "somebody has been fooling you, I see. I owe you nothing, you simpleton; and have been careful enough to square my accounts with you, and that, then and there, right on the spot. No arrears, mind you; nothing to pay back."

"But, Lord of Mercy" sobbed out the broken-hearted one, in utter despair, "have I not sung to thee day and night, all these years?."

"True, my son; but have you forgotten that I have danced to you every time?"

"Woe is me!" cried the poor man, "I am undone."

"Not so, my child" spoke back the Lord, soothingly, "take thy refuge in the holy Sanyâsin that has opened your eyes to your blind folly. With *him* there is no impossibility."—(*G.L.R.*)

1 Near Mylapore.—(*R.D.C.*)

"I suppose you have had a safe and happy journey?" kindly inquired the Lord.

"How could it be otherwise," replied the Master, "when the Lord is ever present with me? Closer is He than breathing, nearer is He than hands and sight. When were the servants of the Lord ever known to fail or regret?" He was then given leave to depart, and returned to his Maṯẖa amidst universal rejoicings and congratulations.

CHAPTER XVI.

Paràṣara Bhaṯṯa—Âḻvàn the Saintly.

Of all his disciples, Âḻvân was dear to the heart of the Master, by reason of his great learning, extreme holiness of life, and unexampled self-surrender to the will of the Master. The world and its ways troubled him not; he lived a life apart—

> "Remote from men, he ran his godly race,
> Prayer all his pleasure, all his business praise."

He regulated his daily life on the strictest lines of simplicity and discipline laid down in the Sacred Book of Rules. He divided the day into five parts;[1] the early hours were devoted to the performance of his daily ablutions and prayers; in the second portion of it, he went round for alms to the houses of a certain member of householders, food from whose hands he could take without the least suspicion of impurity; he then came home, and during the third period, offered the five Great Sacrifices and waited for guests; the afternoon was spent in the recitation and study of the Sacred Scriptures; and the day closed with the meditation on the Supreme One whose nature and glory they seek to unveil.

1 Abhigamana, Upâdana, Ijya, Svâdhyâya, and Yôga. Refer to Pancha-kâla-prakâṣa by D. T. Ṣrînivâsachârya, Madras, 1904.—(*G.L.R.*)

Âṉḏâl Speaks Out.

One morning it rained cats and dogs. It was too late to go for alms; and it was quite unusual for him to have with him any remains of the previous day's alms. He conducted the daily worship of the household god, and, contenting himself with placing at its feet a fruit as an humble offering, fasted throughout the day. The shades of night fell, and he paid his usual visit to the Lord's House, whence he returned to his humble dwelling and fell asleep, reciting the Sacred Collect. Some hours later, the priests were placing before S̱rî Ranganâtha the midnight offering (பெரியஅவசரம்) and the usual blare of trumpets announced it to the expectant worshippers. Âṉḏâl, the wife of Âîvân, heard it too, and glancing at her Lord, who was sleeping peacefully by her side, said to herself:

"Verily, my Lord Ranganâtha, you are having a nice time of it, while your servant and devotee sleeps fasting. Of course, *you* have not to go for alms and no one dare interfere with *your* hours of dinner or supper."

She spoke out of a heavy heart; for, what was S̱rî Ranganâtha or S̱rî anybody to her above her husband and lord? To her *he* was the Perfect Man, her Refuge and Support, her God of Gods, her Guru here and hereafter for all eternity; and what sort of a master was he serving who allows his devoted servant to go without the bare means of sustenance—a thing which the very owners of cattle deny not to their dumb slaves? *She* was right and Lord Ranganâtha thought with her.

He appeared to Uttama Nambi (the master of the temple kitchen) in his sleep, and said: "My friend Âîvân sleeps fasting. Take this supper that has been served me just now and bear it to him on your head with all the marks of honour due to me on such occasions."

Âlvân was roused from his sleep by the noise of the temple music and hastened out to worship the Lord, who, he thought, was coming in procession. Curiously enough it was a procession, but he could see no image of the Lord therein; and to his wonder and surprise it stopped right at his door. He saw Uttama Nambi come towards him with something on his head and say: "The Lord has sent you this, the last offering in the night; be pleased to accept it."

Âlvân could make nothing of it. "I never asked Him for this" muttered he to himself. "He has given me everything I wanted, even when I first took refuge in Him! and I have nothing else to desire. So this is something new and I believe I will have to pay for it."

The Birth of Parâṣara.

He took just what was wanted for himself and his wife, and sent away the rest with humble thanks. Then turning to his wife, he said:

"What was it that you asked of the Lord?"

"Nothing; I simply said to myself: 'There is the blare of the trumpets announcing the last offering. The servant sleeps weary and fasting and the Master sups gaily and in pomp?'"

"You fool!" cried Âlvân, "and you dared say this to my Master! What a—!"

"*Your* master he may be; but he is no master o *mine*. *My* Master is here, my Lord, my Life, my All; when *he* lies asleep fasting, what care I for any other God or man?"

And the two portions of the midnight offering played an important part in the appearance later on into the world of Parâṣara and his brother Vêda Vyâsa.[1]

---

1. The Lord appeared to Âlvân in a dream and intimated to him that he meant to take birth in his family.—(*G. L. R.*)

(*a*) They were the manifestations (amṣa) of the sages Parâṣara

A Teacher from the Cradle.

Âlvân displayed more than his usual indifference in the case of Parâşara and left everything to be done by the Master. After the period of pollution was over, the Blessed One proceeded to Âlvân's house, accompanied by Gôvinda and directed him to bring the infant to him. Embâr did so and on the way, as a safeguard against any evil eye, recited over the infant the Two Truths. The Master received it in his hands and with tears of joy streaming down his face said: " A very wonderful child, Gôvinda, is it not ? What Tèjas (spiritual radiance) and what latent power ! But what is this ? How has it come to be permeated with the refulgence of the Two Truths ? Gôvinda, you have a hand in this, it seems."

" Even so, my Lord. On my way to you I recited the Sacred Syllables over the infant to ward off any evil influences."

The Master gently smiled at Gôvinda's solicitude for his future disciple and said : " You have anticipated me in this; and so continue what you have begun by taking care of his spiritual education." He made the signs of

---

and Vêda Vyâsa.

Parâşara's birth :—
Sâlivâhana Era—983.
Kali Yuga—4163.
Year—Şubhakrit.
Month—Vaişâkha.
Fortnight—The full-moon; Star—Anurâdha.

Vêda Vyâsa's birth :—
Week—Wednesday.
Star—Anusha.
Vêda Vyâsa was named Şrî Râma for his extreme loveliness.
(*Prap.*)

Sudarşana Bhatta, the author of Şruta Prakâşika, the celebrated gloss on the Şrî Bhâshya, was the grandson of Vêda Vyâsa.

Parâşara's Works :—

(1) Şrî Ranga Râja Stava ; (2) Şrî Gunaratna Koşa ; (3) Sahasranâma Bhâshya ; (4) Kriyâdîpa ; (5) Ashtasloki ; (6) Tanişlôki ; (7) Chatuşlôki ; (8) Dvayaşlôki. Died in the year Jaya, in the month of Kârtika, on the 12th day of the bright fortnight.—(*Per.*)

He was directed by the Master to compose the Sahasranâma Bhâshya.—(*V.G.*)

the sacred weapons of Vishṇu over the infant's body; but when the infant was given a name, he directed *Gôvinda* to mark it with the Sacred Badges. Râmânuja named the future teacher, Parâṣara, after the Great Sage through whom we have the Vishṇu Purâṇa; and thus he carried out the *second* of the last wishes of his Master.

Some time after, Gôvinda's brother was blessed with a child, and Râmânuja proceeding thither, named him, Parânkuṣa, after the Great Saint Srî Saṭhakôpa; and thus fulfilled *the third and the last* of the unspoken wishes of Yâmunâchârya.

The Lord's Godson.

Said the Lord to Âlvân: "We have adopted your boy. Bring him to us; his cradle shall be placed right here, and we and our consort will bring him up." The worshippers at the sanctuary beheld, with awe and surprise, the strange sight of the child creeping on his knees to the food placed there before it was offered to Him; stranger still was it to see it climbing up the knees of the Divine Pair, playing with the ornaments about the sacred Person and laughingly call them "Papa" and "Mamma."[1]

---

[1] One day the ruler of the place made a splendid offering to the Lord, and the children were toddling up as usual to help themselves to their share, when the priests stepped forward and officiously hauled them away, even beyond the temple precincts. That night the Râja had a terrible dream. The Lord frowned upon him with brows black as thunder and cried:

"This day you have grossly insulted me, you and your servile priestly crew. You would drive my children away from their meals, and yet you would have me taste of your proud offering. Thank your stars that they are children, else they will blast you with a glance of their eyes. I eat not before my children. I prefer to fast."

The poor man, almost dead with vague terror, rushed out of his palace, on, on to the Lord's House and found that Ranganâtha had not exaggerated matters. He pitched into the trembling priests and gave it to them so hot that they were glad to escape with their

The Little Great Men.

Five revolving years had changed Parâșara into a fair-headed chubby-cheeked boy full of life and spirits, but with a far away look in his eyes that spoke of things not of this Earth. One day, Âḷvân was reciting out of the Sacred Collect the decade beginning with "நெடுமாற் கடிமை" and when he came to the expression "சிறுமாமனிசர்"[1] (the little great men) young Parâșara struck in with:

"Papa, how is it that the Âḷvâr has used the expression? How is it possible for the two contradictory attributes of littleness and greatness to coexist in one and the same person?"

Âḷvân's breath was taken away by the aptness of the question; and that, too, coming from a boy of five! He looked hard at Parâșara and remembered what his master had told him in secret about the mysterious one whom he called his son in this incarnation.

"A very good question that, my dear," replied he. "You have not yet been initiated, else I would prove to you that the Holy Saṭhakôpa was right and that from the strictest Șastraic point of view. Well, I shall place it before you in a more concrete way. Do you remember to have seen here Dêvarâja Muni and Bâlârya (சிறியாழ்வான்)? Good; you see how small they are physically, but the greatness of their souls and of their wisdom is something unthinkable. There you have the Little Great Men."[2]

---

lives. Thenceforth, with them it was the Bhaṭṭars first and then the Lord—a long way behind.—(*G. L. R.*)

1 Nammâḷvâr—viii., 10, 1.

2 This incident occurred during the anniversary of the birthday of Parâșara. Âḷvân offered him no explanation as he was not yet invested with the Sacred Thread and hence unable to comprehend the Vedic explanation.—(*Prap.*)

Parâșara was five years old then.—(*R.D.C.*)

The Omniscient Pandit.

Another day, the boy was playing in the street with his friends, when he saw a large crowd coming that way and a Pandit on a gaudy palanquin in the centre of it, who caused himself to be announced as "The Pandit from whom nothing is hid (Sarvagña Bhaṭṭa)." Parâṣara could not put up with this absurd bravado and said: "Where have they gone to, the Lord Râmânuja and his mighty disciples, that this Sun of Wisdom should perforce come here to enlighten us, poor benighted worms."

He took a handful of dust from the road, and, approaching the Pandit, asked with a smile: "Wise Sir, deign to tell us how much this is."

The Pandit was taken back at this; he was not prepared for this sort of questioning. Plainly it did not come within the range of his studies, and he hung his head in confusion.

"A new sort of Omniscience this," laughed the boy in his face; and clapping his hands, he said: "Even a blind ass would not hesitate to say that it is a handful of dust. *You* are omniscient, and no doubt of that."

"Boys" cried he, turning to his mates, who stood jeering by to see their champion discomfit a learned man, "pluck his feathers from off this gay peacock. And you, bully and fool, *get away from here*, before my masters hear of it and something worse befalls you."

"Who is this boy? and yet he is no boy," asked the Pandit humbly of the bystanders.

"The son of Ṣrîvatsânka, the disciple of Râmânuja."

"Ah! that explains it; when was the eaglet ever known to crawl?" and he placed the boy in his lap and proceeded in his palanquin to the house of Âlvân.

Hêmâmbâ, (ஹேமாம்பா) the wife of Dhanurdâsa, happened to be coming out of it, and hearing of the strange adventure, she clasped the boy to her breast, recited over him the Two Truths to ward off any evil eye, and, covering him with the ends of her garment, took him in, soundly rating his parents for being so careless as to leave him about in the streets, where some evil-minded person might cast his eye upon him. She then caused him to be sprinkled with the Holy Water and wrung her hands in grief, muttering, " Woe is me ! Parâșara, we will not have you long among us. You are too great and too good for this Earth ; and your fiery spirit will consume its frail vehicle out in no time."

His First Day at School, and The Last.

In time he was invested with the Sacred Thread and began the study of the Vêdas. The first day he recited the hymns after his teacher; and when the boy went to him the next day, the teacher began with the hymns as on the previous day ; but, young Parâșara only laughed in his face and scampered off to play in the streets.

When he came home, his parents asked him, " How is it, my dear, I hear you refused to recite the day's lesson along with the other boys ?"

" Even so ; but I found them going over the same ground and ran away ; it was so very dull."

" Then let us hear you recite the lesson."

" Why, it is nothing" said Parâșara, and he reeled off hymn after hymn with perfect accuracy of word and rhythm.

The parents trembled with awe and said to one another : " It would not be safe to allow him to go to the class for some time to come."

Hence it came about that Âlvân and Gôvinda, the one his father in flesh and the other his father in spirit, took charge of him and perfected him in all knowledge, secular and religious.[1]

The Divine Godfather.

One day, Parâșara proceeded to the Temple and was about to enter the Sanctuary where the curtains were drawn around. The Lord, in feigned anger at his daring to intrude on his privacy, ordered him in harsh tones to get out. Parâșara had not gone many steps when the Lord said, "Bring him back here. Ho! Parâșara."

The godson obeyed and stood with folded hands before the Lord.

"How did you regard us when I ordered you to go away from here?" asked the Lord with a smile.

Parâșara answered sadly, "As the Lord Ranganâtha and his Divine Consort."

"Till then?"

"As my father Âlvân and my mother Âṉḏâl."

"What! so soon offended! Really, my dear, you are a little too sensitive. Swear it upon my head that you will from this moment regard us in the old light."

"Happy am I," replied Parâșara, in the gladness of his heart, "to have found favour once again in the eyes of my father."

His Marriage.

Now Parâșara had grown up a fine young man, and Âlvân thought it time enough he should take up the

---

1 Once the Master asked Parâșara to explain a stanza and when he had finished, said to those assembled there: "Regard him even as you would myself."

On a similar occasion Embâr said: "He will be the Glorious Sun of the True Doctrine."

On another occasion the Master happened to listen to a discourse delivered by the boy Parâșara and invested him with the title of Vêdântâchârya.—(*Pal.*)

duties of a householder. So he placed the matter before the Master and said : " But my people, my kith and kin, are still very, very backward in the scale of spirituality, and a girl from them is not a fit mate for the boy."

" Well then, why not select a girl from the relatives of Mahâ Pûrṇa ? It would, I think, meet all our wishes."

Âlvân talked the matter over with his wife and approached the parties through Râmânuja. But, though they made no objections to the boy, they hesitated to form an alliance with a new line, of whose status they were not well assured.[1]

One day, Âṇḍâl said to her husband : " Our boy is growing ; should we not find a wife for him ? "

" It is no business of mine," exclaimed he. " I have had enough of it ; Let the Lord look after his own family."

That night, when he was leaving the Presence of the Lord, he said : " She says that the boy has grown up and ought to be married. "

" What is it to *you* ? " retorted the Lord, " mind your business." That very night, he directed the refractory parties to offer their girls to Parâṣara, and that, without delay. The very next day they were at Âlvân's door and entreated him, on their knees, to honour them by accepting their girls for his son.[2]

---

1 Kûrêṣa belonged to the Vaḍama clan of the Smârtava Brâhmaṇas and Mahâ Pûrṇa was a Puraṣṣikha (forelock) Brâhmaṇa of the Brihaccharaṇa class. Hence the hitch. But now the Bhaṭṭars freely intermarry with the discendants of Mahâ Pûrṇa.

2 The girls were named Manni (மன்னி) and Akkacchi (அக்கச்சி).

" What distinguishes a Vaishṇava from a Smârtava, that you should so highly affect the former ?" once asked a Smârtava Pandit of Parâṣara.

" Look here ! " said Bhaṭṭa, I have no time to waste over useless dialectics on this head. It is good enough for my father and it is good enough for me. Time enough to cast it off, when I become wiser and

CHAPTER XVII.

Râmânuja, the Self-exiled.

KRIMI KANTHA.

There was at the time a Chôla[1], ruling over that part of the country, who was a bigoted Saivite. He saw that the new teachings were spreading far and wide and taking hold of the people, young and old, pandit and peasant He was afraid of the ever-increasing influence of the Teacher, whose divine virtues and mighty powers roused his keenest envy while they struck him with awe and reverence. The priests of his religion censured his deplorable lack of warmth in the cause of the Faith and urged him on to

holier than *he*. You have been in a mighty hurry to forget the first rule of morality. What says the holy Âpastamba? 'The life our wise and righteous elders have led is our first rule of conduct. And *then*, the Vedas.'" The Pandit slunk away, sadder—but wiser.—(*G. L. R.*)

1 When the Master took charge of the Lord's work, he meant to do his very best, and the Lord knew it. So he eased his mind of all anxiety on the score of the welfare of Humanity and spent his time happily in the company of his consort. The Master scattered broadcast the seeds of Wisdom and Devotion, to all who cared to ask for it, prince or peasant, man or woman, young or old. His 74 disciples with their countless followers carried the Good Word to the remotest corners of the land, to hill and dale, palace and cottage, desert and city. A wave of spirituality and devotion spread over the hearts of men, and very soon Hell was deserted and the Halls of Vaikuntha crowded to excess. The grim Lord of Death grew grimmer at the thought of his empty Chambers of Torments and his idle dispensers of Woe; and he gnashed his teeth in impotent fury when he saw that the earth was like the very White Island, the inhabitants of the sin-laden world excelling in spirituality and devotion the very angels around the Throne of the Most High. Heavy of heart, the dread Yama sought his brother-guardians of the Quarters and they went in deputation to wait upon Vishnu to lay their complaints before him.

The Holder of the Discus heard them out and his eyes were opened to the danger he himself had brought about. He turned his attention to the Earth and was filled with extreme anxiety not unmixed with admiration. Râmânuja had done his work well—only too well. He had accomplished what all before him had failed in, God and man. Verily it was time enough to handicap this spirited man, else there

the very congenial task of using his kingly power to make Ṣaivaism the State Religion and, as a natural corollary, fiercely persecute those who held on stubbornly to the new Faith.[1]

They devised a plan to force all the Pandits and the learned men in his kingdom to give their assent in writing to the fundamental article of their faith—'There is nothing higher than Ṣiva?' Some few, afraid of being deprived of their worldly possessions, signed the declaration.

One day, Nâlooran[2] said to him: "These signatures you have been at so much trouble to get are not worth the paper on which they are written. These are but timid sheep; but when I see the names of the holy Râmânuja and his colleagues on this paper, then, and then alone, will I be convinced that your faith is the true one."

"Is it even so," replied the king, and despatched his officers to fetch Râmânuja.[3]

They arrived at the Maṭḥa and asked for the Master, when a certain Vaishṇava ran in and whispered the news to Âlvân who was getting the water ready for the Master's bath.

---

would be no distinction between Earth and Heaven. He was sorely put to avoid a meeting between Yâmuna and Râmânuja, lest the same thing should come about. And here the latter had brought it about, all by himself. He could not allow the harmonious workings of the Universe to be thrown out of gear, even to please his well-beloved Râmânuja. And so he directed one of his servants to be born as the Chôla King, whose capital was at Chidambaram—a bad, bold man, wicked and powerful.—(*Prap.*)

(*a*) The father of Vikrama Chôla (1113-1128 A. C.)—(*G. L. R.*)

(*b*) Chidambaram (Gangaikoṇḍa Chôlâpuram).—(*G. L. R.*)

1 The Master remained 60 years at Ṣrîrangam, preaching the Good Law before the infamous Chôla interfered with him.—(*R.D.C.*)

2 The disciple of Âlvân and the Judas Iscariot of his Master. He was the minister of the wicked Chôla.—(*R.D.C.*)

3 The Chôla's capital was at Rajêndrachôlâpuram.—(*R.D.C.*)

ÂLVÂN, THE FAITHFUL.

The faithful disciple at once dressed himself in his master's garments and accompanied the messengers of the king, having arranged to keep it from the ears of Râmânuja.[1] He had not gone far when, to his great surprise, he was joined by Mahâ Pûrṇa, who got wind of the matter and was proceeding on the same errand.

THE EXILE.

Soon after, the Master had his bath and asked for his garments. Âṇḍân, feeling assured that his friend would

---

[1] The Master asked him: "What is it?" and Âlvân acquainted him with the news.

"Good," exclaimed the Master, "a very nice chance to root out the infamous nest of the Ṣaivaite bigots and sceptics. Let us not lose a moment in going there."

"Nay, not so," interposed Âlvân, "mine it is to save you that trouble; they shall not reach you until they have done with me. Grant me permission to don thy robes and I will go forth to meet the unholy and deal with them as they deserve. Let not this my first prayer be refused."

"Be it so, my dear," said the Master, reluctantly enough, and changed garments with him.—(*R.D.C.*)

Âṇḍân and Varada Vishṇavâchârya of Naḍâdoor were the first to hear the news, as they were proceeding to their midnoon bath in the Cauvery. Âṇḍân resolved to bathe quickly and warn the Master; but the latter quickly went back and acquainted the Master with the unpleasant intelligence. "Ah! my dear," exclaimed the Blessed One, "thou wert ever my favourite nephew."

Then Âlvân suggested that as the Chôla was a very monster of iniquity, he would do well to seek shelter somewhere else, and requested permission to proceed himself to the Court of Chôla to give the Master time to make good his escape.—(*V.G.*)

When they made their appearance before the Chôla, he asked his ministers, "Is this Râmânuja?"

"No," said they, "his pupil, and almost his equal."

He flew into a rage, cursed his minions for their stupid mistake and sent others to bring Râmânuja. When the disciples came to know of this, they advised the Master to remove himself from Ṣrirangam till the storm blew over.—(*Hari Samayadipa*).

be far away by that time, acquainted him with the particulars.

"Alas," cried the Master in great grief, "that evil should come upon them through my unworthy self. Verily, my friends have very little to congratulate themselves upon their acquaintance with me. Well, give me Âlvân's clothes." Then his disciples humbly submitted that it was not safe for him to remain at Srîrangam any longer. As for Âlvân and Peria Nambi, they would surely come back safe and victorious, when the Chôla found out that his messengers had caught hold of the wrong man. The Master took the hint, and, proceeding to the Presence of the Lord Dêvarâja, the object of his daily worship, said :

"Lord, it is not seemly I should punish the Chôla openly as he deserves. It was all right for the Âlvâr to say 'It shall be the duty of every servant of the Lord to destroy those that hate him and revile him.'[1] I am not a militant Hindu, but I shall compass my ends by other means, less open and hence less liable to be defeated. Lord, permit me to stay away from here for some time until the storm blows over." Then with a small band of disciples, who could not be persuaded by any means to desert their Master, he proceeded west.[2] Very soon the king's men were after them in hot chase, observing which, the Master took a handful of dust and said to some of his friends :

---

1 Tirumâlai (8) Toṇḍaruḍippoḍi Âlvâr—([illegible]).

2 "Lord," said the Master, "I leave it to Thee to punish the Chôla as he deserves."—(*R.D.C.*)

The Master asked Ranganâtha what he should do about the invitation of Chôla. "Rest easy," replied the Lord, "I have some work for you to do in the west. Do thou proceed thither and leave me to look after the Chôla." Âlvân offered to go and dispute in his place. The Master gave him his garments, and instructed him how to proceed. Âlvân then set out with most of the disciples of the Master.—(*Hari Samayadîpa*).

"Scatter this across their path, accompanying it with the words, 'Lord of the flaming Discus! Divine Archer! The dread God of Death trembles at the sight of the staff in thy hands.'"[1] They did so, and the king's men were not able to step across the line of sand.[2]

"This is some devil's magic of yonder Brâhmaṇas," exclaimed they in impotent rage, and were forced to look on helplessly while the Master and his friends were lost in the distance.

With Nallân's Disciples.

There were some hunters at the foot of a hill, near the Nîlagiris whom Nallân of the Holy Mount[3] had converted to the True Faith. One day some of them were ploughing a field, when there came unto them a Vaishṇava seeking the Master.

"Where do you come from?"

"From the Great Temple."

"We hope it is all right with the Holy Master. What is the latest news?"

"A nice place, indeed, the Holy Temple, and a nice Lord is Ranganâtha, the owner of it. Our Master has fallen upon evil days and has gone away from among us, no one knows where, and I have wandered far without

---

1 A stanza of Periâlvâr Tirumoḷi (V. 4-4—[Tamil]).—(*Hari Samayadîpa*).

2 A mountain sprang up.—(*Hari Samayadîpa*).

3 Nallân ([Tamil]) was a disciple of the Master. Once he chanced to observe the corpse of a Chaṇḍâla floating along the river Vaigai, near Madura, and finding that it had the caste-marks of a Vaishṇava on its body, brought it to the bank and cremated it with all due rites. Whereupon the Lord Varadarâja happened to remark: "This is an excellent land; and you are more so in my eyes." Hence the name Nallân (Tamil Nallân = a good man).—(*Prap.*)

Another version has the remark thus:—The people of the place resented this act of sacrilege, but Lord Varada silenced them by saying: "He is a bad one to *you*, no doubt of that; but methinks he is good enough for *me* ([Tamil])—*Comp.*

coming upon him." And he then recounted the sad details.

They threw up their work, and with tears in their eyes and grief in their hearts, prayed night and day for the safety of their Master, fasting all the while.[1] Six days passed away; that night it rained heavily, and the cold was something to remember. It so chanced that the Master and his small body of followers lost their way in the neighbourhood and wandered here and there in the dark, drenched to the skin and shivering with cold. Suddenly they caught sight of a gleam of light in the distance and, guided by it, they came upon the small hamlet of the hunters. Râmânuja, too tired in body and too heavy of heart to walk far, had to be conveyed thither by some of his disciples. These cried out to the hunters within the ring-fence:

"Good men, may we trouble you to set us on the right path?"

"As I am alive," exclaimed one of them "they are Brâhmaṇas."

"And did you notice," added another, "that one of them is tired unto death, his voice is so weak and weary?"

They all ran out hastily and led in the guests, dripping wet and caked with mud. They were relieved of their wet clothes and seated round a roaring wood fire, and were not long in making themselves as comfortable as was possible under the circumstances. Then, and then alone, did one of the hunters venture to ask:

"Whence are you, reverend Sirs?"

"From Ṣrîrangam."

---

[1] *Prap* and some other books make no mention of this incident.—*Comp.*

"Ah," cried all of them eagerly, "then you can give us some news of our Lord Râmânuja."

The disciples were amazed to find themselves not unknown at this far away corner of the land; still they said, "What know you of the Teacher?"

"Very little indeed; but our Master Nallân of the Holy Mount (blessed be his name) when instructing us, has enjoined us to remember that the Lord Râmânuja was the Great Master, the Teacher of Teachers, and has ordered us to take our refuge in his illimitable grace. And ever since, he has been our God, our Lord, our stay here and our hope hereafter. Some days ago a holy Vaishṇava had been here and left us with saddened hearts by his account of the recent doings at Ṣrîrangam. It is now six days, and we are observing a strict fast and beseeching the Lord to watch over the Master and bring him safe to us." Such unlooked for welcome and such unparalleled devotion were too much for the disciples and they cried out: "The Lord has indeed heard your prayers and has answered them. He has brought to you, as you desired, the Master; and here he is."

The honest souls gazed with wonder and awe at the Blessed One and could not believe their good fortune. But they had heard their teacher describe the Master too often not to recognise in the person before them, the lofty brow and the eagle eyes that had looked undazzled at the Light of Lights, but that were ever suffused with the compassion that welled up from the heart. They flung themselves at his feet and with sobs and tears bewailed their own miserable fortune that did not allow them to see and entertain the Great One in his happier days. The Master gently rebuked their want of spirit and reassured them that it was but a temporary obscuration he was passing through, and would come out of it all the brighter.

Besides, who knows the Lord might not have some work for him to do in places which he would never have thought of visiting but for this contingency.

The hunters brought them honey and wild grain, upon which they supped heartily. The next morning the Master sent back one of the hunters and one of his men (Mâruti Aṇḍân) to the temple and, with the forty-five disciples that remained with him, proceeded further west. The hunters accompanied them for 50 miles and left them at the house of a friend of theirs. [1] He was out hunting and came home at sunset, when his wife informed him that a number of Brâhmaṇas were awaiting his arrival. Having ascertained that they had not as yet had their supper he called out to a servant and said to him:

"Look here. Take these friends of mine to the Brâhmaṇa quarters of the village, and direct the keeper of the rest-house to have them entertained hospitably as befits their rank. I shall send over the necessary articles."

An Old Disciple.

He then took a respectful leave of the self-invited guests, who proceeded to the rest-house. They had not long to wait, when the lady of the house came to announce to them that supper was ready. The disciples expressed, by their silence, their disinclination to take food from the hands of strangers. The woman, guessing their thoughts, exclaimed, "Doubt not; I too have sat at the feet of the Master."

---

1 They journeyed for about 6 days and reached a certain fastness in the Nîlagiris, where the chief of the forestmen lived.... They entrusted the party to the mistress of the house and said: "These holy men are our Gurus; we commend them to your care. Pray attend to all their wants, and whatever it may cost, debit it to us and write off the same in the accounts against the wages due to us by your master."—(*G.L.R.*)

The disciples were slightly amused at this simple cunning of the woman (as they thought) and her apparent solicitude on their behalf.

" How did you come to be a disciple of the Master ? " asked they, enjoying, in anticipation, her utter discomfiture and collapse.

" Well," replied she, " it is a long while ago, and if you care to hear the story, here goes. It was dreadful famine in these parts, and I and my husband wandered from place to place until we finally settled at the Temple. I have often seen the Master when on his daily rounds for alms,[1] and I have also seen Akaḷanka[2] and many others, high and low, embrace his feet in veneration on such occasions. One day, he came for alms to the house in which I and my husband put up ; and I hastened down to the door and stood across the passage.

---

1 ...." She beheld
One slow approaching................
A yellow cloth over his shoulder cast,
Girt as the hermits are, and in his hand
An earthen bowl, shaped melonwise, the which
Meekly at each hut-door he held a space,
Taking the granted dole with gentle thanks.
And all as gently passing where none gave.

* * *

But he who bore the bowl so lordly seemed,
So reverend, and with such a passage moved,
With so commanding presence filled the air,
With such sweet eyes of holiness smote all,
That, as they reached him alms the givers gazed
Awe-struck upon his face, and some bent down,
In worship, and some ran to fetch fresh gifts
Grieved to be poor; till slowly group by group,
Children and men and women drew behind
Into his steps, whispering with covered lips,
Who is he ? who ? Where looked a Rishi thus ?"—*Light of Asia.*

2 A disciple of the Master and a very influential noble of the land; in fact the ruler, as it were, of Ṣrīrangam and the neighbourhood —*Comp.*

'What would you have, my daughter'? asked the Master.

'Nothing, your Reverence,' replied I, 'I have seen you day after day going round the streets receiving alms from the house-holders; and men of all classes, princes and peasants, touch your feet in reverence. What is your influence over them?'

'Nothing in fact,' replied he, 'I but speak to them now and then about the Lord and His doings and they are kind to me in consequence.'

'Is it given to such as I to hear it, Lord?'

'Why not, daughter; you have as much right to it as any, if not greater,' and forthwith he spoke to me of things strange and sweet that sank into my parched soul like a refreshing shower. And when the famine passed away and the fields were green and the water-courses were full, we started to return to our country. But alas! I found that I remembered, but too vaguely and imperfectly, the Great Word. I was a woman and a wife; it would have been considered the height of impropriety for me to go after the Master and pray for instruction; and here I was about to return to my country with scarcely any hopes at all of ever seeing him. This thought drove me mad, and I was cursing the Karma that made me a helpless woman; when, joy of joys! I saw the Master coming towards the house. I flew down and embracing his feet, said:

'Lord, we go back to our land, and I see no chance of my ever coming back here. I am sorry to say that I but imperfectly remember the Good Word you spoke to me the other day.'

'No matter,' replied the Master with a smile, 'it is a real pleasure to me to be given an occasion to speak again on such a subject,' and he instructed me again in the Two Truths in the name of the Grand hierarchy of Teachers.

He was moving away, when, I fell at his feet and said, 'Grant me something that will ever preserve thy remembrance to me; it will keep me from all evil and all evil from me.'

'Really, I see nothing that I can give away,' said the Master 'but stay, here are my sandals. Take them and may they do you good.'

We left the place the very day, and it was never given me to set my eyes since on the godlike features of the Master."

She ended amidst perfect silence; the disciples, from whose faces the smile of incredulity and pity had long ago vanished, looked with wonder and admiration at one who was a truer disciple of the Master than any of them. The Master was the first to speak; he directed her to lay out the supper, having previously instructed one of his men to watch her closely and report. The woman exchanged her garments for others newly washed and pure, and entered the place of worship with the words "I take refuge in the feet of the Master" upon her lips. She then reverently washed the sandals of the Master and offering to them the meal she had prepared for the guests, remained for some time in deep meditation. She then came out to her guests and invited them to walk in.

THE TESTS.

By that time the Vaishṇava had made his report to the Master, but was unable to describe what she did in the room. "It was something black and long to which she offered the food; certainly it was not the image of the Lord." Accordingly the Master said to her:

"What were you doing within the room?"

"I simply offered the meal, as I always do, to the Holy Sandals."

"May I have a look at them?"

"With great pleasure."

The Master glanced at them and was not surprised to find them his own, but still for the benefit of those of his disciples who might still doubt her, said:

"Whisper into my ears the Good Word the Master said unto you; if it agrees not, the Vaishṇavas here take no food of yours." She looked surprised that any one should ask her to pronounce to him the Most Sacred Word; but there was that in the frank eyes of the questioner that reassured her; and there was a voice deep in her heart telling her she was approaching the greatest hour of her life. So she laid herself at the feet of the Master and with awe and trembling whispered the Word of Power into the ears of the stranger.

"You have spoken the truths," said he, and the woman rejoiced to have come to the end of the investigation. But lo! she was not to be let off so easily; there was another test, the last and the hardest.

"Well then," continued the same mild voice, "see if you can recognise the Master in any of us here." She brought a light and carefully scanned the features of the group. She halted before the Master and said: "The feet are those of the Master, but the features I do not recognise. It is long since I saw him; he was dressed in orange robes, and even then I dared not raise my eyes to his face."

The Master could hold out no longer. "Come unto my heart, true friend and faithful follower. And you, sirs, might thank your stars that it has been given you to set your eyes on this holy lady. You might travel far and not come across any such example of utter lowliness of heart and heart-whole devotion. Get yourselves ready to partake of the food prepared; for verily, I say unto you, it is holy and sweet in the eyes of the Lord. She recalls to my memory the famous occasion when the Great Shepherd deigned to grace the humble abode of the Great Saint Vidura."[1]

Supper was over and the guests retired to their comfortable beds, rendered doubly so by their long travel during the day.[2]

ANOTHER CONVERT.

It was now midnight; the guests were all asleep, and silence deep as death reigned over the place. The lady gathered the remains of the supper and, arousing her husband, made him partake of it, but took nothing herself. He noticed it and said:

"What is the matter with you that you eat not?"

"The holy Râmânuja and his disciples have come down from the Temple; and would not take food from our hands."

"Why, are we not Brâhmaṇas?"

"True, but you are not of the True Faith. What curse has fallen on us that the Holy men should come to our house and fast? Say not the Holy Books, 'A Brâhmaṇa guest enters a house like the Vaiṣvânara fire. Good men make him peace offerings of water to wash

---

1 Mahâ Bhârata, Udyôga Parva, 91 chapter.

2 His disciples had their supper, but Râmânuja ate not.

"How so, my Lord, have I offended you in any way" anxiously inquired the good hostess.

"Nay, nay, my daughter" replied the Master, "how could that be? It is not seemly that I should partake of the food offered to my sandals. Bring me milk and fruits to place before the Lord Varada and *that* is more than enough for me."—(*G.L.R.*)

his feet, a seat to sit on, and food to eat. If, however, the foolish host allows the Brâhmaṇa to remain in his house fasting, verily he is accursed ; the fiery guest consumes the merits that the house-holder had laboriously acquired by acts of charity, gifts, association with holy men, sympathy towards others, sacrifices, nay, even his sons and daughters ?"[1]

"What shall we do ?" enquired the terrified husband.

"Nothing, but to take refuge in the Master and trust to his infinite grace to be forgiven."

"I swear to you, by everything I hold sacred, to do it the first thing in the morning." The lady waited upon the Master before day-break and touching his feet, said :?

"Lord, deign to grace my humble abode yet another day, and take my husband too under the shadow of your feet."

"Be it so," replied the Master, and so taken up was he with her purity of heart and perfect devotion that he, of his own accord, stayed there for some days. [2] He provided himself with the garments of his order and, placing them before his Lord Dêvarâja, received them from his hands as he did when he first took the vows.

AT SÂLAGRÂMA.

They then took reluctant leave of the weeping pair,[3] and proceeded still west until they reached a place named Sâlagrâma.[4] They had come upon an unholy place.

---

1 (Kaṭhopanishad, Valli, 7. 8).

2 The party reached the house of the woman Chêlânchalâmba, called in Tamil [Tamil]) on the evening of the 7th day. The husband was given the name of Srî Ranga Dâsa, on his initiation. —(*Prap.*)

3 The next day the Master sent Mâruti the younger and Ammangi Ammâl, two of his disciples, to Srîrangam to bring him news of Âlvân.—(*R.D.C.*)

4 The place was originally known as Jâlagrâma ([Tamil]) but the Master named it Sâlagrâma, in memory of the purification of

There were none of the True Faith, but plenty of secret enemies. The Master and his friends met with but scant courtesy at their hands, observing which he said to Âṇḍân:

"Seat yourself for some time at the place where people come to draw water with your feet immersed in it." Âṇḍân obeyed, and the inhabitants unconsciously partook of the water purified by the holy magnetism of the Great One. Very soon the scales fell away from their eyes; they felt themselves strangely attracted to the Master and to his teachings. They were mightily ashamed of their own previous indifference; and very soon the Master had them before him entreating to be admitted into the True Faith.

It was in that out of the way place that the Blessed One came upon that strangest of men Ândhra Pûrṇa (வடுகநம்பி) who represented in himself the most perfect ideal of devotion of a disciple to his Guru.[1] The Master then proceeded to Nṛisimhapura and stayed at the place (Nṛisimha's shrine) for some time, earnestly instructing Ândhra Pûrṇa in the doctrines of the Faith.

The Punishment of the Chôḷa.

When there, he saw that the unfortunate Chôḷa ruler had come to the end of his karma in that life; his cup of

---

the inhabitants by the water that had the feet of Âṇḍân—the name suggesting itself to him from the Vaishṇavas partaking of the water that had washed the Sâlagrâma or Holy Stone that forms an object of daily worship.—(*R.D.C.*)

[1] The exact route that Râmânuja took is not known to us; but he seems to have followed the course of the Kavery as far as Satyamangalam, near Erode, then taking a chord line, reached Kavery again, at Râmanâthapuram, (Vahni-Pushkariṇi), 40 miles west of Mysore. Sâlagrâma (Mithila-Sâlâgrâma) now known as Mirle and Sâligrâma, 2 villages about 30 miles west of Mysore.—(*G.L.R.*)

In memory of the same a small shrine is erected at the spot, in which are installed the holy Feet of Râmânuja for devout worship by all; the fountain is close by, connected with the shrine by a flight of steps. It belongs, of right, to the descendants of Ândhra Pûrṇa. The village is reputed to be unaffected by cobra-poison, for Râmânuja is Ṣêsha.—(*G.L.R.*)

iniquity was full to overflowing and would not hold another drop. Râmânuja afflicted him with a terrible disease that ate into his throat and rendered him a loathsome mass of corruption. He anticipated the horrors of the grave, in that the worms preyed upon him *even when he was alive*; hence he is known to posterity as Kṛimikaṇṭha (worm-throated); raised by his own demerits to that bad eminence, he became a mark for the finger of scorn for all time to come.[1]

---

[1] From the house of the holy woman the Master travelled by way of Vanhipushkariṇi, Mithilâ, Sâlagrâma, to Toṇḍanoor.—(*Prap.*)

The priests of the temple at Nṛisimhapura, having informed themselves of the cause of the Master's journey from Ṣrîrangam, were beside themselves with rage, and performed a magical ceremony to bring about the death of the infamous Chôḷa, (Parântaka, by name). (*V.G.*)

The very next day after the Master despatched Mâruti to Ṣrîrangam, he took water in his hand and offered it with due mantras to the Lord Vênkaṭêṣa. Now, the Brâhmaṇâs never fail, during their Sandhyâ prayers, to offer to the Lord Nârâyaṇa, that dwells in the Solar Orb, water accompanied by the recitation of the Gâyatrî. The holy water goes to strengthen the spiritual energy of the Spirit of the Sun and enables him to destroy the Mandêhâs, the evil spirits that attack him every day. Even so, the water offered by the Master served to turn the Lord against the Chôḷa. He had gone round the land destroying His places of worship, had thrown the sacred image of the Lord Gôvindarâja at Chidambaram into the sea and was even then on his way to Ṣrîrangam, to finish his work of destruction by levelling to the ground the House of Rest of the Lord—the centre of the True Faith.

One night, as he was encamped some miles off the holy city, the Lord appeared to the Chôḷa as a huge figure, black and terrible, and the trembling king faltered out:

"Who art thou, dread Image of Death?"

"I am the Dweller of the Holy Mount, Vênkaṭêṣa by name."

"And why hast thou come unto me?"

"To punish you as you deserve for your manifold impieties. Take that and that." And he pierced through and through the throat of the unfortunate Chôḷa with the short sword he held in his hand. The king screamed out in agony, crying, "Vênkaṭêṣa has stabbed me," and fell down senseless. His attendants rushed in at the noise and found their master bleeding from numerous wounds in his throat,

Vitthala Dêva's Conversion.

The Teacher then proceeded to Tondanoor,[1] at that time ruled by Vitthala Râya. He had an only daughter, whose manifold graces of mind and person were but sources of misery to her parents, in asmuch as she was possessed by an evil spirit and ran about naked. The king had tried one exorcist after another and had finally settled down into blank despair. One day Tondanoor Nambi, one of the disciples of our Master—he whom the Master made over to Dêvarâja Muni—came to the palace on his daily rounds for alms and was so much struck with the air of sadness that pervaded the palace and the people, that he could not help saying to the queen:

"Noble lady, if you would not consider me inquisitive, I would like to know why there is such an unbecoming gloom hanging about the palace. Is it owing to any recent bereavement?"

---

deep and ghastly. They were as wide awake as possible and had seen none going into the royal tent or coming out of it. And yet there were the frightful wounds to assure them that it was no mortal hand that had dealt the blows. Meanwhile the Chôla came to himself and his first words were: "Take me away from this horrible place. Hide me from that terrible figure." And so raving, he was conveyed back to his capital, where he lingered on for a time, a living corpse.—(*R.D.C.*)

When at Nrisimhapura, the Master resolved to make a clean sweep of the enemies of the True Faith and directed his discipie Âcchân (Yagñêsa) to perform a magical rite therefor.—(*R.D.C.*)

1 And stayed with Tondanoor Nambi, one of his disciples. He was a poor man and lived the life of a religious mendicant. The Master found that he could ill-afford to entertain him and his party, so he sent word to the Disciple of the Sandals, and her husband at once brought him a thousand pieces of gold.—(*R.D.C.*)

Tondanoor, the capital or a capital outpost of the Hoysâla Ballâla kings of the Jain persuasion, who ruled at Dwâra Samudra or Halêbid. It is now known as Tonnûr, and is 16 miles north of Mysore, on the way to Mêlkote. Even so late as 1316 A. C. the kings used to retire to Tondanoor.—(*G.L.R.*)

"Happier would we have been if it were that," replied the queen, (Ṣântaḷa Dêvi—*G.L.R.*) bursting out into tears. Then, after some time, she added, "We have an only daughter, through whom we are punished, in that we are forced to be helpless spectators of her hourly misery. Her loveliness, the countless graces of her body and mind do but cast a more glaring light on the ghastly life she is leading—life!—a living death."

"It is a thousand pities that I did not know it before. My Master, the Holy Râmânuja, is now fortunately here, and a glance of his holy eyes is enough to strike terror into the hearts of the worst of the lot and cause it to flee in agony. Let me tell you what he did long, long ago at Kânchî," and he narrated to the wondering queen the story of the Master and the Brahmarâkshasa. She, in her turn, acquainted her husband with it, who at once exclaimed :

"Why, if Râmânuja but restores our daughter to health and sanity, he is our God, our Lord, our Master; and where else shall we take refuge?"

Meanwhile, he had sent out invitations to the priests of his own faith for a dinner in the palace; his wife remonstrated with him on his imprudence, saying :

"They are sure to disappoint you and will throw the blame upon you for being a mutilated man and as such impure."

"Let us see. They will not dare to insult me thus; and that too in the presence of a rival Teacher."

After all, his wife proved herself a truer prophet, for, none of them turned up, and that for a very good reason. When his kingdom was overrun by the emperor, he was taken prisoner to Delhi and was mutilated of a finger (to show that he had lost his independence and sovereignty—

G. L. R.); and it was against the rules of their order to take food from a deformed or a mutilated person. The king was enraged beyond bounds, and his wife took the opportunity to set him against his priests and turn him towards the Master.

An Invitation to The Master.

And under her influence, he sent a pressing invitation to him to come over to the palace.

"The rules of my order are against my entering any city, much less the capital," the Master sent back word; but Toṇḍanoor Nambi and the other disciples represented to him that the king would be an invaluable acquisition to the Faith and would advance its interests immensely; and earnestly entreated him to make an exception in his favor. The Master gave a reluctant assent and they all joyfully proceeded to the palace, where they were welcomed with great honour.

The Royal Pair embraced his feet and stood before him with folded hands, their anxious features but too plainly expressing the unspoken wishes of their heart. The Master at once turned to one of his disciples, who immediately sprinkled over the princess the holy water that had washed his sacred feet. A strong shiver ran through her delicate frame; and awaking as from a long trance, she gazed wildly around and was deeply ashamed to find herself without her clothes and before strangers. She immediately ran away, but as soon came back modestly dressed as becomes a princess and fell at the feet of the Master to whom she owed her life, her happiness here and hereafter.

Though the king was prepared for something like this, his hopes fell far short of the reality. He and his friends became the ardent disciples of the Master and did excellent service in spreading the teachings of the Good

Law far and wide. The Master gave to the regenerated king the name of Vishṇuvardhana[1] (his former name, Viṭṭhala Dêva Râya, being but a corrupted form of Biṭṭi-Dêva or 'The Finger-Lord.'—*G. L. R.*)

The Master and the Jains.

The priests of the old faith did not quietly put up with this altered state of things. Their king, the pillar of their faith, was turned against them and a proselyte to the faith they hated. Their places, their honours, their power and their prestige were all in the hands of their enemies and it was only a question of time when they

---

[1] The Indian Antiquary, Vol. II, May 1873, quotes a passage from Śramaṇa Belagula Sthalapurâṇa thus:—"In the Śaka year 1039 (Durmukhi = 1117 A. C.), Beṭṭa-Vardhana, under the taunts of his favorite concubine (?) and the arguments of Râmânujâchârya, received Tapta-mudra (mark of religion) and thus became a convert to the Vaishṇava religion. He then changed his name to Vishṇu Vardhana and with a bitter hatred against this (Jama) religion, discontinued or abolished all the inâms, destroyed 790 Basti temples, and set up Pancha Nârâyaṇas—Chennigi Nârâyaṇa at Bêlûrû, Kirti Nârâynna at Talakkâḍu, Vijaya Nârâyaṇa at Gaḍugu and Lakshmî-Nârâyaṇa at Haradanahalli, transferring to these all the Svâsthyas or inâms that had formerly been given to the Basti temples. He built the tank at Toṇḍanûru from the stones of the destroyed Basti temples, and called it Tirumala-Sâgara. Having abolished different kinds of Jama inâms, he established, below this tank, a chatra for the feeding of the Râmânuja-Kûṭa. He gave the name of Mêlukôṭa and Tirunârâyaṇapuram to the village of Doḍḍaguruganahaḷḷi."

Rice's *Mysore Gazetteer*, Vol. II, p. 274 (1879):—Moti Talâb or Tank of Pearls, a large tank at Tonnûr, in Seringapatam Taluk. It is formed by an embankment carried across a gap between two rocky hills which stem the water of the Yâdava Nadi and other mountain torrents that there unite their streams. The mound is 78 cubits high, 150 long, and 250 broad at the base.

Ibid p. 295:—The Royal convert conferred upon his apostle and his followers the tract of country on each side of the river Cauvery at Seringapatam, known by the name of Ashṭagrâma, over which he appointed his own officers under the ancient designation of Prabhus or Hebbâra.

Rice's Sravaṇa Belagula Inscriptions, p. 48:—The father of Śantala Dêvi was the Senior Preggaḍe Narasinga, a Śaiva, and her mother Mâchikabbe, a devoted Jaina.—(*G.L.R.*)

would feel the iron claws of persecution at their throats. So they took counsel of one another and sent a challenge to the Master :

"You pride yourself on having converted our king and congratulate yourself on the easy victory you have got. But you have reckoned without your host ; it is not such a walk over as you imagine ; meet us in argument and defeat us, and you would have fairly earned the place you now occupy. But you have taken a mean and unfair advantage of a misfortune in the royal family to entrap an ignorant layman. Come on like a man and have it out with us."

Râmânuja was not slow to accept the challenge ; it was long since he had a bout, a square set fight, and he wanted some excitement to divert the sad current of his thoughts. So a day was fixed for the disputation and about 12,000 Sramanas, the most learned priests of their religion, assembled in the palace to fight for their faith.

"Argue with us one after another, and when you have overthrown the last, we shall acknowledge ourselves beaten and place ourselves at your mercy."

The Master smiled ; it would be tedious work, this disputation, and would extend over many years. He would go through it in no time and show them who he was—a very nice opportunity for it.

He assembled the Sramanas in a vast hall, and in the privacy of a curtained space, assumed his divine form —the thousand-hooded Sêsha, the symbol of Boundless Wisdom and Eternity. He called out to them and said :

"You there, every one of you, may put to me what questions you like, one by one, or to save time, all at once ; and you will let me know when any one fails to get a reply."

This took their breath away; it was too tough to go down; they took it as a sheer bravado, and poured a simultaneous volley of questions, the knottiest they could prepare. The noise was something awful and the scene could better be imagined than described. But there came to the ears of each, a voice clear and sweet, with the reply treading hard upon the heels of the question. Each thought that he had tackled Râmânuja and rendered him *hors-de-combat* as regards others; but lo! in a very short time, too short to be believed, there was silence, almost oppressive, over the place. Each had his fill and had shot his last arrow.

"Have you done, ?" came the voice from behind the curtains, "if so, I leave you free to depart. Join the True Faith; for this is no place for the obstinate and the self-willed."

Many accepted the boon and became Srî Vaishnavâs.[1] This considerably enhanced the reverence and devotion of the king towards the Master and gave a

---

1 A king named Ballâla or Bitti-Dêva, who reigned at Dvârasamudra, independently of Krimikantha, was the ruler of the Mysore territory. He professed the Jain faith, with the priests of which the Master disputed and whom he convinced by argument. The king, being convinced of the truth of the system taught by Srî Râmânujâchârya, became a Vaishnava and was given the new name of Vishnu Vardhana.

There is an inscription near the modern Halebîdu, built on the ruins of Dvârasamudra, the capital of Vishnu Vardhana (1114—1138 A. C.) treating of his conversion and dated 1117 A. C.—(*V.C.*)

He caused the refractory Jains of Padmagiri to be ground in stone mills.—(*R.D.C.*)

The king was named Vishnu Vardhana Nârâyana.

The Jains themselves proposed that the defeated party should be ground to powder. During the disputation, one of the Jains, marvelling at the wonderful quickness of the answers and their aptness, ventured to have a peep behind the curtain and beheld a serpent, huge and radiant, and thousand-hooded. He shrank back in terror and whispered the news to his friends. They slunk away one by one and the vast all gradually emptied itself. But they could not escape the watchful

considerable impetus to the progress of the True Faith. He then went back to the temple of Nrįsimha and resumed his duties towards his disciples.

CHAPTER XVIII.

AT TIRUNÂRÂYAṈAPURAM.

All at once, the Master found, to his dismay,[1] that his supply of the Sacred Earth was running short. That night he went to his bed with a heavy heart and prayed to the Lord of Kânchî to avert such a dire misfortune.

The Dream.

The Lord Nârâyaṇa appeared to him in his dream and said : "My dear, I am awaiting your arrival every minute on Yadugiri over there. Come to me at once and I shall take you where you will find a never-failing supply of what you want." The next morning he laid it before his disciples, who were all for instantly proceeding to the holy place.

Vishṇuvardhana despatched a large body of men in advance to clear the way; and the party very soon approached Yadugiri. The Master bathed in the holy waters of the Vêda Saras and changed his orange robes at the slab sanctified by the Divine Dattâtrêyâ[2] when he took orders as a Sanyâsin. He sought far and wide, in and out of the dense undergrowth upon the mountain, but could not come upon the spot indicated by the Lord. The sun set on his fruitless

king, who prepared to deal with them as they so richly deserved. But, the Master, out of the infinite compassion of his heart, interceded for the poor misguided souls and saved them from their horrible fate. Many took refuge in the Good Law, and went to swell the ranks of the True Believers; some few fled the country.

The Master then returned to Sâlagrâma.—(*V.G.*)

1 No Vaishṇava would worship his household deity or perform his daily prayers without his caste-marks.

2 An incarnation of Vishṇu and the teacher of the Yôga Vidya.

search and he passed a restless night, half suspecting that he was not pure enough to be blessed with the sight of the Divine One.

Yet Another.

Once again the Lord appeared to him in his sleep, and said: "Mark well the grove of Champaka trees to the south-west of the Kalyâṇa Saras hard by; you will find a solitary Vakula tree; proceed due south and you will come upon an over-grown Tulasî plant; look among the roots and an ant-hill will meet your eye; look well into it, for there I am; and the Sacred Earth that you so badly want is to be found in a spot due north-west of the tank. It has been brought from the White Island by Garuḍa[1] and never grows less (such is the potency of the mantra connected with it.) Never lose heart, man. I shall give another proof that these directions are not the creation of your over-excited fancy. From here to the ant-hill where I am, you will find broken twigs of the Tulasî plant scattered all along the path."

The next morning the Master rose with a gladder heart; and the king and the disciples augured the success of their search from the expression of superhuman joy that played over the features of Râmânuja.

Tirunârâyaṇapuram.

He followed the track of the Tulasî twigs and very soon came to the ant-hill; reverently they removed the earth around and soon the House of the Lord came to view. A shout of joy arose from the wondering multitude; Vishṇuvardhana was sent for, and gazed with open mouth and staring eyes at the great marvel; with divine honours and after the prescribed purifications, a splendid temple soon sprang around the place at the

1. The Divine Bird, the vehicle of the Lord. The White Island or the Śvêta Dwîpa is one of the abodes of the Lord.

king's command, who superintended the work night and day.[1] The Master worshipped the Lord three days with his own hands; established the Divine Service as laid down in Pâncharâtra Sâtvata Samhita,[2] and placed Srî Ranga Râja Bhatta, (Dêva Râja Bhatta—*V. G.*) one of his disciples and the best ritualist of his time, at the head of it. He lost no time in proceeding to the other place indicated by the Lord, and a blow from his staff sent up streams of the Sacred Earth, of which there seemed to exist an inexhaustible supply. Right gladly he gathered it and stored enough of it to last for a long time to come. As the spiritual son of Srî Sathakôpa and his most beloved disciple, the Master had a right of inheritance to the Divine Find; and he sanctified the Lord Srî Nârâyana at Yadugiri by offering him the decade of the Sacred Collect beginning with திருமாலுக்கம்,[3] as being the most appropriate.

But the Master's joy was dashed with a shade of sorrow when he reflected that there was no Utsava Vigraha[4]

---

1 The date of this important event is :—

The 1012th year of the Saka Era, on a Thursday, the 14th day of the bright fortnight, under the constellation Punarvasu.—(*T.G.*)

Saka Era 1020, (1090 A.C.) year Bahudhânya, month Pushya, the 14th day of the bright fortnight, Thursday, asterism Punarvasu.—(*Prap.*)

Saka Era 911. Thursday.—(*R.D.C.*)

Saka Era 1021. Bahudhânya, Phâlguna month.—(*V.G.*) According to the Bêlûr inscription 1039 S = 1137 A.C.—(*G.L.R.*)

2 The Pâncharâtra Âgamas are certain occult treatises, 108 in number, said to have been taught to Nârada by the great initiates of the Svêta Dwîpa, the Supreme Guru of which was Vishnu in his double incarnation of Nara and Nârâyana. Each of these Samhitas (treatises) is divided into Kriyâpâda (methods for erecting a temple and making an idol), Charyâpâda (worshipping it), Gñânapâda (philosophy) and Yôgapâda (practical occultism).—(*V.C.*)

3 Thiruvaimoli 31 Decade-1.

4 There are always two idols in every temple—the Mûla Vigraha (the root idol) that is generally of stone and never removed out of the Sanctuary; and the Utsava Vigraha (the festival idol) that, as its name implies, is used for being taken out during festivals.

for festival purposes. He went to sleep over the idea and was gratified to see the Lord appear to him again in his dreams and say: "My Utsava Vigraha, Râmapriya,[1] is at Delhi in the palace of the Muhamadan Emperor. Take him thence."

The next morning he consulted with his disciples, who unanimously advised him to start forthwith on his sacred mission. Vishnuvardhana would not hear of the Master journeying there without a royal escort; and in a

---

[1] When Vibhîshana, the brother of Râvana, took leave of Râma to go to Lankâ, the latter gave him the Lord Ranganâtha, the object of his daily worship.

Sometime after, Brahma came to him and offered him an idol, which he said, was of the same amsa as the one he had given away and was equal to it in holiness. Râma received it right gladly and continued to worship it all his life. Hence it derived its name of Râmapriya (dear to Râma).

The Lord gave it to Hanumân to worship, who in his turn, handed it over to Kusa, the son of Râma. He had a daughter named Kanakamâlini, who was extremely devoted to Râmapriya; and when she was married to a prince of the Yâdava race, she took it away as her dowry. And it was worshipped by the kings of that line.

Once, Balarâma, while on a pilgrimage to the various shrines of India, visited Nârayanâdri and was much struck with the sanctity of the place and the spiritual splendour of the image of the Lord there. He informed his brother Krishna of it, and persuaded him to take their own image to the Sacred Hill. They found the two almost indistinguishable, so much alike were they in every respect. Hence the place was named Yâdavâdri.

Later on, during the Kali Yuga, some rebellious nobles erected a fort on the spot and named it Mêlkote. The Muhammadans of Hindustan attacked them and destroyed the fort; and their leader Emmâdu Râya (Mahmud) took away all that was worth taking; and among them, the image of Râmapriya.—(*R.D.C.*)

It might have been carried away from Mêlkote by one of the generals of Mahmud of Ghazni, whose depredations extended all over India. Emmâdu Râya might be a corruption of Mahmud. The foundation of the Mahomedan Empire at Lahore (1022-A. C.), the sack of Sômanâth (1026-A. C.) and the death o Mahmud (1030 A. C.) are contemporaneous. Buchanan (Vol. I, 351) reads :—"Near Tondanoor, there is a monument dedicated to one of the fanatical followers of Mahmud Ghazni."—(*G.L.R.*)

short time the Blessed One was at Delhi, and caused his arrival to be announced to the Emperor. Strange to say, the Muhamadan, on his part, felt himself attracted to the Master and came to him at his camp. Something in him made him render the Master the highest honours that were due to the head of their faith; and in respectful accents, he asked the Master wherein he could be of service to him.

"Long may you reign and happily," said the Master. "Strange it is to see so much toleration and real devotion in one of your faith; you are an ornament to your country and to your religion. I am come to ask of you permission to seek in your palace for a sacred idol that I sadly want."

"Honoured am I," replied the Emperor, "by such a request."

He took the Master to the palace and directed his ministers to accompany Râmânuja to the building where the idols from the conquered lands were kept. Long did the Master look among them for what he wanted, but found it not. He returned to his camp with a heavy heart; he never for a moment doubted Râmapriya's presence there, but attributed his failure to his want of purity of heart, that prevented the Lord from manifesting Himself to his eyes. That night he was surprised and overjoyed to find Râmapriya before him in his dreams; who addressed him with a smile of pleasure, as if enjoying his confusion and said:

"My son, you have looked for me where I am not. The Emperor's daughter keeps me in her room and is very devoted to me; come there if you would see me."

The next morning the Master communicated the intelligence to the Emperor, who naturally wanted to test it, for, the stranger had evidently no way of ascertaining by ordinary means the whereabouts of the idol in that

Sanctum Sanctorum of the Muhamadans, the Imperial Seraglio. So he requested permission to accompany the Master, which was gladly given. They proceeded to the princess' apartments, and the Master, bowing himself to the Earth, prayed with folded hands:

"Lord of my heart, if Thy servant has found favour in Thy eyes, deign to gladden his eyes, dim with weary watching, with a sight of Thy Blessed Presence."

No sooner were these words out of his mouth, than behold! a sound of twinkling bells was heard, that fell upon the ears of the entranced spectators like dream-music; and following it, was seen the image of Râmapriya advancing towards the Master with leaps and bounds—like a dear child towards his beloved father whom he had not seen for a long time. The amazement of every one there could better be imagined than described, when they saw the image jump upon the knees of the Master and fondly nestle itself close to his breast.

But the Master, O! where was he? In the regions of Supreme Bliss, before the Throne, pouring forth his prayers and thanks to the Lord for His unlooked for grace. Soon he recovered himself and warmly embraced the Divine Infant, saying: "Child of my heart, (Sampatkumâra, செல்வப்பிள்ளை) long hast Thou been away from me and miserable have I been in consequence; but now that I have Thee, I have everything."

The Emperor and his suite looked on at this strange spectacle and could not shake themselves free from the belief that they were enjoying a pleasant dream, which they would give anything to last for ever. They found themselves in a strange atmosphere; strange sensations came over their bodies and strange thoughts in their hearts. Somehow or other, before they knew it, they found themselves at the feet of the Master, who broke the spell with the sweet words:

"Lord of the happy millions! Grant me permission to go back to my country and take with me what I came to seek."

"Strange man!" cried the Emperor, "I see nothing I can refuse you; yet I think you had better be away from here and *that* as soon as you can. You have strangely bewitched me and I feel that if you remain here longer, I would prove but a renegade to the faith I am born in and am bound to maintain."

The Master took the hint and was very soon on his way back to Yadugiri, where he was welcomed with divine honours by the king and his people.[1]

---

[1] The princess could not long survive the separation from her beloved Râmapriya. He was to her a living entity, the Lord of her heart, and no other would she ever think of, even in her dreams. She worried her father into sending men after the Master to bring back the image. The Master heard of this and refused to give back the image, whereupon the princess set out after her beloved, resolved never to be separated from him. The king, finding it useless to dissuade her from her purpose, sent his son with a large escort to accompany his sister on her way. She overtook the Master and entreated to be allowed to serve her beloved in her own way. The Master, from whose sight nothing was hid, past or future, placed her in the same palanquin as the image, and the cortège rode on. But, one day, the bearers of the palanquin reported that their burden was extremely light and the Master, who appeared as much surprised as any, examined the palanquin and found no princess in it. She had been absorbed into the essence of her Beloved, such was her devotion and such was the favor she found in the eyes of her Divine Lover. The beholders were struck with awe and reverence at this marvellous incident and looked at the Master for an explanation, who replied with a mysterious smile that left them no wiser than before. The brother of the princess accompanied the Master all the way and was present during the ceremony of installation of his sister's Divine Lover. The Master placed a golden image of the princess between the feet of Râmapriya and declared her as much entitled to worship as her Lord.

(Prabhâkara has written a work, 'Yavanî-pariṇaya,' about the marriage of Sampatkumâra and the Sultani. The bridegroom, as the son of Râmânuja, belongs to the Harita Gotra; the bride belongs to the Gargya Gotra. Gargya is the father of Kâlayavana, and hence the patriarch of all Yavanas or non-Hindus—*vide* Vishṇu Purâṇa, V. 23, 4 and 5, and Harivamsa, 115, 15.—*G.L.R.*)

The Master then arranged for the due observance of the various festivals, daily, fortnightly, monthly, half-

---

The prince could not but be impressed with the sincerity, the holiness and the magic influence exercised by the Master, and on his return to Delhi gave a glowing account of his journey to his astonished father.

Out of the extreme love the king bore to his daughter and out of the great reverence in which he held the Master, the former came over all the way to Tirunârâyaṇapuram. The Master received him with all honours and conduced to make his stay there a happy one. The king, not to be outdone in generosity, presented to his divine son-in-law priceless jewels and untold wealth.

One of his sons, Kabîr by name, was with him all the time, but, the decrees of Karma that gave him the body of a Mlêccha for temporary use, could not put back by a single second the hour of redemption and awakening. He remained behind while his father and his retinue returned to Delhi and with a view to purify his physical encasement, as far as possible, that had been defiled by unclean ways of living, the Master advised him to make a pilgrimage to the various shrines of India.

One day he came to Ṣrîrangam and so rapid was the reawakening of that advanced Ego to his former spiritual heritage, that he drew nearer and nearer to the throne of the Ancient of Days—nearer than many others.

"Lord, if I have found favour in Thy Eyes and if I have served Thee to the best of my abilities, take me from this dark Earth unto Thyself," said Kabîr.

"Nay, not so, my dear," replied Ranganâtha ; "here I take unto myself only those who, by their good Karma have been born as Hindus, and are capable of entering into the True Faith. They should either be touched by my Sacred Discus in the way of caste-marks as disciples, or obtain their death through it as my enemies. But at Jagannâth, they come to me by merely looking at my Discus. So you had better come to me at Jagannâth."

Kabîr did so and served the Lord long and devoutly at His seaside resort. One day, the Lord bethought Himself of taking His faithful servant unto His bosom and presented Himself before His devotee as a dog. Kabîr noticed it not, until the animal suddenly snatched away the basket that contained the pûries (wheaten cakes) for his dinner. Kabîr awoke from his deep meditation and seeing the dog run away with the dry pûries, *hastened after it with gheê to soften it.* But he could not overtake the strange dog until they were well on the sands of the sea-shore. And there the Lord gathered the faithful and patient servant unto His bosom. Not content with that, He informed His high priest of the event and directed him to proceed thither and pay high honours to the body that enshrined the pure soul of Kabîr.

yearly, and annual.[1] He had a maṭha erected in the place for the accommodation of the faithful and selected fifty-two of his disciples to settle themselves in that holy spot and serve in the temple. He gave them the proud name of 'The Fifty-Two' and each had his own baptismal name when he was born in the Faith.

His father at Delhi came to know of the glories of his sainted son, and as a mark of his appreciation of the great honor done to his family, sent valuable presents of money and jewels to his Divine Son-in-law.

When the Master was returning from Delhi, he was attacked by robbers and was in danger of losing his dear Son, so miraculously recovered. Some low-caste men, Pariahs, who dwelt thereabout, offered to assist him, beat off the robbers and took the Master and his men to a place of safety; nor did they leave him until he was well on his way and out of danger. And in token of the disinterested help rendered him at that critical moment, the Master gave them a recognition—a rare one in those days, and one that shows the broad heart and the allembracing love of the Great One. During the grand festival at Tirunârâyaṇapura, the Pariahs are given free access into the sacred precincts of the temple. They bathe in the Kalyâṇasaras, wear the sacred caste-marks, penetrate into the temple as far as the High Altar (Balipîṭha), make the circuit of the courtyards, present their offerings of rice and oil, worship the deity from afar, and depart after having been sumptuously entertained. Then the temple is purified and the festival goes on. And it holds even to this day.—(*Prap.*)

Râmânuja gave them the name of Tirukkulattâr (திருக்குலத்தார்) 'the Blessed Caste.' He gave them the privilege of entering the temples of Bêlûr, Srîrangam, and Mêlkote, once in a year; and the Brahmaṇas cannot complain of pollution, should they happen to be touched by the Pariahs on those occasions.—(*G.L.R.*)

1 One day the Lord at Toṇḍanoor appeared to Toṇḍanoor Nambi in his sleep and said: "We desire to be taken to the house of Sampatkumâra and hunt with him." The Nambi communicated the wishes of the Lord to His followers, who accordingly took Him in sacred pomp to the shrine of Râmapriya. The Master received Nambi kindly; caused the highest honors of the place to be shown him; and presented large offerings of various kinds of food to the Host and His Divine Guest. The fifty-two disciples of Nambi prayed for permission to partake of this; and the Master, who ever loved a joke, directed them to take it by force from the servants of the temple; whereat the fifty-two disciples of *his* clamoured loudly.

One day, the Master held a large gathering in the maṭha; there were present his disciples, who were themselves Spiritual Teachers of many in the land. There were the Jeers, the Êkângis, the famous Fifty-Two, the Srî Vaishṇavâs, and the Sâthânis, the Nuns (Kôthis) and others who waited upon the Master, ready to do his least bidding. The Master raised his hand and there was profound silence.

"I am directed to say," said he in slow accents, "that the true sons of the Faith residing in this holy spot, have, of right, a place by the Throne of the Eternal in Srî Vaikunṭha." The vast audience bowed themselves at the feet of the Master and wept with tears of silent joy. Ah! Blessed were they who lived in the time of the Master and heard it assured in his own words.

In the Kṛita Yuga, the Divine Sanatkumâra brought the hill from Satya Lôka, the world of Brahma, along with the Vimâna of Bliss, and established the worship of Srî Nârâyaṇa on it; hence the Great Ones call it "The Mountain of Nârâyaṇa."

In the Trêta Yuga, the Divine Dattâtrêya, an incarnation of Vishṇu, spent his time on the banks of the Vêda Saras and the old hills echoed to the sweet and majestic chant of the hymns by the Teacher and his disciples; hence it was called "The Mountain of the Vêdas."

In the Dwâpara Yuga, Srî Kṛishṇa and his elder brother Balarâma worshipped at this Holy Shrine long and fervently; hence the wise ones know it as "Yâdavagiri."

In the Kali Yuga, Râmânuja, the Great Teacher, recovered the long lost temple from amidst the ruins, and

"Why, if you can, nothing prevents you from taking it away from your brethren of Toṇḍanoor," said the Master with a sly, humorous twinkle of the eye. And then there ensued a pleasant fight, all in sport, and much pushing and scrambling for the sacred offerings; and the stronger won. And it goes on even to this day.—(*R.D.C.*)

had re-established the worship of the Lord Nârâyaṇa; hence it is even known as "Yati Ṣaila."

The Master then proceeded to Padmagiri, a strong centre of the Bauddhas; and after long and arduous disputations, he expelled them from the land and spread the True Faith far and wide. He remained for twelve years at Tirunârâyaṇapura, completing his work and discharging his manifold duties with unflagging zeal and rare ability.

One day a Ṣrî Vaishṇava touched the feet of the Master and gave out that he was come from Ṣrîrangam. "What news of the Lord?" exclaimed the Master in unfeigned eagerness.

"The best news possible," replied the Brâhmaṇa "except for the great void created by your absence."

"What of Mahâ Pûrṇa and Âḻvân that proceeded to the Chôḻa?"

"They were taken before him and were asked to sign their names to the declaration—'There is none higher than Ṣiva.'[1]

'Nay, not so,' replied Âḻvân in gentle but firm accents. 'The Vedas, the Smṛitis, the Purâṇas and the Itihâsas proclaim in no measured tones Ṣrî Nârâyaṇa as higher than the highest; from Him proceeds the universe; through Him it lives and in Him it is absorbed; He is the goal of our knowledge; Brahma and Rudra stand to Him as son and grandson and are guided by Him. Here is a puzzle; make it out if you can. One stretched out his feet, another washed them reverently with water from his gourd, and a third sprinkled himself with the holy

1 "Is this the Great Râmânuja of whom you spoke so high," asked the Chôḻa of Nâloorân.

"Nay, his disciple and his equal," replied the Hindu Judas. —(*R.D.C.*)

water. Now which of them is the Highest, O Lord of Men.'

The king remained silent, unable to reply. Âlvân continued:

'Nay, one more point for consideration. Ṣiva was so named in as much as he was purified of his heinous sin of Brahminicide by the holy water that washed the feet of Trivikrama. Now, is there none higher than Ṣiva?'[1]

The king and his pandits sat tongue-tied and shame-faced; but the king was more obstinate and self-willed than Âlvân had bargained for. He adopted the maxim—'when there is no case, abuse the plaintiff's attorney'—a dictum sanctified by long usage and great authorities.

'You are a great Pandit,' cried he; with uncontrollable anger. 'You are skilled in the subtleties of dialectics and can make two and two appear five; but I am an honest straightforward man and know nothing of your wiles and crooked ways. Here is the declaration which says, 'There is none higher than Ṣiva.' I pin my faith to it and I want you to give your assent to it, yes or no?'

'Needs must, when the devil drives,' replied Âlvân, laughing. 'Well, hand me over the declaration.'

He wrote something and handed it back to the king, who no sooner ran his eyes over it, than he sprang at Âlvân with a cry and roared out, 'This to me! Dare you beard the lion in its den? Look here, lords, what the infamous wretch has written—Drôna[2] is certainly larger than it. What, ho, there!

---

1 Âlvân criticised the tenets of the Ṣaiva faith by 25 unanswerable arguments.—(*Hari Samayadîpa.*)

R.D.C. attributes the latter part of the speech to Mahâ Pûrṇa.

2 The word 'Ṣiva' also means a measure of corn; and Âlvân punned upon the word and said, 'yes there is something higher than Ṣiva and that is Drôṇa (another measure, larger than Ṣiva).

take these recreants away and have their eyes torn out of their sockets.[1] '

Alas! his evil karma was driving him headlong into committing this most outrageous act of cruelty—an act that no follower of the Faith ever hears without feelings of unutterable grief and horror. Well, it was over—the terrible deed; the helpless pair were turned out to find their way back to their homes.[2]

It was too much for Mahâ Pûrṇa, enfeebled by age and infirmities; he declared himself unable to proceed further and in a forlorn garden—ah! what a resting place for the Great Teacher!—he laid himself down on the bare ground, with his head on the lap of the devoted Âḻvân and his feet on the lap of his daughter Attuḻâi, who followed him and would never be persuaded to go away. She humbly submitted that it would be better if he would allow himself to be conveyed to Ṣrîrangam, that he might breathe his last there.

'Nay, not so,' replied Mahâ Pûrṇa, 'it would create a false impression in the minds of those that follow me. They wiḻḻ conclude that it was absolutely necessary for all Ṣrî Vaishṇavâs to breathe their last at Ṣrîrangam.' He then concentrated his soul on the feet of his Master, Yâmunâchârya, and withdrew himself from his mortal

1 "Nay not so," replied Âḻvân, "you have but suggested the right course of action I should take; these fleshly eyes of mine cannot be more justly punished for their having looked upon you and your infidel crew." And he plucked out his eyes with his own hands.

He then called out: "Is there none among this heretic assemblage that claims membership with the True Faith?" Forthwith, a woman-servant of the Chôḻa, who carried his sword before him, threw it away and cried, "Here am I, my Lord, dispose of me as thou wilt."

"Lead me hence," said Âḻvân; and they left the hall. She took him to a deserted garden on the far outskirts of the town and tended him the live long day.—(*R.D.C*).

2 Mahâ Pûrṇa was led by his daughter to the same garden —(*R.D.C.*)

encasement. Some Srî Vaishnavâs privately cremated his remains there; and had Âlvân conveyed by easy stages to Srîrangam. Âlvân reached his home and bewailed his misfortune in not being allowed to follow Mahâ Purna."[1]

---

[1] His feet on the lap of his wife Ândâl.—(*Prap.*)

Jatâyu had the supreme happiness of breathing his last on the lap of Srî Râma, who was on his way to destroy the infamous Râvana. Likewise, Mahâ Pûrna was blessed in departing from this body on the lap of the sainted Âlvân, who was on his way to destroy the wicked Chôla.—(*R.D.C.*)

That spot was sanctified by being the Samâdhi of the Great Nâtha Yôgi and his disciple Kurukâdhipa.—(*R.D.C.*)

Pasupati Koil, a village 7 miles from Kandiyûr, near Tanjore. —(*G. L. R.*)

Meanwhile some persons that made their living by cremating the homeless and the forsaken, offered to do the same in the case of Mahâ Pûrna; but Âlvân broke forth indignantly and said: "What! know you not that the Master of the Universe and his servants are ever ready to wait upon a Vaishnava, nay, esteem it as a favor; your chances are almost nothing. Go, you have been forestalled."

Then, the Srî Vishnavâs of Parântaka, a village hard by, came up and assisted Âlvân in cremating the holy remains of the Great Teacher according to the Brahmamêdha rites—who more deserving than he? They conveyed Âlvân on a litter to their village and nursed him tenderly.

The Lord Ranganâtha expressed his recognition of the great services rendered by Nâvalkodi Ammâl, who took a leading part in the affair, by conferring upon him and his descendants the highest honours of the Temple and the envied title of Âchârya, Teacher of Men.—(*R.D.C.*)

Mahâ Pûrna was 105 years old when he died.—(*Prap.*)

His friends conveyed Âlvân to Srîrangam. The warders at the gate stopped the escort.

"Who are you?"

"Âlvân and his friends."

"Are you not the disciples of Râmânuja, late of Srîrangam?"

"Even so. Do you not know it?"

"We know it; and hence you cannot go in. We have suffered enough through Râmânuja and his teachings. But for him we would not have had the tyrant Chôla upon us, threatening to level the time-honored temple to the ground. What horrors! What persecutions! And all through that Râmânuja. What care we whether Vishnu or Siva be the first or the best? Enough. You do not get in."

"Nay, not so," interposed another, "this is quite another sort of man. He was ever known as a quiet, uninterfering, holy man;

Tears of rage and grief stole down the cheeks of the Master; he calculated upon his iron-will to keep down his rising emotions; but he very soon found out that he had over-estimated his strength of mind. He broke down completely and sobbed like a child :—

"Lord, Lord, why am I reserved for such a fate? What heinous sin have I committed that I should be made the unhappy spectator of this horrible act of sacrilege?" He fell down senseless, and was revived, but with very great difficulty, by his disciples, who, themselves with hearts breaking with grief, tried their best to console the Master.

"Fortunate are we in that our Âlvân is spared to us," said they.

The Master celebrated the obsequies of his Teacher with extraordinary pomp; and despatched one of his disciples, Mâruti the younger, to Srîrangam to bring back fuller and more recent information.[1]

It was about this time that the revered Gôshṭhî Pûrṇa left this earth for his Seat of Bliss around the

the people like him much and have nothing against him. I think we can safely allow him in."

"As you deem it fit," replied the first.

"Not so fast, my friends," struck in Âlvân, "you dispose of me too quickly and without any regard for my own feelings in the affair. I am an humble follower of the Great Teacher and my only claim to any consideration I base upon that and that alone. And since you feel so kindly towards the Master, it is but just that you should extend the same consideration towards the servant. I shall enter the place with the Master or never."

And he turned away from the inhospitable spot to go to Thirumâlirumsôlamalai (திருமாலிருஞ்சோலை) where he was welcomed warmly. It was there he composed his famous works and there he stayed all the years the Master spent abroad.—(*Prap.*)

Âlvân stayed at Srîrangam and seemed to be none the worse for his loss of sight.—(*V.G.*)

[1] Mâruti the younger and Ammangi Ammâl were sent to Srîrangam when the Master was enjoying the hospitality of the hunters. —(*R.D.C.*)

Throne of Light. One of his disciples ventured to ask him at the last moment :

"May we know what your Holiness may be thinking of just now?"

"Nothing .pleasant. A bird spoiled the peace of mind of the Divine Man, Srî Râmachandra."[1] He only meant that the Lord could not console Himself for having done so little towards the crow, Jayanta, that took refuge in Him. Such is the grace of our Lord—need we any other source of comfort now or ever !

Meanwhile Mâruti, like his namesake, proceeded on the wings of speed to the holy temple and flung himself at the feet of Âlvân with tears of grief and joy. Âlvân warmly embraced him and asked eagerly, "How is the Master? And his disciples, my brothers? I have seen him in that I have seen you, the repository of his confidence."

"The Master is plunged in inconsolable grief at hearing of what took place here in his absence and sent me to ascertain the facts of the case."

"Alas! that the holy Mahâ Pûrṇa should be made to suffer by the wanton cruelty of that misguided Chôla. The world will never see his equal. But, as for me," said he, "that is another thing. Tell him that I am supremely happy in the thought of the Master's safety and extremely sorry at not being able to sacrifice something more valuable than these worthless eyes of mine."

Then came to them the pleasant news that the infamous Chôla had paid a heavy penalty for his horrible

1 "I have laid my burden at the feet of the Lord and am happy. Nay, I was wrong. I need not even formally take refuge in him."—(*Prap.*)

Srî-Saila-Pûrna, Vara Ranga Gâyaka, Mâlâdhara, and Kânchî Pûrṇa went back to their homes about this time.—(*G.L.R.*)

crimes[1]; and they proceeded to his capital to assure themselves of the truth of the news. On his way back, MÂrtui came upon Ammangi AmmÂl, a co-disciple of his, and the pair returned to the Master.

They found him on the banks of the KalyÂṇa Saras in the act of taking his bath. Throwing themselves at his feet, they communicated to him the joyful intelligence that the persecutor of MahÂ PÛrṇa and ÂlvÂn was no more, but died in horrible agony. The Master and his disciples shouted for joy; and warmly embracing the pair, he bathed them with tears of gladness and gratitude.

"What shall I give you in return for this news that comes to me like manna in the desert—I, a poor wandering mendicant. Yet, the Lord rejected not when SudÂma gave him his all—though it was but a handful of parched grain.[2] I pray you, good friends of mine, to take the will for the deed and accept my all, though it be but little."

He then initiated them into the holy mysteries of the Sacred Two Truths—that was his all and in truth the Be-all and End-all of human aspirations.

The Master then repaired to the shrine of Nṛisimha, and throwing himself at the feet of the Lord, cried out in tones of joy:

"Life of my life! In the far past Thou deignedst to destroy with Thy own hands, the great Daitya, Hiraṇyakaṣipu, inasmuch as he hated Thee and Thy servants. And now Thou hast stretched forth Thy hand and smitten the sinner ChÔla, who wantonly tortured the innocent MahÂ PÛrṇa and ÂlvÂn."

---

1 He was seized with a cancer in the throat and horrible pains in the stomach and died the very night he was taken away from Ṣrîrangam.—(*Prap.*)

2 BhÂgavata, Tenth Skandha, SudÂma ÂkhyÂna.

He next sought the presence of Ṣrî Nârâyaṇa and with tears in his eyes, requested permission to return to Ṣrîrangam ; no reply proceeded from the Lord ; when, the Master, correctly guessing the great reluctance on the part of the Lord to part with him, gently suggested, " I was ordered by my Lord to remain in His southern mansion as long as I lived ! "

" Ah ! yes. It is even so. You have our leave to depart ; and may all good go with you."[1]

No sooner was he out of the sacred precincts, than the Fifty-Two fell at his feet and, with heart-rending sobs and tears, declared their inability to keep away from his presence. The Master was lost in thought for some time ; then, recovering himself, he said :

" I shall leave with you an image of myself, impregnated with myself as it were. I shall ever remain with you thereby and shall assist you in all your difficulties.[2] But, more important than this, let me give you some parting words of advice and request you to earnestly

---

[1] The Master proceeded west as far as Chengâmi (Chengama), defeated the Sectarians therein and built a Maṭha in honor of the event. He then deputed Âṇḍân to complete his work, who visited Belûr (Vêlâpura) and returned with the news of the success of the Good Law wherever he went. He installed the Lord Nârâyaṇa in that place. [S. 1039=A. C. 1117.]—(*R.D.C.*)

[2] They where loth to believe it and cried. "How can your image take your place among us ? We want a living Teacher to guide us. Give us such a one."

Then said Râmânuja, irritated beyond his wont by this blindness of spirit : "Oh, ye of little faith ! When have you called on me and I replied not ? Is my word of so little value that you will not give it a decent trial, a chance to vindicate itself ?"

They slunk away abashed at their temerity; yet the spirit of scepticism was strong in their hearts and they stood before the image and called out "Lord ! Râmânuja ! "

At once came back the sweet reply "Lo ! here am I, now and for ever. What would you of me ?"

The unbelieving ones had enough of it.—(*G.L.R* .)

follow them. Take care of my beloved Râmapriya and serve Him well, or, one of these days, He will prove Himself a sad truant and you will see Him no more. Let the rites in the Temple be fully and duly observed; entertain strangers to the best of your ability; love ye one another; and let every thing you do, secular or otherwise, be founded deep on the spirit of service to the Lord. Swear it with your hands upon my feet."

But he had a harder task to go through; do what he may, he could not tear himself away from Râmapriya whom he somehow came to regard as a son. But the iron-hands of Duty dragged him away and with a bleeding heart and many a longing look behind, he proceeded on his journey to Srirangam.

CHAPTER XIX.

Râmânuja, the Saint.

The whole town turned out to meet their beloved Teacher, brought back to them safe and victorious from his long self-imposed exile.[1] He made the round of every sacred shrine and holy spot, rendered dear to his heart by numerous pleasant associations, and immeasurably so by his long absence away from them, and stood in the presence of the Lord with folded palms and streaming eyes.

"You have long been away from us, my son," came forth the sweet accents of welcome, "and seem weak and weary."

"Nay, nay, my Lord" replied the favored servant, "those to whom it is given to worship the Divine One

[1] According to a Bêlûr inscription, Dâsarathi founded the Bêlûr temple in 1039 Saka (A.C. 1117), so that, taking Râmânuja's entry into Melkote as about 1099 A. C., it gives 18 years for his sojourn and 2 years for travel, making in all 20 years as the interval between his departure from Srirangam and his rejoining it.—(*G.L.R.*)

between the Two Rivers and those who have been promised the sovereignty of this world and the other, can never want ; they are ever happy and bask in the Glory of the Great Father. And am I not, by your grace, such a one ? "

" When were thy words other than sweet ? " rejoined the Lord. He then directed the highest honors to be paid him, and gave him leave to depart to his Maṭha.

The Master hurried to the house of the disciple of his heart, Âlvân. But the latter had heard of his approach and met him outside his residence. He lay at the feet of his Master, whom he could not see with his eyes of flesh, and bathed them with tears of joy. The Master folded him to his heart and wept over him in silent grief.

" My son, my son, " cried he at length, " and was I, the Miserable Sinner, the means of depriving you of your sight, you, the light of my eyes, you, the Eye of the True Faith ? "

" Grieve not, my Lord ; you had nothing to do with it. It was a just punishment for my sins. Long had I prided myself on the purity and innocence of my life, and my pride had a fall, a deserved one. What ! is it possible that I had never thought, even for a moment, that a Srî Vaishṇava wore not his caste-marks aright ? "

" Alas ! my dear Âlvân, you but intensify my grief when you speak of your demerits. How could any one think of speaking of Âlvân and demerit in the same breath ? It is all my black heart, that has denied me even the privilege of suffering for my evil Karma. *That* would have been just and deserved ; but—to make *another* pure and innocent soul suffer cruelly for what *I* have done—it is something atrocious, unheard of, and unspeakably wicked ; " and the Master wept aloud in the great agony and bitterness of his heart.

Now, it was all that they could do, Âlvân and the rest, to console Râmânuja and convince him he was not so much to blame as he thought. At length the Master was persuaded to return to his Maṭha and took up his old round of duties.[1]

His Trip to Tirupati.

Some time after, news was brought to him that the Mûla Vigraha at the shrine of Chitrakûṭa (Chidambaram)

1 Straight from the house of the Lord, he proceeded to the residence of his teacher Mahâ Pûrṇa. Puṇḍarîkâksha, Attulâi and the others came out to welcome them. The Master consoled them as well as his great grief allowed him.—(*R.D.C.*)

Being informed that Alvân was at Vânamâmalai, he at once sent word to him to come over to Ṣrîrangam with all speed.—(*R.D.C.*)

The Master took Âlvân before Ranganâtha, who out of his great mercy, said: "My dear, you gave your eye for the Faith; and it is but bare justice that I should restore it to you."

"Nay, nay," replied Âlvân, "I desire not the eyes of flesh that had looked upon the unfortunate sinner Chôla. I rejoice in the Eye of Wisdom that my Master has blessed me with."

The Master was struck dumb with wonder at the unfathomable devotion of Âlvân, whom he was ashamed to call his pupil.

"What an irony of fate that you should suffer thus?" broke out the Blessed One, in great grief.

"I must have deserved this, else it had not come unto me"

"What! you, of all, to sin even in thought! Nay, let me hear something more credible."

The Lord broke in upon this strange dialogue and said: "We unreservedly give the illimitable bliss of Heaven to all that take refuge in the grace of this Great Saint."

"I pray, my Lord, that you include Nâloorân too in the happy group" suggested Âlvân in humble tones.

"Be it so."

The Master knew not which to admire most—Âlvân's devotion to himself or his utter selflessness and devotion even to his bitterest enemy. "Fortunate am I in that I am in some way related to this Holy One: for then I am sure to have a place in the House of the Lord," and, in the excess of his joy, he threw his head-dress in the air and caught it again.—(*R.D.C.*)

Said Âlvân, in sorrow; "I well remember, before my eyes were opened to the light of the True Faith, to have laughed at the Ṣrî

was destroyed and that the Utsava Vigraha was removed to the Holy Mount (Tirupati). Râmânuja proceeded thither, installed both the images at the foot of the Mount, and restored the sacred offices of worship. He took this opportunity of offering his worship at the shrines on the way, and returned to Srîrangam.[1]

Vaishṇavas for the curious painting of their bodies. Hence this deserved punishment."—(*Prap.*)

[1] The infamous Chôḷa destroyed the temple of Gôvinda Râja and scattered it into the sea. The priests fled to Tirupati with the Utsava Vigraha, and a woman of the place, a Vaishṇava, named Tillai, cast an illusion over the Chôḷa and had the Moola Vigraha too conveyed to the Holy Mount. The Master commemorated the miraculous preservation by naming the Lord of Chidambaram, 'Tillai Govindarâja.'—(*Prap.*)

R. D. C. gives the date of the destruction of the shrine at Chidambaram as 1009 Saka=1017 *A.C.*

One year, owing to heavy rains, it was impossible to convey the image of Nammâḷvâr from Tirunagari to Srîrangam; the Master thereupon had an image of the Saint installed in the Temple and carried out the festival of the Sacred Recital as directed by Nâthamuni.—(*V.G.*)

Once when the Aḷvâr was coming from Tirunagari, robbers fell upon the party and took away the holy Sandals, named Madhurakavi. The Master thereupon went over to Tirunagari and had new Sandals made, naming them Râmânuja. He had an image of the Saint placed in the Temple, to be used during the Sacred Recital, and thus avoided similar accidents in future.—(*Pal.*)

Srî Rangâmṛita (திருவரங்கத்தமுதனார்), one of the devoted disciples of Âḷvân, composed one or two poems in honor of his Master and placed them before the Blessed One, who carefully went through them and found them but of inferior merit.

"Well, my dear" said he with a gentle smile, "if you are so much bent upon versification, you had better busy yourself with some work that might more aptly express your feelings to your Mâster, Âḷvân, our Masters, the Holy Âḷvârs, and the Holy Shrines sanctified by their approval."

Rangâmṛita bowed in obedience; and after some time, placed before the feet of the Holy One the now famous Râmânuja Nûttantâdi (இராமாநுச நூற்றந்தாதி.) It was read out before the assembled pupils and received the approbation of the Master, who recommended it to all posterity as worthy to be recited every day.

It is named Prapanna Gâyatri. The Brâhmaṇas recite the Holy Gâyatri 108 times every day; in fact, upon it depends their spiritual

The Eyes of Âlvân.

One day, the Master said to Âlvân: "You know that the Lord of Kânchî never refuses any prayer of his servants. Pray to him, in sweet words, for the restoration of your sight."

---

life; now, to those that have taken refuge in the Master, this poem, with its 108 verses, is the Sâvitri, to be daily recited with heart-whole devotion. Madhurakavi's poem is like the Long Sâvitri, 10 in number; the composition of Rangâmṛita is like the Short Sâvitri, 108 in number. In the Gâyatri, the name of the Lord Nârâyaṇa is recited and meditated upon; here the name of the Lord Râmânuja takes its place. —(*R.D.C.*)

Rangâmṛita took Madhurakavi's poem as a model and expanded the sentiments therein, ten to one, as it were, and composed his famous Antâdi. But the Blessed One would not hear of its being read before him. Then, the disciples urged that the poem was no ordinary one and was in fact broadly hinted at in the Stanza *Poliga* (பொலிக), when Nammâlvâr handed down the Sacred Collect to Nâthamuni; that the Yôgi was shown the mortal form of the Future Teacher and informed that this poem would be included in the Sacred Four Thousand. Meanwhile, the Lord Ranganâtha sent word through the High Priest to the same effect; whereupon, the Master allowed the Antâdi to be placed at the end of the Iyarpâ (இயற்பா) and conferred the privilege of reciting it on Ṣrî Rangâmṛita.—(*V.G.*)

Ṣrî Ṣaila Pûrṇa's son brought word to the Master that his revered father had departed from this earth to his place in the House of the Lord. Râmânuja had the usual rites performed over his Teacher with unusual pomp. He then proceeded to the Holy Mount and by the way re-installed Gôvindarâja. He set up at the foot of the Mount, images of the Âlvârs and the Great Teachers, and arranged for the yearly celebration of the festival of the Sacred Recital.—(*V.G.*)

He got a Yâdava prince, named Kaṭṭiya Dêva (his capital was Nârâyaṇapura.—*G.L.R.*) to build the temple.

He bought of him the village of Iḷamaṇḍayam (இளமண்டயம்) and portioned off among his favorite disciples, Tirumalai Nambi, Nallân, and Eechambâdy Jîyar, the most fertile parts of it; he also had houses built for them near the temple; and gave them, and later on to 71 other disciples, the image of Nṛisimha for daily household worship. He assigned the superintendence of the worship on the Holy Mount to the Yâdava prince.—(*R.D.C.*)

The town round the temple he named Gôvindarâjapaṭṇam (Pâdapuri)—*G.L.R.*

Âlvân would not consent to trouble the Lord for such a trifle; but the Master was so importunate and persistent that he got from him a reluctant promise to try; and Âlvân began to sing the famous Varada Râja Stava. In one of the stanzas, he earnestly prayed the Lord to endow him with the Divine Eye, whereby he could for ever gaze on the Divine Beauty as it delights the eyes of the mighty Angels around the Throne of Glory. That very night, the Lord appeared to him in his dreams, and said:

"My dear Âlvân, you have your wish. I am sincerely glad to be of any service to you, for you very rarely ask anything of me."

Next morning he finished the Song of Praise and recited it to the Master.

"Charming!" exclaimed Râmânuja; "Varada can refuse nothing to such a sweet singer."

"You speak true" replied Âlvân, "he has given me what I asked of him, even last night."

"What! has your sight been restored? I see it not."

Here it was that Ramanuja instructed his disciples Kûrêṣa and Hanumad-dâsa in the secrets of the worship of the Household God. Just then broke upon them, another of the Master's disciples, Vankipurattu-Nambi, whom he had promised to teach it first, and placed the Holy One in a dilemma.

"My dear Nambi," said the Master "kindly excuse me this seeming breach of promise to teach you first. I see now how the Lord of the Universe was bound by the strong, but silken ties of Yaṣodâ's love. And I, a poor mortal, cannot pretend to have a stronger will than He. But if you have no objection, the knowledge you wanted of me is even now at your service."—(*G.L.R.*)

Kulottunga Chôla II, son of Kṛimi Kaṇṭha, sought out Râmânuja, begged him to forgive the manifold crimes of his father and had the good fortune to be handed over to Dâṣarathi, as his disciple. He made over the management of the Temple to the Master, who made a gift of it to Dâṣarathi and his line.—(*G.L.R.*)

"Well, I never prayed to Him for the eyes of flesh, but for the Divine Vision that would enable me to see Him as He shines in His glory to the Angels in Ṣrî Vaikuṇṭha."

"You have sadly disappointed me" rejoined the Master, in tones of deep sorrow, "come with me to the Lord's House at Kânchî, and I will see that He does you the needful."

And they proceeded to Kânchî and stood in the presence of the Giver of Boons. At the direction of the Master, Âlvân recited the poem he had composed in His praise. But, alas! Râmânuja was unfortunately called away to give his attention elsewhere. Asked the Lord of Âlvân:

"Is there anything else I can do for you?"

"Yea, my Lord, I pray that my disciple Nâloorân, be blessed as I am."

"*He* too shall have it" said the Lord.

By that time the Master was back, and catching the reply of the Lord, guessed what had happened.

"Lord of Kânchî," cried he in accents of grief and despair, "are You sure You have acted aright in this? You are said to be All-Knowing, and yet You cannot know what lies next my heart or You would have granted it;" and turning to Âlvân: "And *you*, friend of my heart, have I fallen so low in your eyes, that you should disregard my earnest desire and take it upon yourself to act thus? I begin to see that I am not fit company for either of ye," and he walked out of the Sanctuary with a breaking heart. It was too much for the Lord Varada; He could bear anything—but to see His dear son Râmânuja go away offended with Him! As for Âlvân, he was so overcome with shame and repentance that he rushed forward and fell across the path of the Master, crying, "My Lord, my God, pardon your son his first offence—and the last. Thou art the Soul of Mercy and shall I not find refuge in Thee?"

And close upon this, came the words of the Lord, half command, but more of entreaty: "Come back, Râmânuja. What a hot-headed man you are! You shall have anything you ask. Come back now, will you?"

"Lord, I will pray for anything you command me to," came in piteous tones from Âlvân, "but let my Master never turn away his face from me, and let me ever hear but the sweet and soul-calming tones of his voice."

The Master stopped short, came back and stood before the Lord, ashamed of his temerity.

"And so, you would have, for ever, turned your face from us, is it not? And all this, because I failed to give you what you wanted, the moment you asked for it. Really, what an exacting Master I have to serve and one so easily offended! Well, you shall have what you want. *I* cannot afford to be so hard-hearted."

"Nay, my Lord, I sue for humble pardon and forgiveness. If I were as perfect, where would be the difference between me and my Master? Never shall it be said that the Lord went back upon His word for my sake. Let Âlvân have his wish."

"He has it. But he shall also behold yourself and Myself with his eyes of flesh." And, directed by the Lord, Âlvân began to describe in detail the appearance of both. The Master was overjoyed at having succeeded so far in his object, and returned to Srîrangam.[1]

---

[1] Âlvân desired the Lord to give him the Divine Eye, but Varada restored him even his eye of flesh.—(*Prap*).

But the Master was not yet satisfied; he wanted to do something substantial to his dear friend that would be of material use to him. So

One day, while explaining the Stanza நாறு நறும் பொழில் (Nâchiâr Tirumoḷi, IX. 6, 7) it occurred to the Master that it was his duty to carry out the wishes of the Divine

---

one day, he proceeded to the house of Ṣrî Rangâmṛita, all alone, in the burning sun of midday. It was strange, it was unsual; the Master had long ago given up going out for alms; whence this mysterious return to his old routine? Ṣrî Rangâmṛita lay at the Master's feet, inwardly guessing to what he owed this wonderful piece of good fortune.

"We desire to have for ourselves your rights as a Purôhita in this place" said the Master.

"Thrice blessed am I" replied the delighted Rangâmṛita "in that I have something that can be of any use to my Lord" and forthwith he formally made a gift of his office of Purôhita, mentally fixing upon his teacher, Âḷvân, as the recipient. For he knew that the Master wanted nothing for himself, and none other than a teacher can accept anything as a gift at the hands of a disciple —and Âḷvân was his teacher. The Master thereupon conferred upon Âḷvân the office of Purôhita; directed him to read every day and expound before the Lord Ranganâtha the Sacred Purâṇas; and conferred upon him the title of 'Parâṣara' in consequence.—(*R.D.C.*)

He had two houses built opposite one another for Âḷvân and the members of Mahâ Pûrṇa's household.—(*R.D.C.*)

Then it was that he finished the last portion of the Ṣrî Bhâshya and lectured on it in the presence of Ṣrî Ranganâtha. The Lord directed the temple servants to have the honors of Brahmaratha and Ṣatakalasâbhishêka conferred upon his favorite. "As my Lord willeth" said the Master.

Thereupon the favorite disciples of the Holy One, honored in honoring the Master, fetched water from the sacred streams and watering places, and poured them over the head of the Blessed One, with appropriate Mantrâs and Chants, a hundred vessels of them, and at the close of the rite, installed Parâṣara as the heir-apparent to the Spiritual Throne.

And then, his disciples, his friends, his admirers and his followers, crowds untold, placed the Master on a chariot and had him taken in procession along the crowded streets of Ṣrîrangam, now grown too small to hold those to whom the Master opened the gates of Life Eternal. The Sanyâsins and the Holy Brâhmaṇas fought one another for the honor of yoking themselves to the conveyance that they might have at least a share in the great service. And thus with chants of Vedic Mantras, with the sonorous strains of the Sacred Collect, with the jubilant shouts of the heralds proclaiming the Master and his deeds of fame in all pomp and splendour, was the Brahmaradha gone through.—(*Prap*).

Bride. Accordingly he proceeded to Vânâdri,and made an offering to the Lord there of a hundred vats of butter and a hundred vats of sweet food. He then proceeded to the Shrine of the Divine Bride at Villiputtûr.

" Well have you done," spoke the Soul of Compassion to him, "and you have our thanks for your kindness in carrying out the wishes of my heart, so long unfulfilled. None but an elder brother has the right, and you are " the Elder Brother of my House." (நம்கோயிலண்ணன்.)

"As the Divine Mother willeth " replied the Master, and obtained permission to return to Srirangam.[1]

---

1 The Divine Bride made a vow that She would offer Her lover 100 vats full of sweet food and 100 vats overflowing with ghee, if He would come there and accept Her offering. (*Vide* Nâchiâr Tirumoli, the decade beginning with சிந்துரச்செம்பொடி, Stanza 6).—*Comp.*

She made the vow if the Lord should marry Her. She gave the Master the name of ' Godâgraja'—the elder brother of Goda.—(*Prap.*)

The *R. D.* makes no mention of this incident, but the title was conferred upon the Master when he visited the place during his grand tour of pilgrimage.—*Comp.*

a He next proceeded to Tirunagari and from there to Tirukkoloor, ever associated with Madhurakavi. On his way thither he met a woman coming out of it. "Whence are you, good lady ?" asked the Holy One.

"I come from Tirukkoloor" replied the woman.

"Ah ! that is strange " rejoined the Master "Every one desires to *go* there, but you are *coming away* from it."

"It is even so, good Sir" was the ready reply ? "who am I that I should pollute the holy place with my unhallowed presence ?" ; and forthwith she proceeded to recount to the astonished Teacher 73 examples of good men and holy that have done something to deserve the grace of the Lord and a place by his side. Râmânuja saw that he had caught a Tartar ; but he had the good grace to confess himself beaten, took back the good lady to Tirukkolur, stayed with her and considered himself honored by partaking food at her hands.—*G.L.R.*

When at Kurukoor, which he visited next, he prayed to Sathakôpa that his sandals might thenceforth be named ' Râmânuja ' instead of "Madhurakavi," and it was accordingly granted. The Master was thinking of how to express his gratitude for the great honor shown him.

"I wish I could find some one, pure and holy, whom I could name after the Great One," said he, half to himself.

Âlvân permitted to Go Back.

One day Âlvân repaired to the Lord's House, unknown to the Master and stood silent before Him. Said the Lord to him: "My son, it seems you would like to speak to me somewhat."

Piḻḻân, the son of Ṣaila Pûrṇa, stood forth and said "Lord, may I make bold to offer myself?"

The Master accepted him and he was named Kurukêṣa. "Strange indeed," said the Master, "that Piḻḻân should unite in himself the names of the Holy Ṣaṭhakôpa and my Master Goshṭhipûrṇa." He was thenceforth looked upon as the spiritual son of Râmânuja.—(*R.D.C.*)

The Master regretted his inability to express his gratitude of Nammâlvâr for the great boon he had conferred upon Humanity and said: "Oh that I had a son of my own, to name after him!"—(*Prap*).

One day the Holy One was walking about in his room and reciting to himself a stanza from the Sacred Collect. Piḻḻân who was watching him through the keyhole, inferred from the play of his features and gestures the stanza he was meditating upon, and unable to contain himself called out:

"It seems my Lord is engaged upon the stanza திருமாலிருஞ்சோலை மலையென்றேனென்ன?" (Tiruvâimoli, 98th Decade 1).

"Is it my Piḻḻân outside" asked the Master in reply. "It can be no other."

He mentioned the incident to his disciples and said: "My Master Ṣaila Pûrṇa was not wrong in saying that Piḻḻân was the fittest person to receive the inheritance of spiritual knowledge from me." Râmânuja adopted him as his son and named him after Ṣaṭhakôpa, thus fulfilling his last promise to Âḻavandâr. (He had the son of Bala Gôvinda named Parânkuṣa Nambi after Nammâlvâr).

Later on the Master called Piḻḻân to him and said: "My son, I have refrained from commenting upon the Sacred Collect, as the people would stick to it as the only and sole interpretation of the words of wisdom. But it is otherwise with you; you are of the line of the Great Nâthayôgi; you unite in yourself the names and the grace of the Holy Nammâlvâr and my Master Goshṭhipûrṇa; you have been the means of fulfilling the last wish of Âḻavandâr; you are naturally attracted to the Sacred Collect, and you are deservedly the highest authority upon it. So compose a commentary upon it in 6,000 grandhas after the Holy Vishṇu Purâṇa." Piḻḻân accepted the task with great diffidence and laid his work at the feet of the Holy One who went through it and declared himself satisfied with it. He named it the 'Bhagavad Vishaya' and enjoined its daily study.—(*V.G.*)

"Even so, my Lord" replied Âlvân; and, selecting a saying of the Great Ones [1] as his text, he proceeded to explain it so beautifully that the Lord was in rapture over it and exclaimed : "Ask of me what thou wilt, and thou shalt have it."

"But, my Lord, Thou hast, of Thy infinite Mercy, given me *every thing*, long, long ago, when I took refuge in Thee."

"Gainsay us not" rejoined the Lord, in tones of evident displeasure ; "I am now in a giving mood, and it is my will you ask of me *anything* you want, and by my

---

The other commentaries upon the Sacred Collect are :—

(*a*) The 'Nine Thousand' of Nanjîyar, the disciple and successor of Parâşara.

(*b*) The Thirty-six-Thousand of Nampiḷḷai, the disciple and successor of the former. It was more a lecture on the Sacred Stanzas than a regular commentary ; and was written out by Şrî Krishṇapâda (வடக்குத் திருவீதிப்பிள்ளை).

(*c*) The 'Twenty-four-Thousand' of Periavâcchân Piḷḷai.

(*d*) The 'Twelve-Thousand,' a word-for-word commentary by Vâdikêsari Alagia Manavâḷa Jîyar.—(*Pal*).

Once when the image of Nammâlvâr was being taken to Şrîrangam for the festival of the Sacred Recital, robbers fell upon the party and the Sacred Sandals were lost. The image was taken back to Tirunagari. Soon after, the Master went there, and had new Sandals made, which he was allowed to name after himself. Returning to Şrîrangam, he installed the image of Nammâlvâr and the rest within the precincts of the temple.—(*Pal*).

After his return from Tirunagari the image of Nammâlvâr was prevented from coming over to Şrîrangam on account of heavy rains and the Master took advantage of the occasion to have his image set up in the Temple.—(*V.G*).

[1] The stanza was from his own Varadarâja Stava. It runs thus :—I take my refuge in the Holy Feet of my Master, the Lord Râmânuja ; the Holy one was a servant of the Great Yâmuna ; he again was the disciple and descendant of Nâtha Yôgi ; he again sought the feet of the Saint Şaṭhakôpa ; and he, more fortunate than the rest, drank of the fountain of Life and Light, the Divine Mother ; and Thy Feet are enshrined in Her heart of hearts. Then, Lord, have I not some claim to Thy grace ? —(*R.D.C*).

Consort and by my dear Râmânuja, you shall not fail to have it."

Âlvân remained plunged in deep thought for a moment; then he raised his head and said: "Grant me to shake off this fleshly vesture that stands between me and Thee and enable me to revel in the Bliss of the Divine Presence."

"Anything but that," put in the Lord, evidently confused," We cannot spare you so soon."

"Ah" sighed Âlvân, "it is as I feared. I knew all along You would disappoint me and wisely refrained from asking You anything. But You spoke so surely and pressed me to ask so persistently, that I was half tempted to change my mind about You. It shall never be said of You that *You* went back upon Your word, nor shall I go back upon *my request*—that or nothing. I have never troubled You to do anything for me and You cannot afford to refuse me my first petition to You and—the last."

Ranganâtha was stung to the quick with self-reproach; and what was worse, He went out of His way to seek it; for did He not force His boon upon Âlvân? So He turned to him with a gracious smile (He could not but make a virtue of necessity) and said: "My dear Âlvân I give you and those related to you the free and undisturbed enjoyment of the bliss of the World of Brahman."[1]

---

1 "Then," said Âlvân "may the misguided Nâloorân too be similarly favored?"

"What" cried out the Lord. "He! the Judas, the thing below contempt! I made a reservation as regards the traitor and you should have known it."

"*I* did not and I do not like to know. What! Shall it be said that Âlvân, the worst of sinners, forgave him that did him harm and sought for him the highest good attainable, and the Lord Ranganâtha, the Father of All, sinner and saint, bore a grudge against him for a crime that the injured one had freely forgiven. Never, if I can prevent it. Again, *You* could afford to do anything and take the consequences; but *I* am a man lower than the lowest, and cannot bear to

"Âlvân thanked the Lord in fitting terms, and proceeding straight to the shrine of the Âlvârs, waited outside.

ÂLVÂN GOES BACK.

The Master was informed of this; and in the height of his joy, he threw his upper garment in the sky and caught it as it fell.

"What is this, Lord" cried the disciples in amazement at what they considered a childish freak.

"Rejoice with me," exclaimed he, "in that we are sure of a place in the high heavens since we are somehow connected with Âlvân."

He then proceeded straight to where Âlvân was[1]; and in the presence of all his disciples said :

---

hear my name coupled with this act of injustice. So either grant me this, not for me, but for another, or Thy gift remains with Thee. You force me to be obstinate and I am sorry for it."

"Be it so, then" said the Lord, reluctantly enough.—(*R.D.C.*)

1 Âṇḍâl was the first to hear of it and proceeded straight to where her Lord was, followed by her sons. He gave them his parting instructions before the others came up.

"You, my dear, do not require to be told by me that you should consider it as the goal and object of your existence here to take refuge in the feet of the Master and serve with your heart and soul the servants of the Lord." He directed Parâsara to take his refuge in Embâr and Râmânuja and regard the disciples of the Master as he would regard Âlvân himself. He enjoined Vyâsa his other son to take his refuge in Parâsara; that was enough for him. And to his disciple Piḷḷai-piḷḷay-âlvân he said: "Keep watch over thy tongue; as for your bodily acts, the fear of the enemy and the law of the land will keep you within bounds; but your thoughts, what will you do with them when they turn against you? I shall point out to you a speedier and easier method to control them than the tedious and difficult one laid down by Srî Krishṇa. He recommends repeated efforts and dispassion, but do thou take thy refuge in the Lord of my soul and you will find yourself before the Throne of Glory sooner and by an easier path than the followers of Srî Krishṇa's method."

Lastly he turned to his other disciples and said "Lay this to your hearts. The Sayings of the Âlvârs form the Means and the End."

"My son, was it right of you to do this?" Âḷvân replied not.

"How was it you wanted to precede me?" again urged the Holy One, in tones more entreating still. Still no reply.

"Thou speakest not. How have I incurred your displeasure?"

Âḷvân was struck dumb. He was misunderstood and his own words turned against him.

"It was only out of an earnest desire to avoid the breach of the etiquette which, I hear, holds in Vaikuṇṭha."

"Explain yourself, my son" rejoined the Master in bewilderment.

"The Sacred Collect,"[1] replied Âḷvân humbly, "teaches us that the Eternally Free Ones and those that reach Vaikuṇṭha earlier, come forth to welcome the new-comer. If I go there after you, I should place you in the awkward position of advancing to welcome me; and further, it would pain me to the quick, were I not there to welcome my Master and wait upon him."

"But the Books also instruct us that *there* there is no distinction of high and low, master and servant, teacher and disciple. All are equal before the Throne of Glory; but you would still like to carry these distinctions even there. Well, please yourself."

He then remained silent for some moments; and, rightly guessing the current of Âḷvân's thoughts, whispered into his ears the Sacred Two Truths.

Meanwhile the Master was in his Maṭḥa explaining to his disciple the stanza சிற்றஞ்சிறுகாலே, (Tiruppâvai 29), when some one casually mentioned before him what took place between Âḷvân and Ranganâtha.—(*R.D.C.*)

[1] The last stanza in the Tiruvâimoḷi.

"Where is the necessity of it now ?" said some of the disciples, " he is not a new comer into the Faith. "

"Oh ye of limited vision and faint hearts, see you not that the Prince feels dry in the mouth, when the camphor has run out.[1] ? Âlvân's tongue is parched, since the ambrosia of the Two Truths had not touched it for a long time."

But all on a sudden the human side of his nature came out; and the thought that the friend of his choice was to be removed from his sight in no long time, so overcame him that the Master fell upon Âlvân's neck and wept aloud in the grief of his heart.

"Light of mine eyes ! first and best acquisition to the Faith !" cried the Master, " have you no pity upon my sufferings, that you refuse to take me with you ? Have I become so hateful in your eyes that you should rejoice to go away from me ? The Lord of Vaikuṉṯẖa has greater charms for you than my Lord Ranganâtha ; so much so that you have chosen to forego my company. Ah ! blessed indeed are the Lord of S̲rî Vaikuṉṯẖa and the holy Angels therein ; and luckless indeed are the Lord Ranganâtha of the Great Temple and His worshippers here. I would be the last man to disturb you in your last moments and I do not want any one to regard me as envying you your good fortune. Fare you well and may all good go with you."

The Master then passed his hand down the back of his favourite disciple, and with streaming eyes gave him leave to precede him.[2]

Âlvân, too much affected to speak, fell at his feet and reverently placed them on his eyes, breast and head.

---

1 Persons of high rank always keep in their mouths aromatic pills made of camphor and other spices to render them fragrant and cool.

2 He, as a great occultist, facilitated by that Yôgic process, the separation of the higher from the lower Upâdhis.

He then received the Holy Water from the hands of the Master himself and exclaimed in the fullness of his heart :

"I take my refuge in Thy Holy feet; and now, my Lord, I would request you to come no farther."[1]

But Râmânuja found it impossible to tear himself away from his beloved; so he continued to follow Âlvân as far as the Northern Cauvery. Âlvân noticed this and said humbly but firmly :

"I *will* not allow you to come any farther. Nay, I insist upon it. Would you, the Light of the World, unman me and make me forget myself?" He then walked on until he came to a lovely spot, where, seating himself, he turned to his wife and said :

"Well, my dear, what may you be thinking of just now?"

"Nothing new, my Lord; one idea and one only runs in my mind, waking or sleeping, alone or in company—to serve the Lord of my heart to the best of my might."

Âlvân smiled sweetly and spoke to Parâsara and his brother Vyâsa. "You have your Divine Father and Mother who will see that you want for nothing. But take heed that your heart be not puffed up with the pride of having been brought up by the Divine Pair. *That* will serve you little; take your refuge, as I do, solely and wholly in the Holy One. Take counsel of your mother in everything; for she is good and intelligent. Guard yourselves against any offence towards the servants of the Lord, in thought, word or deed. Wait upon them and find favor in their eyes."

---

1 He recited the verse यो नित्यमच्युत, which was thenceforth regarded by the disciples as the Saranâgati Sloka (Stanza of Refuge) to be recited by a person in his last moments.—(*R.D.C.*)

He then raised them up and brushing away their fast falling tears, said to them sternly :

" If you grieve for me, as being connected with you through this garment of flesh, you but bring disgrace upon your relations with the Master. If you, on the other hand, grieve for me, as being related to you in spirit, you but forget the eternal and inalienable bonds that bind us together.[1] "

He then laid himself on the ground, facing the Temple ; his head was on the lap of his disciple Putrikâputrâchârya (Piḻḻai-piḻḻai-âḻvân) [2] and his feet on that of Âṇḍaḻ; and with his whole soul concentrated on the feet of his Master, he rose from his tabernacle of flesh and went back to his seat by the Lord.

---

[1] Meanwhile Rangâmṛita, the chief disciple of Âḻvân, was informed of all this and bewailed his misfortune in being the last to hear of it. He ran up to where his beloved Master was, and, falling at his feet, sobbed aloud in the bitterness of his grief. Âḻvân calmed him, and gently but firmly persuaded him that to serve the Holy One here was a greater boon to any one, than to follow his worthless self to the Highest Heaven.—(*R.D.C.*)

[2] He was the disciple of Âḻvân and was well known all over the place as one who spared not the Vâishṇavâs but calumniated them right and left. Of course the people laid this upon Âḻvân ; so, to put a stop to the scandal, the Master took from the disciple, as a voluntary gift, his use of speech, body and thought. PiḻḻayâḻvÂn went to his house and lay like a log, for he was deprived of everything. But nature proved stronger and, in a moment of forgetfulness, he went out into the street, and casting his eyes upon a Vaishṇava, thought ill of him. Like a flash came to him the promise he had made to his Master and he repented bitterly of his indiscretion. " Wretch that I am, I have stolen that which I had given away as a free gift to my Master. It is an unpardonable sin and I shall not survive it."

Âḻvân came to hear of this and proceeding to where the foolish one was making ready to take away his life, gave him back his mind and said : " For the sins of the body and the speech there is the law to punish you and the one whom you have injured. But for the sins of thought, I know of no other remedy than to take refuge in the feet of the Holy One."—(*Prap.*)

The Master thereupon proceeded to the spot with all his disciples and had the funeral ceremonies performed by Bhaṭṭar. [1]

The Installation of Parâṣara.

The next day Râmânuja led the young Parâṣara into the Sacred Presence and formally made him over to the Lord. Ranganâtha graciously accepted him as His dear son, and said: "Grieve not that you have lost your parents. Know you not that We stand to you as such?"[2]

---

[1] He had the 12 day's rites performed as Nâthamuni had directed, and at the end, in addition to the usual recital of the Samhita portion of the Vêda, as laid down in the Gautama Smriṭi, he instituted the recital of the Sacred Collect to finish with Râmânujanûttantâdi; and had the Sambhâvana (first honors) paid to Nammâlvâr. It was accordingly done; but his disciples, made an addition of their own—another Sambhâvana to the Master himself. He accepted it after great reluctance and allowed the usage to be followed on all future occasions. —(*V.G.*)

(*a*) The Master would not accept the Drâvida Râmânuja-nûttantâdi, of Dêvarâjamuni, because it contained no reference to Kûrêṣa and the author had to insert Verse 7 before the Holy One would allow it a place along with the Four-Thousand.—(*G.L.R.*)

Six months after the death of Âlvân, his friend and co-disciple Âṇḍân followed him to Vaikuṇṭha. (He lived 105 years). Some days later, Dhanurdâsa, who was wandering about, like a forlorn spirit, after his bosom friend Âlvân left him, took leave of the Master to go back; and his wife Hêmâmba did not survive him even a few hours. The Master directed Parâṣara to conduct their funeral rites.—(*R.D.C.*)

One day some of the disciples approched Hêmâmba and said "Lady, we have drawn what we know from many sources, the Master and his elect. But whom shall we look up to as our Saviour, in whom we can take refuge and be saved?"

The lady smiled and gathering her long fair hair into a knot passed a red thread round it to keep it in its place. The teachers were as numerous as the hairs on her head, but the Holy One was the Synthesis of them all; he keeps them in their place and but for him they would be but as the scattered rain drops on the vast bosom of the Ocean. He and he alone is the Saviour.—*G.L.R.*

[2] He conferred upon him the title of 'Vêdantâchârya Bhaṭṭâ'. —(*R.D.C.*)

The Master instructed him once in the Sacred Two Truths, taught him a Ṣlôka, and turning to those around, said: "Look upon this

"True" broke in the Holy One. "Do Thou permit him to remain long on earth, and I will look to it that he lacks not learning nor wisdom."

No reply came forth from the Lord; and the Master, upon whom was not lost the hint, took leave of the Dweller between the Two Rivers and proceeded straight to his Maṯẖa. Parâṣara was entrusted to the charge of Gôvinda to be trained to take upon himself the heavy responsibilities of the Future Teacher.

The Master's Image.

One day, Âṉḏân's son, Râmânuja, approached the Master and humbly said:

"Lord, do I ask too much in suggesting that your image be put up in the temple at Ṣrîperumbûdûr, where you first saw the light? It might serve as a beacon of faith for the elect and an object of loving worship for all time."

"Well, I see no reason why you should not do so," replied the Master.

Then Âṉḏân had an image of the Master carved by the best artist of the day, and placed it before Râmânuja, who embraced it warmly, and impregnated it with all his energies and powers. Âṉḏân departed to Perumbûdûr to instal it with due rights and pomp. The Holy One fixed an auspicious day for the event; and Âṉḏân carried out his directions to the very letter. That day, Râmânuja felt a curious depression of vitality and lowness of spirits steal over him; [1] he was at a loss to make it out, when the

---

Parâṣara as you would myself." He then took him into the presence of the Divine Mother who graciously renewed Her protection and kindness.—(*R.D.C.*)

(*a*) This was after the Master had taught his disciples for the last time.—(*T.G.*)

[1] Blood flowed from his eyes.—(*Prap.*)

(*a*) Nammâlvâr gave his disciple Nâthayôgi the image of the Great Teacher to come. It was handed down reverently through

truth flashed upon him. He remembered that it was the day when his image, into which he had infused all his self, was to be installed there. So he at once despatched a messenger, in hot haste, for Âṇḍân to come back to him at once; and he came.

The Future Teacher.

Some days later, Râmânuja took Bhaṭṭar to the presence of Ranganâtha and caused the usual honors to be done *him* first; then turning to those assembled, he exclaimed in a loud voice: "Behold your Future Teacher and my successor."

Then addressing himself to Parâṣara, he said: "I hear there is a great Vêdântin out in the West. Seek him out and bring him within the fold. *He* shall be *your* successor.

CHAPTER XX.

THE PASSING OF RÂMÂNUJA.

Râmânuja Prepares to Go Back.

The Master proceeded to his Maṭha,[1] and, gathering

Puṇḍarîkâksha, Râma Miṣra, Yâmunâ, Gôshṭhîpûrṇa, and Dêvaki Piràṭṭi. Then Prâṇatârtihara waited upon her long and was given it as a favor So, the following alone are the original images :—

(1) The one given to Nâtha Yôgi.

(2) The one given to the disciples at Tirunârâyaṇapura by the Master.

(3) The one given by him to Âṇḍan the Younger, to be put up at Ṣrî Perumbûdûr.

(4) The one put up over the place where his body was buried, by Âṇḍân the Younger, by the order of the Master and the Lord Ranganâtha.—(*Pal.*)

[1] The Holy One lived a long life, a hundred years and twenty, of which sixty were spent at Ṣrîrangam. One day, he proceeded to the Sanctuary of the Lord and, with clasped hands, said :

"Lord of Life! I have carried about this fleshly vesture of mine long enough. I am tired of it; allow me to lay it by and rest. The years of mortal man are a hundred at the most; so say the Scriptures. And have I not exceeded that by twenty years ? Lord, deign to grant

his disciples unto him, said to them : [1]

"Mark me well, friends and well-wishers of mine. Beware how you do any act of foolishness, when I go away from among you. I swear by the names of the Holy Ones that have preceded me, that you shall for ever be cut off from me, and what is worse, from the holy feet of Yâmunâchârya and Mahâ Pûrṇa ; the chances of your ever taking your place among the Ever Free Ones, around the Throne of Light, shall be lost to you. You would have gone against the express wishes of Sri Saṭhakôpa ; and you shall secure to yourself an eternal lease of the lowest of hells. I command every one of you to swear to it with his hands upon my feet."

---

my prayer, the more so that my work here is over and there are good men and true, to hand down the Torch of Wisdom to future generations."

Ranganâtha replied not; he was too much taken aback by surprise. The Master pressed the point again and again, until the Lord, out of sheer annoyance, forgot his resolve not to commit himself to any words and broke out with :

" What is that to you ? *I* am the Lord of Time. *I* know when to relieve you of your responsibility. I have some more work for you; do thou stay here a little longer and complete the glorious edifice you have built."

"Nay, my Lord" rejoined the Holy One, "allow me to be the best judge of my own poor abilities. I have worn out this poor body of mine with too much work and I am, above all, (pardon me for saying it) home-sick."

The Lord knew the iron will of Râmânuja; that he never set his heart on a thing but he got it. So, to avoid a scene, He reluctantly gave him permission to go back.

"Not so soon " added the Master, "I go not from here until I have your solemn promise that all who are in any way connected with me or mine, yea, even unto the last degree, share my world and all its delights."

"Be it so; the Kingdom of Heaven is for those whom you choose to admit into it. I place in your hands the Keys of Life and Death now and for ever."—(*Prap.*)

[1] 'I go away from among you the fourth day from this.'—(*Prap.*)

'There was held
A high assembly, where the Teacher spake
Wisdom and power, winning all souls which heard.

They did so with heart-rending sobs and tears. Whereupon the Teacher made them take their meals and assemble before him. Calling to his side the most advanced of his disciples, Âṇḍân, Dêvarâja Muni, Embâr, Kurukêṣvara and Madhyamârya, (நடுவிலாழ்வான்) he entrusted the others to their keeping.

Turning to Bhaṭṭar, he said with a smile : "Âṇḍân and Âlvân were the first of my disciples—my Staff and my Ring. Their love towards one another, exceeded, if possible, their love towards me. You, Parâṣara and Râmânuja, sons of the Inseparable Pair, love one another in the same way and hand it down as a sacred trust to those that come after you."

His Exhortations.

Thereafter he exhorted the disciples then assembled, as to how to conduct themselves, towards one another, towards their Master, and towards the world.

'The Master sate
Eminent, worshipped, all the earnest throng
Watching the opening of his lips to learn
That wisdom which hath made our *India* mild;
* * * I cannot tell
A small part of the spendid lore which broke
From the Lord's lips; I am a late-come scribe,
Who love the Master and his love of men,
But have not wit to speak beyond the books;
And time hath blurred their script and ancient sense
Which once was new and mighty, moving all.
A little of that large discourse I know,
Which the Teacher spake on that soft Indian eve;
So, too, I know it writ that they who heard,
Were more—lakhs more—crores more, than could be seen,
For all the Dêvas and the Dead thronged there,
Till Heaven was emptied to the Seventh Zone.
And uttermost dark hells opened their bars;
Also the daylight lingered past its time
In rose-leaf radiance on the watching peaks,
So that it seemed Night listened in the glens,

The 72 Golden Words of Râmânuja.

1. Make no difference between the worship you render to your Spiritual Teacher and to the Srî Vaishnavas.
2. Have earnest faith in the teachings of the great Teachers of yore.
3. Continue not the bondsmen of the senses.
4. Do not remain content with the acquisition of secular knowledge.
5. Delight in the study of the writings that glorify the Lord and his works.
6. Once that your Master has opened your eyes to the Light of Lights, never again be seduced by the fatal charms of the senses.

And Noon upon the mountains! Yea, they write,
The Evening stood between them like some maid,
Celestial, love-struck, rapt; the smooth-rolled clouds
Her braided hair; the studded stars, the pearls
And diamonds of her coronal; the Moon
Her forehead-jewel, and the deepening dark
Her woven garments. It was her close-held breath
Which came in scented sighs across the lawns
While our Lord taught, and while he taught, who heard,—
Though he were stranger in the land or slave,
High caste or low, come of the Aryan blood,
Or Mlech or jungle-dweller—seemed to hear,
What tongue his fellows talked. Nay, outside those
Who crowded by the *Matha*, great and small,
The birds and beasts and creeping things—'tis writ—
Had sense of the Teacher's vast embracing love,
And took the promise of his piteous speech;
So that their lives, prisoned in shape of ape,
Tiger, or deer, shagged bear, jackal or wolf,
Foul-feeding kite, pearled dove, or peacock-gemmed,
Squat toad or speckled serpent, lizard or bat;
Yea, or of fish fanning the river-waves—
Touched meekly at the skirts of brotherhood,
With man who hath less innocence than these,
And in mute gladness knew their bondage broke.—*Light of Asia* (adapted.)

Ranganâtha gave him permission to depart from this earth on the seventh day. He taught his disciples for three days; and on the fourth he told them that he was going away.—(*T.G.*)

7. Learn to regard all sensations with equal indifference.

8. Do not be too much addicted to the use of sandal, flowers and sweet scents.

9. Recite the names and glories of the servants of the Lord with as much delight as you would His own.

10. Let it be engraven upon your heart that no one reaches the feet of the Lord sooner than he who ever remains devoted to the service of His servants.

11. The wisest of men perishes hopelessly if he devotes not himself entirely to the service of the Lord and His Elect.

12. Never regard the life of the Vaishṉavas as a means to the end.

13. It is, verily, the Goal you should try to reach.

14. Never address any servant of the Lord in other than respectful language.

15. Whenever you cast your eyes upon a Vaishṉava, fail not to salute him first.

16. Never sit stretched at your ease in the presence of the Lord, or His Elect or other holy men.

17. Never sleep with your feet towards the house of the Lord, or of your Teacher or of the Lord's Elect.

18. As soon as you awake, recite the names of glorious Spiritual Hierarchy

19. When you approach a body of S̱rī Vaishṉavas gathered together before the Lord, prostrate thyself before them, reciting the Two Truths.

20. When the Vaishṉavas are singing the names and glory of the Lord or of His Elect, worship them to the best of thy might. But never get up in the middle and go away from their midst ; this is the worst of sins against them.

21. When you hear of a Vaishnava coming over to you, fail not to advance to welcome him. When he departs,

accompany him a part of the way. A neglect of these rules of etiquette subjects one to grievous sin.

22. Maintain thyself by taking humble service under Srī Vaishṉavas. But to wait upon persons that have not been touched with grace, to frequent their houses, to put their name before thine and seek thy livelihood at their hands—this will, verily, degrade thee in no time.

23. The moment you cast your eyes upon the temples of the Lord, the domes or the spires thereof, join thy hands together in profound reverence.

24. Gaze not wonder-struck at the temples of strange gods, however beautiful they may be as works of art.

25. Do not be amazed when you hear of the wonderful doings of strange gods.

26 It is a great sin to interrupt and argue with the Srī Vaishṉavas when they are engaged in the delightful task of reciting the glories of the Lord or His Elect or the Teacher.

27. Do not cross the shadow of Srī Vaishṉavas.

28. Allow not your shadow to fall upon them.

29. If you touch one out of the Faith, touch not a Srī Vaishṉava before you are purified.

30. If a poor Vaishṉava salutes you first, treat him not with disrespect, for it is a great sin.

31. If a Srī Vaishṉava should salute you first, and say 'I am thy servant' show him not any disrespect; for it is a heinous sin.

32 If you should happen to be aware of the defects of any Srī Vaishṉavas—sleepiness, idleness, low birth, &c.—proclaim them not to others. Keep them to yourself and give out only their good characteristics.

33. Never partake of the Holy Water that had washed the feet of the Lord or of His servants, in the presence of the uninitiated.

34. Never partake of water that had washed the feet of those who know not the Three Truths and the Three Mysteries.

35. Fail not, at any cost, to procure and partake, every day, of the holy water that had washed the feet of those that follow in the ways of wisdom and are of pure lives.

36. Raise not thyself, in thy own estimation, to the level of the Lord's Elect.

37. If, by oversight, you happen to be defiled by the touch of an unbeliever, bathe with thy clothes on, and purify yourself by the Holy Water that had washed the feet of the Srī Vaishṇavas.

38. Regard the Great Ones who are adorned with such virtues as dispassion, wisdom and devotion as Holy Beings that have assumed their last pure fleshly vestures; and serve them to the best of your might.

39. Let not thy mind dwell upon their birth, or any other detracting element, but look upon them as beings sent to you to serve and follow.

40. Partake not of the Holy Water that had washed the feet of the Lord in the houses of the unbelievers.

41. Nor offer worship to the idols of the Lord in their houses.

42. But in the holy places sanctified by the presence of the Lord do not hesitate to partake of the Lord's offerings even in the presence of the unbelievers.

43. If, in the presence of the Lord, a Srī Vaishṇava should ask you to partake of the offerings of the Lord, refuse it not on the ground of its being a fasting day with you.

44. Regard the offerings of the Lord as holier than the holiest; it burns all your sins. Say not "It is not pure; it has been offered by such a one."

45. Never extol thyself in the presence of the Srī Vaishṇavas.

46. Nor put another to shame.

47. Let every moment of your time be occupied with singing the glories of the Lord's Elect or serving them.

48. Devote some portion of your day, say an hour at the least, to the singing of the Virtues of your Spiritual Teacher;

49. And to the earnest study of the sacred writings of the Holy Saints (the Âlvârs) or of your Teacher.

50. Associate not with those that centre their affections on their own selves.

51. Nor with the hypocrites who but assume the external marks of Srī Vaishṇavas.

52. Nor converse with slanderers and scandal-mongers.

53. Free yourself from the sin of having conversed with the followers of other faiths, by talking with holy Vaishṇavas.

54. Look not upon those wretches, that insult and scandalise the Lord's servants, nor upon those tigers in human shape that have insulted their Guru.

55. Ever seek the company of those that are Masters in the Science of the Two Truths.

56. Avoid those that recognise other means of salvation; ever dwell with those that live out the Doctrine of Surrender (Prapatti).

57. And that are well versed in the Mysteries of the Three Truths and the Three Secrets.

58. Seek not the company of those that are ever intent on the pursuit of wealth and pleasure; but remain, as much as possible, with those that are devoted to the Lord.

59. If a Vaishnava should do you any harm, harbour no thought of evil against him, but keep thyself under control.

60. If you should ever desire to win a seat in the House of the Lord on High, ever seek to benefit the Vaishnavas.

61. The wise One that had taken refuge in the Lord should never engage in any undertaking that is against the rules of conduct for the Elect, though it might bring him great profit.

62. Never partake of any food or use any sandal paste, flowers, betel-leaves, clothes or drink, until they have been offered to the Lord.

63. Accept nothing at the hands of those that seek wealth and pleasure, though they offer it voluntarily.

64. Partake of food prepared by people of pure birth and clean lives.

65. Offer not to the Lord objects that are pleasant in your eyes (unless they be specified as objects to be offered).

66. But offer to the Lord only such things as are laid down in the Sacred Books.

67. Look upon the food and the fragrant objects offered to the Lord, as objects purified by his acceptance, but never as things to be enjoyed.

68. Perform the duties enjoined in the Sâstras as service to the Lord.

69. Spiritual suicide is brought about speediest and surest by disrespect towards those High Beings that ever remain in the contemplation of the Three Holy Mantras, and Eternal Life is attained speediest and surest by finding favor in their eyes.

70. Know that service to the Lord's Elect is the End and the Aim of your existence ; their displeasure, in any way, brings about the death of the soul.

71. You can recognise him as a permanent dweller in the lowest and darkest of hells, who regards the images of the Lord as mere blocks of stone; his Spiritual Teacher as a man like any other; the Chosen Ones as men of the world, high or low, according to their accidents of birth; the Holy Water that washes away all sin as mere water; the sacred Mantras as nothing but so many collections of sounds; and the Lord of All as in no way higher than the other gods.

72. The worship of the Chosen Ones is more efficacious than the worship offered to the Lord himself; disrespect towards them is a sin more terrible in its consequences than an insult to the Lord; the Holy Water that had washed their feet is holier by far than what had washed His feet. Lay this to your heart and ever remain intent on the service of the Holy Ones.

"Lord of wisdom," said the disciples: "Deign to tell us how we may order our lives in future, till we quit this body."

"Be it so" replied the Master, and he gave them the followiug Ten Commandments or Rules of Life.

1. One that had taken refuge in the Lord should never think of his future; for it is in the hands of the Lord; if he should trouble himself about it, in the least degree, his having taken refuge is a myth and a farce.

2. His present is the result of his past karma: so he should never bewail it. A Vaishṉava is to be free from any anxiety as to his present or future.

3 Never perform your duties as Means to an End.

4. Regard them as so much service offered to the Lord.

5. Study the S̱rī Bhâshya and spread its teachings far and wide; this is service pleasant to the Lord. If you cannot do this;

6. Study the Sacred Writings of S̱rī S̱aṯhakôpa and the other Holy Saints and hand them down to deserving disciples; or

7. Spend your time in service to the Lord at holy places (feeding the hungry, supplying offerings to the Lord, lighting His temple, preparing beautiful garlands for Him, sweeping the temple and adorning it with beautiful figures in colored powder, &c); or

8. Build a cottage at YAdAvadri (the dearest spot to me on earth) and dwell there in perfect peace and content ; or

9. Remain where you are, and having cast thy burdens on the Lord or on your Guru, ever meditate upon the meaning of the Two Truths; or

10. Seek out some Vaishnava, adorned with the virtues of wisdom, devotion and dispassion, who would regard you as something dear to him, as his own, efface all idea of egotism from your nature and obey his behests. This is the last and the only means ; and I see none other.

Such a one should carefully distinguish between three kinds of men in this life—friends, enemies and indifferent ones.

His *friends* are the Srī Vaishnavas. His *enemies* are those that hate the Lord. The *indifferent ones* are *the worldly*. When you meet with the *friends*, thy heart shall rejoice as at the sight of any object lovely in thy eyes—flowers, sweet scent, betel leaves.

When you meet with *the enemies*, thy heart shall shrink as at the sight of any object frightful and dangerous—serpents, tigers, &c.

When you meet with the *indifferent ones* you shall regard them with supreme indifference, as you would logs of wood, slabs of stone, &c. [If they show any leaning towards the subtle, instruct them in the knowledge of Brahman ; if not, pity them.—*T.G*].

Thus shall you, that have taken refuge in the Lord, conduct yourselves.

Keep company with the Vaishnavas; supreme Wisdom shall illuminate your heart and you will attain final beatitude.

Avoid carefully the company of the enemies; never talk to them.

If you disrespect the friends and out of worldly motives, reverence the enemies, you shall verily cause the heart of the Lord to grieve, even as the heart of an Emperor grieves at an insult to his beloved son in his presence. So let not any worldly benefits tempt you to show any reverence to the enemies; for, the wealth that comes to you from them, is sure to bring about enmity between you and the Lord in no time.

Have you not the Lord, the Giver of all Good, to ask of? If you should pass him by and demean yourself by begging of the enemies, you insult him as keenly as would the wife of an Emperor if she were to go about a begging of vile Kshatriyas.

Nor do thou reverence the indifferent ones out of any worldly motives, for see you no difference between shining gold and dull iron, between a flashing gem and a dark clod? Such a state of mind is worse than useless to you and should never be desired in any case.—(*Prap.*)

"These words the Master spake of duties due
To father, mother, children, fellows, friends;
Teaching how such as may not swiftly break
The clinging chains of sense—whose feet are weak
To tread the higher road—should order so
This life of flesh that all their hither days,
Pass blameless in discharge of charities * *
Living pure, reverent, patient, pitiful;
Loving all things which live even as themselves;
Because what falls for ill is the fruit of ill
Wrought in the past and what falls well of good;
And that by how so much the householder
Purgeth himself of self and helps the world,
By so much happier comes he to the next stage
In so much bettered being.
So all that night he spake, teaching the Law;
And on no eyes fell sleep—for they who heard
Rejoiced with tireless joy * * *
* * * * only gazed
Eye-rapt upon the Master; only hung
Heart-caught upon the speech, compassionate,
Commanding, perfect, pure, enlightening all,
Poured from those sacred lips."—(*Light of Asia.*)

He begs Forgiveness.

He sent for the temple officials and servants, and standing before them with folded hands, said humbly: "If I have, at any time, consciously or otherwise, offended you in any way, I request you to forgive me, ere I go away from amongst you."

"Lord, Lord," cried they in tones of horror and amazement, "to talk of you and offence in the same breath!! God forbid we should ever be guilty of such a sacrilege. But let that pass. What shall we do, dear Master, now that you are about to leave us?"

"Do! Why, one would almost think that you find it rather irksome to serve the Lord between the Two Rivers. Mine is the misfortune that I have to go away from His presence. Serve the Lord to the best of your might, and show every kindness and courtesy to the servants of the Lord that might chance to grace the Temple with their presence. I have spoken."

His Last Moments.

The last scene of the wondrous life-drama drew near;[1] and the Master laid himself down, with his head on the lap of the beloved Gôvinda and his feet on that of

1 During his last illness Kali Purusha, the Spirit of Darkness, came unto him and said:

"For these many years you have driven me out of this holy land; now that you are about to leave this place, what care you what becomes of your people? You have done your work well and earned a name for all time to come. And why look farther? So be a good man for once and let me have my own way now at least. Nay, it is a matter of courtesy that I ask this of you. For if you are so churlish as to deny me this, I will surely assume the garb of one of your men and undermine the Faith with factions."

The Holy One laughed long and loud—a laugh of supreme contempt.

"And so you have known me but ill all these days. I have been able, at all times, to foil you and your works; and shall not the Lord

the devoted Ândhra Pûrṇa. His disciples stood around reverently, reciting the Brahma Valli, the Bhrigu Valli,

into whose hands I leave my children, look after his own? And dare thou say thou wilt find Him easier to deal with than this poor worm? Avaunt! thou spirit of evil! Get thee behind me. Thou hast learnt thy part but awkwardly and blunderest."

At the request of Piḷḷân and Âṇḍan he had three images of himself made. Piḷḷân took charge of the one at the Temple, Âṇḍân the Younger and Naḷḷan, of the one at the birth-place of the Holy One and Âcchân, (Praṇatârtihara) of that at Tirunârâyaṇapura.

"What had Varada done to forfeit the coveted honor," humbly asked Nadâdoor Âlvân (Varada Vishṇu Âchârya.)

"Ah! rightly did Âlvân call you the favorite nephew of mine" replied the Master; and he gave permission to have images of his put up all over the land—to Nadâdoor Âlvân at Kânchi, to Ṣaila Pûrṇa's son at Tripati (Upper and Lower).

He then took Piḷḷân and Âcchân aside and taught them long and earnestly; placed his sacred feet on their heads and said: "The Lord has chosen to continue the teachings through you; rejoice in this and bear the honor right nobly. I fear that through the influence of the Black Kali, some may start secessions and try to ruin the cause. But verily, there shall in future years arise one, who will set things right and restore the rule of the Good Law."

He entrusted the image of Varada, the object of his daily worship, and that of Hayagrîva to the charge of Piḷḷân.

He prepared seventy four Conches and seventy four Discuses and four copies of Ṣrî Bhâshya and placed these and Piḷḷân's commentary on the Collect before the image of Varada. He then gave, with the Lord's permission, the Conches and Discuses to seventy four of his disciples, and named them Simhâsanâdhipatis (Throned Monarchs of the Kingdom of the Good Law); to four of them Varada Vishṇu Âchârya, Praṇatârtihara, Âṇḍân the younger and Piḷḷân the office and privilege of expounding the Ṣrî Bhâshya; and to Piḷḷân alone the Dual Throne—of the Bhâshya and the Sacred Collect.

He directed all to obey Piḷḷân and support him; and with his head on Piḷḷân's lap and his feet on that of Praṇatârtihara he arose from this tabernacle of flesh that had served him long and faithfully for a hundred years and twenty.—(*V.G.*)

He directed Âṇḍân the Younger to take care of his funeral obsequies; and placed Parâṣara over all his disciples.—(*T.G.*)

He gave the Bhâshya Teachership to Varada Vishṇu Âchârya and the office of expounding the Sacred Sayings (Ṣrî Sûkti—his other writings) to Parâṣara.

He died in Ṣaka 1009, Pingaḷa, in the month of Mâgha, the 10th day of the bright fortnight, under the constellation of Ârdra, at about noon.

and that most solemn decade of the Sacred Collect beginning with சூழ்விசும்பணி முகில், when, lo,! the crown of his head opened and the form of the Blessed One rose in a halo of glory. Bands of heavenly choristers discoursed sweet music; celestial nymphs scattered flowers of divine fragrance and sang peans of praise; and the untold hosts of Heaven, Dêvas, Gandharvas, Vasus, Maruts, Siddhas, Sâdhyas, Yakshas, Kinnaras, Kimpurushas, Vidhyâdharas, flocked to welcome the self exiled Great One. And then he advanced higher and higher, through worlds celestial, until he reached the banks of the Sacred Viraja. There were the radiant forms of the Ever Free Ones, ready to receive him back, their brother and chief, so long away from his vacant seat near the Lord; and the gladdest of

---

His body was buried within the precincts of the Temple.—(*Pal.*)

Ranganâtha and his consort bathed and purified themselves, as relatives do.—(*T.G.*)

The anniversary of his birth is celebrated by every Ṣrî Vaishṇava. —(*T.G.*)

He lived for 128 years and died in the year Durmati, in the month of Vaiṣâkha.—(*Per*).

He died in 4238 Kaliyuga (A. C. 1137).—(*V.C.*)

Ṣankara and Madhwa left behind them various Maṭhams or monasteries, presided over by Sannyâsins, who are supposed to continue the spiritual line of descent. But Râmânuja departed from the rule and his disciples were mostly married men.—(*V.C.*)

He died on a Saturday. Before his eyes were the Sandals of Mahâ Pûrṇa and in his heart the holy feet of Yâmunâchârya. The moment the Master left the body, there was heard a voice in the sky, the heart-cry of all Nature—"Lost is Dharma."—(*Prap.*)

The news spread far and wide and his disciples all over the land came to assure themselves of the truth of it. Anantârya, Guhadâsa and the rest from Tirupati; Yajñêṣa and the rest from the east; Yâmuna, the son of Gôshṭhîpûrṇa and many others from the Paṇḍya country; Sundarabâhu, the son of Mâlâdhara; Somayaji Âṇḍân, Marudoor Nambi, Toṇḍanoor Nambi and their friends from the western provinces of Tirunârâyaṇapura. They came in thousands and were kindly received by Parâṣara and Âṇḍân, who calmed their violent grief and sent them away consoled.—(*T.G.*)

all was his beloved Âḻvân who embraced the feet of his Master and washed them with tears of joy.

"Was I not right, Lord of my Heart? Would you have me forego this bliss of welcoming you thus, for a few more paltry years of existence down there in that dark fleshly tabernacle of mine?"

"You were always right, my dear. When was it otherwise? And yet, I could not bide there without you. So I took the earliest opportunity of asking the Lord to spare my services."

And thus, in sweet converse, they passed on to the City of Light, and Râmânuja—or Ananta—stood before the Throne of Glory, and gazed with never-satisfied eyes on the Divine Beauty.

"The time had seemed long and weary, that you have been away from us"; so came forth the accents of sweet love and gladness. "Welcome home, son of my heart. All glory to you, thou victor over Black Kali and his dread hosts. You have succeeded in accomplishing what I and many of My sons had failed to, and had almost given up in despair. Well have you redeemed your promise with us, and gladly do we acknowledge ourselves defeated. Henceforth I shall rest in peace."

"I went forth but as *Thy servant*, Lord. Your grace was ever with me, and made me serve You to the best of my poor ability. All glory be to Thee and to Thy servants."

The Hierarchies around the Throne took up the words, and shouts of joy rose up from among them, the faint far-off echoes of which reached this mortal earth and were felt by the workers therein as an unknown wave of joy and peace stealing over their hearts.

Meanwhile the disciples were prostrated with overwhelming grief that numbed their souls and took the heart out of them. But very soon Uttama Nambi was seen approaching from the Temple with the dress worn by the Lord, His garment, the offerings and all the paraphernalia of the Temple. The disciples were roused from the lethargic stupor in which they were sunk, and were reminded of the duty that lay before them. The mortal remains of the Teacher were then bathed with Holy Water; they adorned the body with the Twelve Sacred Marks, tied round his head the upper garment of the Lord, and hung round his neck the fragrant garland. They reverently placed his holy Feet on their heads, eyes and breasts; and, with due Brahmamêdha rites, had the funeral obsequies performed by Kurukêşvara, whom the Master had adopted as his son in spirit.

CHAPTER XXI.

THE VIŞISHṬÂDVAITA PHILOSOPHY.

There are two branches of the Vişishṭâdvaita Philosophy,—Şaiva Vişishṭâdvaita and Vaishṇava Vişishṭâdvaita.

The former was taught by one Şrîkaṇṭha Şivâchârya. The only difference between the two is that the Vaishṇava Vişishṭâdvaitees (the followers of Şrî Râmânujâchârya) acknowledge the supremacy of Vishṇu over the other deities, and the Şaiva Vişishṭâdvaitees, that of Şiva.

But, at the present day, the term *Vişishṭâdvaita* is generally applied to the teachings given to the world through Râmânujâchârya, while the other sect goes under the name of the *Şaivites* or *Siddhântins*.

The expression *Vişishṭâdvaita* is composed of the two words *Vişishṭa* and *Advaita*. *Advaita* means non-duality or the One Reality; *Vişishṭa* means, 'containing the attributes (Vişêshaṇa), *i.e.*, containing *Chit* and *Achit* as *S̱arîra* (body). Therefore the expression means non-duality or the One Reality—Parabrahman—which is united with Chit and Achit as its attributes; or, in other words, the Viṣishṯâdvaita School of Philosophy is the best exponent of *Qualified Monism*.

PARABRAHMAN

Is in reality the One Truth. It is said to be Eternal (*Nitya*), Unconditional Reality (*Satya*), Eternal and Infinite Knowledge (*Gñâna*), Infinite in point of Time and Space (*Ananta*), Omnipresent (*Vibhu*), Omniscient (*Sarvagña*), and Omnipotent (*Sarvas̱akti*). It is the material cause of the Universe (Upâdânakâraṇa) as also the instrumental and the auxiliary (Nimitta and Sahakârikâraṇas).

Many other names are given to It. The Vêdas call It *Sat* (Self-existent), *Âtma* (Spirit), *Brahman* (Great), *Îs̱a* or *Îs̱vara* (Lord), Vishṇu or Nârâyaṇa (Dweller in the Cosmos). In the other sacred writings one meets It under the names of *Purushôttama* (Supreme Spirit), *Vâsudêva*, &c. It exists in an inseparable union with *Chit* (Âtma) and *Achit* (Anâtma), two other Realities. It is knowable only in that condition, but this does not make It material. It is absolutely different from the Two, and is of the essence of knowledge (*Gñânâtmaka*). It is the only independent Reality, and the other two are dependent upon It. Yet they have no separate existence, but, like a substance and its attributes, exist in an inseparable union with one another. The Vêdas explain this relation by the simile of the Body and the Dweller. *Chit* and *Achit* form the *S̱arîra* (Body) of Parabrahman, the *S̱arîri* (the Dweller); the one cannot exist without the other.

The Upanishads explain the term *S̱arîra* as meaning *attributes* and not *bodies*; and the union between the *S̱arîra* and the *S̱arîri* is called *Apṛithaksiddha*, an inseparable union which has for ever existed, which is not brought about at any intermediate period, and which can never cease. However, there is a real difference between the three; but that difference is neither conditioned (*Anupâdhika*) nor *Mâyâkrita* (illusionary). The Three exist in indissoluble union with one another and are knowable only in that condition. In short, Parabrahman is the centre of the attributes *Chit* and *Achit*, which three, again, are one Reality (*Tatva*).

The following are some of the passages quoted by the Advaitins to support their position :—

1. *Sat* (Be-ness) alone, my dear, this was in the beginning, one only without a second. (Chândôgya Up. VI. 2.1.)

सदेव सोम्येदमग्र आसीदेकमेवाद्वितीयम् ॥

2. 'That, by which the Indestructible is known, is Higher knowledge; that which is invisible, intangible, which has no name, no color, no eyes, no ears, no hands, no feet; that which the wise see as the source of all beings, is the eternal One, all pervading, infinitely subtle, indestructible.' (Mundaka Up. I. 1. 6.)

यत्तदद्रेश्यमग्राह्यमगोत्रमवर्णमचक्षुःश्रोत्रं तदपाणिपादं नित्यं विभुं सर्वगतं सुसूक्ष्मं तदव्ययं यद्भूतयोनिं परिपश्यन्ति धीराः ॥

3. Brahman is Reality, Knowledge, Infinity. (Taittirîya Up. II. i. 1.)

सत्यं ज्ञानमनन्तं ब्रह्म ॥

4. Brahman is Bliss. (Tait. III. 6. 1.)

आनन्दो ब्रह्मेति व्यजानात् ॥

5. For, whenever one perceives even the slightest distinction in Him, then, indeed, he has reason to fear. (Tait. II. 7. 11.)

यथा ह्येवैष एतस्मिन्नुदरमन्तरं कुरुते । अथ तस्य भयं भवति ॥

6. Thou canst not see the Seer of Sight, nor cognise the Thinker of Thought. (Brihadâranyaka Up. III. 4. 2.

न दृष्टेर्द्रष्टारम् ॥

7. That which is all this is Self. (Bṛihad. IV. 5. 7.)

इदं सर्वं यदयमात्मात्मेदममृतमिदं ब्रह्मेदँसर्वम् ॥

8. There is nothing here that is many and varied. He who sees this world as varied, passes from death to death. (Bṛihad. VI. 4. 19—Kaṭha Up. IV. 10.)

नेह नानाऽस्ति किञ्चन । मृत्योस्स मृत्युमाप्नोति य इह नानेव पश्यति ॥

9. But, where there is duality as it were, there one sees another, but where to one all this becomes Self, then who shall see whom and by what? Who shall know which and by what? (Bṛihad. II. 4. 14; IV. 5. 15.)

यत्र हि द्वैतमिवभवति तत्केन कं पश्येत् ॥

10. Modification is but a name arising from speech; but the truth is that it is verily clay. (Chând. Up. VI. 1. 4.)

वाचारम्भणं विकारो नामधेयं मृत्तिकेत्येव सत्यम् ॥

11. He is without parts, without actions, tranquil, without fault, without taint. (Ṣvêtâṣvatâra Up. VI. 19.)

निष्कलं निष्क्रियं शान्तं निरवद्यं निरञ्जनम् ॥

12. He, who thinks that the Brahman is not known to him, knows him indeed. He, who thinks that the Brahman is known to him, knows him not. He is not known to those that believe they know Him. He is known to those that believe they know him not. (Kênôpanishad II. 3.)

यस्यामतं तस्यमतं मतं यस्य नवेद सः ॥

13. That Thou art. (Chând. Up. VI. 8.7.)

तत्त्वमसि ॥

14. He who worships another deity thinking that that deity is one and he another, he knows not. (Bṛihad. Up. I 4.10.)

अथ योऽन्यांदेवतामुपास्तेऽन्योसावन्योऽहमस्मीति न स वेद ॥

15. Let him worship Him as the Self itself. (Do. I. 4.7.)

आत्मेत्येवोपासीत ॥

16. He who knows Brahman becomes Brahman indeed. (Mund. Up. III 2.9.)

स यो ह वै तत्परमं ब्रह्म वेद ब्रह्मैव भवति ॥

17. Whatever I am, that is that deity, whatever that deity is, that am I. (Aitarêya Âranyaka II. 2.4.6.)

तद्योहं सोसौ योसौ सोहमस्मि ॥

18. That which is without attributes, without taint. (Atharva Mahâ-Nârâyana Up. 7.)

निर्गुणं निरञ्जनं ॥

19. That which is neither gross, nor atomic, nor short, nor long. (Brih. Up. III. 8.8.)

अस्थूलमनण्वह्रस्वमदीर्घम् ॥

20. Indeed, the Self, this one only, was in the beginning. (Aitarêya Up. I. 1.) इदमग्र आसीत् ॥

आत्मा वा इदमेक एवाग्र आसीत् ॥

21. He who knows Brahman attains the Supreme. (Taitt. Up. II. 1. 1.)

ब्रह्मविदाप्नोति परं ॥

22. This Self is Brahman. (Brih. Up. II. 5. 19 ; IV. 4. 5. Mând. Up. I. 2.)

अयमात्मा ब्रह्म ॥

23. Not even on account of the peculiarity of situation can the two-fold characteristics of positive and negative belong to the Highest, for He is taught to be without distinctions. (Vêdânta Sûtras III. 2. 11.)

न स्थानतोऽपि परस्योभयलिङ्गं सर्वत्रहि ॥

24. But the world of dreams is a mere illusion, on account of its being of an unmanifest form. (Vêdânta Sûtras III. 2. 3.)

मायामात्रं तु कार्त्स्न्येनानभिव्यक्तस्वरूपत्वात् ॥

25. The Jâbâlas worship the Lord as the self and the Scriptural texts teach us so. (Vêdânta Sûtras IV. 1.3.)

आत्मेतितूपगच्छन्ति ग्राहयन्ति च ॥

26. I exist in the hearts of all beings, as the individual self. (Bhagavad Gîta X. 20.)

अहमात्मा गुडाकेशसर्वभूताशयस्थितः ॥

27. There exists no being, moveable or immoveable, which is without Me. (Bhagavad Gîta X. 39.)

न तदस्ति विना यत्स्यात् मयाभूतं चराचरम् ॥

The following are some of the texts that support the Viṣishṭâdvaitic position :—

1. Knowing the individual self and the Impeller as distinct, and being therefore blessed by Him, he attains immortality. (Ṣvêtâṣvatara Up. I. 6.)

पृथगात्मानं प्रेरितारं च मत्वा जुष्टस्ततस्तेनामृतत्वमेति ॥

2. He who understands all, he who knows everything. (Mând. Up. I. 1.9; II. 2. 7.)

यस्सर्वज्ञस्सर्ववित् ॥

3. His supreme power is revealed, indeed, as varied, natural, as consisting of knowledge, strength and action. (Ṣvêt. Up. VI. 8.)

पराऽस्यशक्तिर्विविधैव श्रूयते स्वाभाविकी ज्ञानबलक्रिया च ॥

4. He whose desires are true, he whose will is true (Chând. Up. VIII. 1. 5.)

एष आत्माऽपहतपाप्मा विजरो विमृत्युर्विशोको विजिघत्सोऽपिपासस्सत्यकामस्सत्यसङ्कल्पः ॥

5. The self is not a produced thing as the Scripture does not say so. (Vêd. Sûtras II. 3.187.)

नाऽत्मा श्रुतेर्नित्यत्वाच्च ताभ्यः ॥

6. It thought. (Chând. Up. VI. 2. 3.)

तदैक्षत ॥

7. This same deity thought. (Chând. VI. 3.2.)

सेयं देवतैक्षत ॥

8. He thought—may I create the worlds. (Ait. Up. I.1.)

स ईक्षत लोकान्नु सृजा इति ॥

9. Eternal among the eternals, Intelligent among the intelligent, He, though One, realises the desires of many. (Katha. Up. V 13 ; Svetas. Up. 13.)

नित्यो नित्यानां चेतनश्चेतनानामेको बहूनांयोविदधाति कामान् ॥

10. The two unborn, the Intelligent and the Non-intelligent, the Ruler and the Non-Ruler. (Svet. Up. I. 9; VI. 7. 8.)

ज्ञाज्ञौद्वावजावीशानीशौ ॥

11. This self is free of sin, old age, death, sorrow, hunger, and thirst. His desires are true, his thoughts are true. (Chând. Up. VIII. 1. 5. ; VIII. 7. 1 and 3.)

एष आत्माऽपहतपाप्मा विजरोविमृत्युर्विशोको विजिघत्सो ऽपिपासस्सत्यकामस्सत्यसङ्कल्पः ॥

12. Fearing Him the wind blows...... He who knows the bliss of Brahman, fears nought. (Taittirîya Up. II. Anuwakas 7. 8.)

भीषास्माद्वातः पवते भीषोदेति सूर्यः । भीषास्मादग्निश्चेन्द्रश्च मृत्युर्धावति पञ्चमइति. सैषानन्दस्य मीमांसा भवति ॥

यतो वाचोनिवर्तन्ते अप्राप्यमनसा सह। आनन्दं ब्रह्मणो विद्वान्। न बिभेतिकुतश्चनेति ॥

13. The successful worshipper attains, along with the intelligent Brahman, all His auspicious qualities. (Taitt. Up. II. 1. 1.)

सोऽश्नुते सर्वान् कामान् सह । ब्रह्मणा विपश्चितेति ॥

14. May I become many and be born (Taitt. Up. II. 6. 1.)

सोकामयत बहु स्यां प्रजायेयेति ॥

15. He who has entered within, is the ruler of all things that are born, and is the self of all. (Taitt. Âranyaka. III. 24.)

अन्तःप्रविष्टश्शास्ताजनानाम् ॥

16. He who, dwelling in the self, is within the self, whom the ṣelf does not know, whose body is the self, who is the inner ruler of the self. He is thy inner ruler and immortal Self. (Bṛihad. Up. III. 7. 22. ; the whole of the Antaryâmi Brâhmaṇa.)

य आत्मनि तिष्ठन्नात्मनोऽन्तरो यमात्मा नवेद यस्याऽत्मा शरीरम् य आत्मानमन्तरोयमयति सत आत्माऽन्तर्याम्यमृतः ॥

17. He who is moving within the earth. . . . whose body is matter, whom matter does not know, He is the internal self of all beings, He is devoid of all sins, He is the One Nârâyaṇa. (Subâla. Up. VII. 1.)

यस्य पृथिवी शरीरं यः पृथिवीमन्तरे सञ्चरन् यं पृथिवी न वेद । सर्वभूतान्तरात्मा अपहतपाप्मा दिव्यो देव एको नारायणः॥

18. Having created the world, he entered into the same world. (Taitt. Up. II. 6. 1.)

सोऽकामयत ....तत्सृष्ट्वा तदेवानुप्राविशत् तदनुप्रविश्य ॥

19. The Lord alone rules over the destructible and the individual self. (Svetas. Up. 1. 10.)

क्षरं प्रधानममृताक्षरं हरः क्षरात्मानावीशते देव एकः ॥

20. He is the Lord of the lord of the senses, the individual self. (Do. VI. 9. 16.)

स कारणं करणाधिपाधिपः न चास्य कश्चिज्जनिता न चाधिपः॥

21. He is the Lord of the individual souls, is eternal, auspicious and inexhaustible. (Mahâ Nârâyaṇa Upanishad XI. 3.)

आत्मेश्वरं शाश्वतं शिवमच्युतं ॥

22. Knowing the Enjoyer, the object of enjoyment and the Impeller. (Ṣvêtâṣ Up. 1. 12.)

भोक्ता भोग्यं प्रेरितारं च मत्वा सर्वं-प्रोक्तं त्रिविधं ब्रह्ममेतत् ॥

23. One of them eats the sweet Pippala fruit, while the other shines in splendour without eating at all. (Ṣvetas. IV. 6.)

द्वा सुपर्णा सयुजा सखाया समानं वृक्षं परिषस्वजाते । तयोरन्यः पिप्पलं स्वाद्वत्त्यनश्नन्नन्यो अभिचाकशीति ॥

24. Prakriti and Purusha are both without a beginning. (Gita XIII. 19.)

प्रकृतिं पुरुषंचैव विद्ध्यनादी उभे अपि ॥

25. Entering into these three deities along with this individual self which is the same as Myself, I bring about the differentiations of Name and Form. (Chând. Up. VI. 3. 2.)

सेयं देवतैक्षत हन्ताहमिमास्तिस्रोदेवता अनेन जीवेनाऽत्मना ऽनुप्रविश्य नामरूपे व्याकरवाणीति ॥

26. Except in the matter of activity pertaining to the creation of the universe, etc., the liberated selves possess all the powers of the Lord, because the texts dealing with this point mention the Lord alone and not the selves. (Vêd. Sûtras IV. 4. 17.)

जगद्व्यापारवर्जं प्रकरणादसन्निहितत्वाच्च ॥

27. Equality between the individual self and the Lord is confined solely to enjoyment. (Do IV. 4. 21.)

भोगमात्रसाम्यलिङ्गाच्च ॥

28. Brahman is that which is approached by the liberated selves. (Do. I. 3. 2.)

मुक्तोपसृप्यव्यपदेशात् ॥

29. Those who depart from here, after having known the Self and His eternal and auspicious qualities, freely move over all the worlds. (Chand. Up. VIII. 1. 6.)

य इहाऽत्मानमननुविद्य व्रजन्त्येताँश्च सत्यान्कामाँस्तेषाँ सर्वेषु लोकेष्वकामचारो भवत्यथ य इहाऽत्मानमनुविद्य व्रजन्त्येताँश्च सत्यान् कामाँस्तेषाँ सर्वेषु लोकेषु कामचारो भवति ॥

30. The liberated self having reached the Lord, whose nature is Bliss, moves about over all the worlds, enjoying whatever thing he likes, and assuming whatever form he likes. (Taitt. III. 10. 5.)

एतमानन्दमयमात्मानमुपसंक्रम्य । इमाँल्लोकान्कामान्नीकामरूप्यनुसञ्चरन् एतत्साम गायन्नास्ते । हा३वु हा३वु हा३वु ॥

31. He moves about there. (Chând. Up. VIII. 12. 3.)

स उत्तमः पुरुषः सतत्र पर्य्येति जक्षत्क्रीडन्रममाणः ।

32. Then the wise man, casting aside merit and demerit and free of all taint, attains the highest degree of equality with Brahman. (Muṇḍ. III. 1. 3.)

तदाविद्वान् पुण्यपापेविधूय निरञ्जनः परमं साम्यमुपैति ॥

33. Bliss and other attributes are to be understood in all the Vidyas, because Brahman, the possessor of those qualities happens to be the same in all of them. (Vêd. Sût. III. 3. 11.)

नस्थानतोऽपि परस्योभयलिङ्गं सर्वत्रहि ॥

34. Having approached the Supreme Light, the liberated self manifests himself in his own free form. (Chând. Up. VIII. 3. 4.)

परं ज्योतिरुपसंपद्य स्वेनरूपेणाभिनिष्पद्यते ॥

35. The knowledge of the knower does not disappear. (Bṛih. Up. IV. 3. 30.)

न हि विज्ञातुर्विज्ञातेर्विपरिलोपो विद्यते ॥

36. By what means shall one know the Knower? (Bṛih. VI. 5, 15.)

विज्ञातारमरेकेन विजानीयात् ॥

The other texts on which the Advaitins base their doctrine are interpreted by Râmânuja to support his views. (*Vide* Ṣrî Bhâshya, Jigñâsa Adhikaraṇa.)

Now these apparently contradictory passages are, however, reconcilable, when we regard *Chit* and *Achit* as the attributes of Parabrahman, the only Reality. The indissoluble union of the three is what is really meant by the non-duality asserted in the passages.

When we meet with passages in the Scriptures that declare Parabrahman as devoid of any attributes or qualities (Nirguṇa) we are not to take it that It has no attributes whatever; for It is a Reality and every Reality must have attributes ; what is really meant is that It is devoid of all undesirable attributes, material limitations and imperfections, to which Jîva is subject, and which are brought about by its association with Prakriti. But It has *Gunas* (attributes) such as :—

1. Omniscience (Gñâna).
2. Omnipotence (Sakti).
3. The power of containing everything in itself (Bala).
4. The power of ruling over everything (Aisvarya).
5. Though It is the material basis of this universe It is not subject to any of the changes (Vikâras) of matter (Vîrya).
6. It is higher than the highest (Têjas).
7. Forgiveness (Kshama).
8. Mercy (Kripa).
9. Love (Vâtsalya).
10. Purity (Sîla).
11. Straightforwardness (Ârjava).
12. Goodness (Sauhârdam) &c.

It has no particular name, but all names denote It either directly, as Nârâyana, Vishnu and Vâsudêva ; or indirectly as Agni, Indra, &c.

It is omnipresent, all-pervading and infinite, and hence formless, colorless ; but It can take any form. But there are five chief manifestations of It :—

1. *Para Vigraha.*—The form in which he manifests himself in the Vaikunthalôka, with his weapons and ornaments ; Sankha, the Conch, that power by which all sins are destroyed ; Chakra, the Discus, which dispels all ignorance ; Khadga, the Sword which symbolises the Gñânasakti ; Padma or the Lotus, representing the Cosmos, of which he is the Lord ; Gadâ or the Mace ; Sârnga, the

Bow; Kaustubha, the resplendent gem on his breast; Srî-vatsa, a mole on his breast, &c., all emblematic of some divine attribute or other. He is then called Vâsudeva.

2. *Vyûha Vigraha.*—The bodies he takes when he manifests in the three Vishṇulôkas (Âmoda, Bhuvana and Pramoda) located in the Satyalôka within the material universe. These forms are named Sankarshaṇa, Pradyumna and Aniruddha, and are worshipped by the Dêvas till the Prâkṛita Pralaya destroys these worlds. Through these manifestations he looks after the evolution and the involution of the Universe, wards off the evils that befall the Jîvas while in bondage, and facilitates the devotion of the Bhaktas.

Vâsudeva is endowed with all the six divine attributes, while the latter possess only two of them.

Sankarshaṇa is endowed with Gñâna and Bala; he teaches truth to the world, and brings about the involution of the Universe, at the end of the Mahâ Kalpa. He is the presiding deity over the Jîvas.

Pradyumna is endowed with Aiṣvarya and Vîrya; he teaches the Good Law (Dharma), creates all pure objects and organises the four castes. He is the presiding deity over Manas.

Aniruddha is endowed with Ṣakti and Têjas; he gives knowledge to the world, he is its Protector, and is the presiding deity over the Miṣra Srishti (Mixed Creation).

3. *Vibhava Vigraha.*—Avataras like Râma and Krishṇa. This is of two kinds: Amṣâvatâra—simply possessing the power of Îṣvara; Sâkshâdavatâra—the direct incarnation.

4. *Archâ Vigraha.*—An invisible body (of the nature of intellect) which enters into idols by the force of concentration and the Vedic Chants; if the idol be polluted or

if no proper worship be paid to it, the in-dwelling energy departs from it.

The Âgamas or Occult treatises define an idol as "an object of stone, wood or metal, usually fashioned in the form of a human being, in which certain spiritual forces are focussed by the concentrated will-power of high initiates, for the purpose of aiding a worshipper in acquiring that stability of mind necessary to him for the contemplation of the ALL, as laid down in the Upanishads."

These are endowed with certain qualities, of which the most significant are:—

1. Creating in the minds of the devotees a spiritual desire for worshipping a particular figure. (Ruchi Janakatva.)

2. Creating in their minds a feeling of satisfaction at the sight of that figure. (Ṣubhâṣrayatva).

3. Attracting all people to worship it. (Aṣêshaloka Ṣaraṉyatva).

4. Capable of being easily concentrated upon. (Anubhâvyatva).

Antaryâmi Vigraha.—The body in which the Lord manifests himself to a person when he meditates upon him. It is located in the Lotus of the Heart, and controls Buddhi. It is likened to 'a flash of lightning in the heart of a blue cloud.' (Now the commentator on Râmânuja's Vêdârthasangraha, remarks upon the expression "Nîlatoyada Madhyastha Vidyullêkhêvabhâswara" that the real meaning should be learnt only through initiation).

When the Lord takes up any of these bodies, Lakshmi, the Divine Mother, follows Him with a similar body.

These forms are not produced by Karma and are not composed of ordinary matter but of Ṣuddha Satva, a peculiar intellectual substance. An Impersonal Deity cannot form an object of contemplation, and the Lord, out of His infinite mercy, takes these forms to facilitate the contemplation of the Yôgins.

ACHIT.

(i). *It is three-fold. It is Time*:—The cause of all changes. It is Eternal, Universal and Unconditioned (Akhaṇḍakâla); and Conditioned (Khaṇḍa), not Eternal, but reckoned by the rotation and the revolution of the planets, *i.e.*, hours, days, yugas, kalpas. It is also called Satvâdiguṇaṣûnya (devoid of the three Guṇas—Satva, Rajas and Tamas).

(ii.) *It is Nature*. It is the material basis (Upâdânakâraṇa) of the universe, as the clay is of the vessels made of it; it forms the bodies of the Jîvas and of everything in the Cosmos. It has no origin, it is Self-existing, Universal, ONE, but in every respect subordinate to Brahman.

In the Sacred Writings it goes under various names—Prakṛiti, Pradhâna, Mûlaprakṛiti, Avyakta, Mâyâ, Tamas, Akshara, Brahman, &c. It is matter in which none of the three Guṇas predominate over the other. It is their heart and root, and produces all its manifestations through them.

EVOLUTION.

The first modification of it is *Mahat*, in which the three Guṇas are not in a state of equilibrium. It is three-fold in its nature—Sâtvika, Râjasa and Tâmasa.

Mahat does not mean 'intellect', as in the Sânkhya system; nor Adhyavasâya or Buddhi (a manifestation of knowledge): but it is a manifestation of matter, and knowledge is an attribute of Jivâtman.

Mahat evolves Ahankâra, (Egotism), also of three kinds, Sâtvika, Râjasa and Tâmasa, derived from the corresponding varieties of Mahaṯ.

It does not signify Egoism, as in Sânkhya; nor Antahkarana or Abhimâna as in the other systems, but is a manifestation of Mahat and cause of the subtle elements and the senses.

Manas is the Antarindriya or the sixth sense by means of which every kind of knowledge is produced in the Âtman.

It is atomic, and is located in the heart along with the other senses; and their functions are carried from the heart to the organs through their nerves.

From the Sâtvika Ahamkâra proceed—

(*a*) The mind (the Manas or Antahkarana).

(*b*) The five faculties of perception (the Gñânêndriyas)—the organ of touch, the eye, the tongue, the nose and the ear.

(*c*) The five organs of action (Karmêndriyas) the throat, the hands, the feet, the organs of excretion and generation.

From the Tâmasa Ahamkâra proceed the five Tanmâtras, the five subtle elements, the essences containing the attributes of the gross elements. They are—sound, tangibility, visibility, taste and odour.

These again produce the five gross elements, the Mahâ Bhûtas—Ether, Air, Light, Water and Earth.

Râjasa Ahamkâra aids the other two, Matter and Mahat, to produce everything according to the will of Îsvara.

(iii) *It is Suddha Satva*—a substance different from matter and not subject to its qualities. It is also called Swaccha Dravya and Nityavibhûti. This goes to form the Vaikuntha, the world of the Lord and the bodies of Vishnu and the Muktas, when they choose to take one.

It is intellectual in its nature, and yet, not being Jîva, is included under Achit.

Matter is not the material basis of the Universe independently of Parabrahman, of which it is the attribute or Ṣarîra. Parabrahman is the material basis of matter.

It exists in two conditions—the Sûkhsma or latent and undifferentiated. It is the cause.

Sthûla—differentiated, the effect. Then it produces a congeries of forms called Jagat or Universe.

In ordinary life we observe the material, the instrumental and the auxiliary causes different from one another, *e. g.*, the clay, the potter, and time. But Parabrahman is the material cause of the Universe as stated above; it is the instrumental cause, because, by its will, matter, its attribute, evolves the Universe out of itself. It is the centre (Ṣarîri) of Time, and as such the auxiliary cause of Jagat.

Creation is of two kinds:—

(1) Samashṭi (General) Evolution of Mahat, Ahamkâra, &c.

(2) Vyashṭi (Special):—The Evolution that results from the correlation in certain proportions of the differentiated five elements, bringing into existence the four kinds of bodies.

(i) Sura (Daityas, Gandharvas, &c.)

(ii) Nara (human beings).

(iii) Tiryak (animals).

(iv) Sthâvara (vegetables or minerals).

The General Creation takes place at the beginning of each Mahâ Kalpa; the Special Creation at the beginning of each Brahma Kalpa (day of Brahma); and the Nitya Srishṭi, goes on all throughout, according to the effects of Karma—the birth and growth of all gross bodies.

INVOLUTION.

When the Universe changes from its present objective or manifested state into a latent or Sûkshma condition, it is said to be in Pralaya. It is of four kinds :—

(1) Prâkrita Pralaya—affecting the entire Universe, when it is resolved into unmanifested Nature, where the Guṇas are in a state of equilibrium. It takes place at the end of every Mahâ Kalpa.

(2) Naimittika Pralaya—when the Solar Systems are disintegrated into their primitive elements—at the end of each Brahma Kalpa.

(3) Nitya Pralaya—which takes place every moment, when the atoms that compose the various forms in the Universe enter and depart.

(4) Âtyantika Pralaya—when a Jîva attains Mukti or liberation, and enters no more the house of flesh.

The Worlds.

(1) Bhûlôka—the Earth.

(2) Bhuvarlôka—extending from the Earth to the Sun.

(3) Suvarlôka—from the Sun to the Pole Star.

(4) Maharlôka
(5) Janalôka
(6) Tapôlôka
(7) Satyalôka
} from the Pole-Star to the limits of the Brahmâṇḍa. These are generally called Ûrdhvalôkas.

The Pitṛilôka, Vishṇulôka and Ṣivalôka are certain regions of these Ûrdhvalôkas.

There are innumerable such Brahmâṇḍas, each containing its 14 Lôkas, its Sun, its Moon, &c., and each ruled by a Brahma. They are all resolved into their primal elements when their Brahma's life-period comes to a close. They have all been produced from one and the same Mûlaprakṛiti, and are distinct from one another, being encompassed by layers of the five elements, Mahat and Ahamkâra in their uncombined condition. They go into Pralaya at different periods. But all of them are pervaded and controlled by one Îṣvara (Parabrahman). They fairly correspond to what are known as Solar Systems or Macrocosm. The Material Universe is said to be unlimited on all sides below, but it is limited above by the region of Ṣuddha Satva—which is limited below by the limited Universe but unlimited on all other sides. Some Viṣishṭâdvaitins hold that Ṣuddha Satva, being substance, is a kind of matter, but having only the Satva element unmixed with Rajas and Tamas.

CHIT.

It is Jîvâtman and is not material, is eternal, is not produced by anything else, and is different from Achit and Îṣvara. Each Jîva is different from another. Properly speaking, the expression applies both to Jîvâtman and Paramâtman, in that it means 'that which possesses knowledge.' But the knowledge of Îṣvara is eternal and infinite, and requires no aid for development; while the knowledge of the Jîva is limited by matter and Karma. Hence the term is usually applied to the Jîvâtman.

It is atomic in form, but possesses infinite knowledge in Môksha; it is pure, blissful, intellectual, immutable; it is at the same time the centre of intellect; it is subject to Karma till it attains Môksha and till then cannot exist apart from Prakriti. Every particle of Prakriti contains the Jîva and forms its vehicle. Every Jîva has the supreme spirit as its Antaryâmi (Inner Ruler); it is the Ṣarîra (body) to the Ṣarîri (Parabrahman) to whom it is subordinate, and who pervades every Jîva as also every particle of matter.

The seat of the Jîvâtman in the body is the heart and in its atomic form it is finite, but its attribute—knowledge—infinite and of various kinds. When it desires to know anything about an object, it proceeds to that object, directly, near or distant, and without being limited by time or space. This knowledge is real and eternal, but its various manifestations (inference, perception, &c.,) require some foreign aid for their action. In other words, knowledge is eternal, but its manifestations (avasthas) are not so.

There are 3 classes of Jîvas :—

(*a*) *Nityas* :—They enjoy supreme bliss for ever and are never subject to Karma or matter. They are omniscient and their home is Vaikuṇṭha. Among them are Ananṭa or Ṣêsha , Garuḍa, Vishvaksêna, Jaya, Vijaya, Nanda, Ṣkanda, Ṣankhakarṇa, Pushkara, Pushkarâksha, Kumudâksha, Gajânana, Priṣni Garbha, Kâḷa, Puṇḍarîka, Kumuda, Vâma, Jayatsêna, Supratishṭha, Sumukha, Amânava Purusha, Sarva Gandhi, &c.

(2) *Muktas* :—Those that attain liberation in this evolution and have become omniscient.

(3) *Baddhas*:—Those that are yet subject to the limitations of Matter and are under the baneful influence of Ignorance and Karma. They are devas, men, animals, &c.

KARMA.

The act of the Jîvâtman entering a body is called Birth ; and its abandonment of the body is called Death ; its change to another body is called Re-birth. Birth, Death and Re-birth are changes that affect the body that is subject to them, but not the Jîva that is changeless.

The Jîvâtma is pure, immaterial and eternal, but yet it is brought into connection with matter, takes a body, and is subject to pleasure and pain. Karma is the cause that brings the Jîva into relations with matter in the shape of Kâraṇa Ṣarîra (human monad) and with misery and happiness; it produces the various kinds of bodies, as also birth, death and re-birth in connection with these.

Now, Karma is the result of the conscious action of the Jîvâtman, good or bad. It is good if it pleases Îşvara, if it accords with his will ; it is bad if it goes against it.

This is produced through Agñâna or Avidya (Ignorance). There are two aspects of it—Anyathâgñâna, which confounds the attributes of one thing with another, and Viparîtagñâna, which confounds one thing with another. The Jîvâtman confounds the body (matter) with itself, and then its attributes of birth, death, &c., with those belonging to itself.

This ignorance gives rise to such undesirable forces as hatred, desire, &c., which ultimately results in certain actions (the cause of karma good or bad). These again create other Karmas through habit (Vâsana) and ignorance. Again, through taste or desire (ruchi) the Jîva becomes connected with other matter of various kinds. The result is ignorance productive again of karma.

This karma has no beginning, and works through ignorance, action, habit, desire and connection with matter. In this sense alone is karma beginningless, like the ever-flowing current of a stream, as also the relation of Jîva to the Kâraṇa Şarîra; this does not come in at any intermediate period, but exists latent in the Jîvâtman, even during Pralaya. When the Cycle of Evolution starts anew, they manifest themselves and produce results as before.

NARAKA.

The effects of bad karma are experienced through suffering in Naraka and misery in this world. Now, Naraka is a state of existence in a certain locality, where the Jîvâtman suffers pain as the punishment for the effect of its bad karma (pâpa). It is governed by Yama (the god of death). During the process of suffering, or more properly purification, in Naraka, the Jîva is clothed in a peculiar body (Naraka Şarîra or Yâtanâ Şarîra) formed from the Sûkshma Şarîra, after its separation from the gross body.

SVARGA

Is a happy state of existence in a certain locality in the Ûrdhvalôkas ; there the Jîva enjoys happiness unmixed with any sorrow, clothed in a body evolved out of its Sûkshma Sarîra. This enjoyment and happiness in this world in future births are the results of good karma.

His stay in either locality depends on the continuation of the karma that takes him there. The course of karma is the same throughout, in this Brahmânda as well as in the others.

Îsvara is omnipotent, but he cannot and does not interfere with any one's karma and prevent him from producing bad karma. For he is not the individual cause, but the cause of everything ; but every Jîva is individualised and is responsible for its own action. Îswara is perfectly neutral ; and since growth depends upon individual experience and knowledge, it would be absurd in the Lord of All to take away the conditions of progress and for the Jîva what he ought to do for himself. It will be but misplaced kindness.

When the Jîva has enjoyed or suffered on the superphysical plans of existence according to the intensity of the karmic causes set up by it, it takes fresh encasements of matter, according to the preponderance of its karmic attraction. This process is repeated until it learns all its lessons and becomes perfect in Wisdom, Power and Love. It attains liberation and is freed from the cycle of karma and re-birth.

THE GODS

Dwell in the Ûrdhvalokas. They are of various grades or ganams,—Hiranyagarbha, Rudra, Indra, Agni, Maruts, &c.,—and perform certain definite functions in connection with the grand work of Evolution, under the orders and supervision of Îsvara. Each has a particular lôka or world of his own, and has various grades of assistants to help him in his work. They live to the end of the life period of Brahma and attain Môksha along with him.

During the next Mahâkalpa, others take their places—such as are progressed enough to be entrusted with the responsibility.

MOKSHA.

There are two kinds of It :—

(*a*) *Kaivalya,* when the Jîva enjoys supreme bliss as Jîva, in its natural state.

(*b*) *Brahmânanda* or Sâyujya, enjoyment of the same by the Jîva as Brahman enjoys it.

Môksha is experienced in Vaikuṉṯhalôka, or Paramapada, but each variety has its own particular locality in it.

Sâyujya includes the *Sâlokya,* living in the same world as Vishṉu and *Sârûpya,* being endowed with a body similar to his formed of Ṣuddhasatva. But never during Môksha does the individual self merge absolutely in the Universal Soul and become one with it.

The essentials of Môksha are entire separation of the Jîva from all connection with matter and complete destruction of karma, good or bad. These are attained before the self enters the Paramapada at a place beyond the limits of this material Universe.

There is no difference among the Muktas themselves in their enjoyment of the bliss of Môksha; or between them and the Parabrahman itself.

It is attainable by every Jîva, provided it possesses the necessary qualifications. When one, whose work down here is done, is about to depart, the Jîva clothed in his Sûkshma Ṣarîra goes from the heart to a spot in the crown of the head, Brahmarandhra, along the Sushumna, a Nâdi or nerve running from the heart. He breaks out through it and is conveyed by the solar rays to the Sûryamaṇḍala (the Orb of the Sun). From thence he proceeds to Paramapada through a dark spot in the sun. Supreme wisdom attained by yôga directs him all along the Path and the Ativâhikas, bearers in transit, lead him on; they are certain holy souls named Archis, Ahas, Pûrvapaksha, Uttarâyaṇa, Samvatsara, Âditya, Chandra, Vaidyuta, Varuṇa, Indra, Prajâpati, and lastly an incarnation of Vishṇu, named Amânava. This path is known as the Archirâdi or Dêvayâna.

Môksha is everlasting. The Muktas are never again subject to karma or to the bonds of matter; but of their own free choice, they may incarnate for the good of the world. Even there they are free and are untrammelled by Matter or Karma.

There is another Path, Pitriyâna, (Dhûmâdi Mârga, the Path of Smoke), along which proceed those who have not as yet attained liberation; but who have, by their good lives, won a right to the World of the Pitris (Svarga.) They return to birth here when the karma that took them there has worn itself out.

The Four Means to attain this Glorious End.

(*a*) *Karma Yôga*: The aspirant should thoroughly acquaint himself with what is taught in the Scriptures on the nature and the attributes of the Three Realities, Chit, Achit and Îsvara, and continue to perform his duties, social and individual, to the best of his ability, but without any sense of egoism or interest in the results of his actions; he should discharge them as carefully and conscientiously as any whose heart is centred on the enjoyment of the results thereof, but cheerfully and joyously as service to the Lord, as a glorious privilege granted him to labour in the Lord's Vineyard.

(*b*) *Gñâna Yôga*: He practises Yôga Vidya under a competent Guru, thoroughly and systematically. Either of these two means, or each by itself, gives him a true perception of the nature and attributes of the Jîvâtman, and secures for him the two kinds of Môksha (Kaivalya and Brahmânanda).

(*c*) *Bhakti Yôga* or Upâsana : The Bhakta discharges the duties laid upon him to the utmost, as so much pleasing service to the Lord ; but all the while his heart and soul is centred in the uninterrupted contemplation of the Lord and his attributes. Gñâna Yôga may be of great help to one engaged in this.

(*d*) The Mantras and the Brâhmaṇas of the Vedas and the Dharma Ṣâstras lay great stress upon the efficacy of Karma Yôga as a means ; the Bhagavad Gîta (Chap. ii-vi.) recommends the Karma and the Gñâna Yôgas ; while Chapters 7-12 glorify the Bhakti Yôga, as also the Brahma Sûtras (Chapter iii.) and the Sâṇḏilya and the Nârada Sûtras.

Bhakti Yôga is the crown of the edifice ; Gñâna Yôga prepares one intellectually for it ; and Karma Yôga destroys undesirable Karmic affinities and purifies one's heart.

Seven are the qualifications that one should strive to acquire before he enters the Path of Devotion :—

(1) He should build up a pure and unstained body, by feeding it only upon pure diet—such articles as are recommended by the Gîta and the Yôga Sûtras as Sâtvic (Spiritual). This gives him a vehicle that interferes not with the concentration of his mind, but receives and responds to perfectly the higher and intenser vibrations that he sends through them, during meditation.

(2) He trains himself to analyse his desires, to purify them and rise above them.

(3) By steady practice and by removing from the path all disturbing influences he progresses rapidly in concentration, until he can nail his consciousness to anything that he fixes upon, and that for any length of time.

(4) All the while, he neglects not the duties he owes to those around him, but performs them to the best of his ability, without in the least being tinged by any desire for the enjoyments of the results thereof.

(5) He earnestly endeavours to possess every attribute that will help him on the path—truth, mercy, charity, &c.

(6) His heart is filled with peace eternal, perfect and undisturbed. Perfect equanimity of spirit under the most trying circumstances, prosperous and adverse, and perennial cheerfulness at his being allowed to serve the Great Father have become a second nature with him.

(7) He quietly falls into his place in evolution, as the one that he had won for himself by his past Karma, and strives to utilise his powers and his opportunities to their utmost.

Such a Bhakta contemplates upon himself as being one with Parabrahman ; not in the sense of perfect identity, for that is never possible ; but as one of the numberless attributes or Sarîras of It.

One mode of it is what is known as Pratîkopôsana—contemplation as Parabrahman, of Pranava, and of certain other objects. The Madhu Vidya, the Udgîtha Vidya, &c., deal with it.

The other, Apratîkopôsana is the direct contemplation of Parabrahman, and includes the Sadvidya, the Dahara Vidya and the Nyâsa Vidya, &c. These Vidyas are 32 in number and are dealt with in great detail in the Upanishads.

They differ from one another but in the attributes of Parabrahman they meditate upon. The first kind of Upâsana gives him everything he desires, except Môksha ; and later on Môksha, through these ; whereas the second gives him either of these, as he may wish for.

PRAPATTI.

But for those who realise their faintness of heart and utter inability to practise any of these three Yôgas, the Lord has graciously pointed out another Path—the easiest and the safest. They have but to lift up their voice and cry from the depths of their hearts:

" Lord of Mercy, I any weak and I have sinned ; I am ignorant and am unable to save myself ; Thou art my Redeemer, my only stay and support. I take refuge but in Thy Mercy Illimitable."

He has thrown the heavy burden of his Karma from off his tired shoulders, he has no more thought of his salvation, for it is in the hands of the Lord. He has no other work in this life than to ever keep before his mind his own powerlessness and the infinite glorious attributes of the Lord.: he has no will but the Lord's, and he remains to the end of his existence in uninterrupted meditation on the Perfections of the Lord.

He is to contemplate on the Lord as the Ṣarîri of Chit and Achit and as endowed with the divine attributes of Gñâna, Ṣakti, Bala, Aiṣvarya, Vîrya, Têjas, Ânanda, Daya, Vâtsalya, Sauṣîlya, Saulabhya, etc ; and upon the forms taken at will by Himself and by the Divine Mother Lakshmi for the regeneration of the world.

The first three Paths are to be trod only by persons of high mental development and spiritual knowledge ; but the last is open to those whose feet are weak and whose hearts are faint, to any one without distinction of caste, creed, color, race or sex. He can do it himself or through a qualified Guru.

But every one that desires to enter any one of these paths should study the Scriptures in any language he can, under a qualified Âchârya and should possess a thorough knowledge of Chit, Achit and Îṣvara. He should have complete faith in the truth of the Sacred Books and their efficacy to save him ; his teacher should be to him everything here and hereafter, for he is the giver of Life Eternal. He should have burnt out his lower nature and all worldly affections and desires pertaining thereto. And he should, above all, so order his daily life and his relations to others, as to attract as many as possible to the Path of Surrender and Service.

Upon him Karma has no more hold ; perfect devotion to the Lord and complete accordance with His will render his actions in this life perfectly fruitless; they will forge for him no further links in the chain of Karma. Constant contemplation on the Divine Glory and entire absorption in his service render for him the exhaustion of past Karma an easy task ; he takes everything that comes to him with perfect equanimity and goes through it cheerfully as service to the Lord of his heart ; peace eternal and unruffled reigns in his heart, though storms may rage all around and lightnings flash about. Such a one does not enjoy or suffer ; that he leaves to his lower self that produced the causes. He is but the calm and silent Watcher. The Karma that brought about his present incarnation exhausts itself at the close of that life, and he goes before his Lord, free for all eternity, Lord of Matter and Master of Karma.

CHAPTER XXII.

RÂMÂNUJA'S DISCIPLES.

A. The Seventy-Four.

1. Choṭṭai Nambi, son of Âḷavandâr.
2. Puṇḍarîka, son of Mahâpûrṇa.
3. Yâmuna, the son of Gôshṭhîpûrṇa.
4. Sundarabâhu, the son of Mâlâdhara.
5. Râmânuja, the son of Ṣaila Pûrṇa.
6. Parâṣara and his brother, sons of Âḻvân.
7. Râmânuja, the son of Aṇḍân.
8. Madhyamârya (நடுவிலாழ்வான்).
9. Gomaṭhârya (கோமடத்தாழ்வான்).
10. Tirukkovaloor Âḻvân.
11. Tirumohoor Âḻvân.
12. Piḷḷai-piḷḷai-âḻvân.
13. Varada Vishṇu Âchârya (Naḍâdoor).
14. Vishṇu Chitta (எங்களாழ்வான்).
15. Marîchyarya (மிளகாழ்வான்).
16. Neyyuṇḍâḻvân (நெய்யுண்டாழ்வான்).
17. Bâlârya (சேட்டலூர் சிறியாழ்வான்)
18. Anantârya (அனந்தாழ்வான்)
19. Vêdânti Âḻvân.
20. Kôil Âḻvân.
21. Utkalârya (உக்கலாழ்வான்).
22. Haraṇapurârya (அரணபுரத்தாழ்வான்).
23. Gôvinda (எம்பார்).
24. Praṇatârtihara (கிடாம்பியாச்சான்).
25. Bâlârya (கணியனூர் சிறியாழ்வான்).
26. Îcchambâḍi Âcchân (ஈச்சம்பாடியாச்சான்).
27. Kongilâcchân (கொங்கிலாச்சான்).
28. Îcchambâḍi Jîyar (ஈச்சம்பாடி ஜீயர்).
29. Naḷḷân of Tirupati (திருமலை நல்லான்).
30. Ṣaṭṭampiḷḷai Jîyar (சட்டம்பிள்ளை ஜீயர்).
31. Tiruveḷḷarai Jîyar (திருவெள்ளறை ஜீயர்).

32. Âṭkoṇḍavalli Jîyar (ஆட்கொண்டவல்லி ஜீயர்).
33. Tirunagari Piḷḷai (திருநகரிப்பிள்ளை).
34. Kârânji Somayâji (காராஞ்ஜீ ஸோமயாஜி).
35. Alankara Vênkaṭavar (அலங்கார வேங்கடவர்).
36. Nambi Karundêvar (நம்பிகருந்தேவர்).
37. Dêvarâja Bhaṭṭar (தேவராஜபட்டர்).
38. Piḷḷai-urandai-uḍayâr (பிள்ளையுறைந்தை யுடையார்).
39. Piḷḷân (திருக்குருகைப்பிரான்பிள்ளான்).
40. Vaḷḷalâr (பெரியகோயில் வள்ளலார்).
41. Âsûri Perumaḷ (ஆசூரிப் பெருமாள்).
42. Âcchân of Kaṇṇapura (கண்ணபுரத்தாச்சான்).
43. Muni Perumâḷ (முனிப்பெருமாள்).
44. Ammangi Perumâḷ (அம்மங்கிப்பெருமாள்).
45. Mâruti the Elder (மாருதியாண்டான்).
46. Mâruti the Younger (மாருதி ச்சிறியாண்டான்).
47. Ṣrî Râma, Kratunâthârya (சோமயாஜியாண்டான்).
48. Jîyarâṇḍân (ஜீயராண்டான்).
49. Îṣvarâṇḍân (ஈசுவராண்டான்).
50. Îyuṇṇi-piḷḷai âṇḍân (ஈயுண்ணிப்பிள்ளையாண்டான்).
51. Periâṇḍân (பெரியாண்டான்).
52. Âṇḍân the Younger (சிறியாண்டான்).
53. Âṇḍân the Younger of Kurinjipuram.
54. Ammangi Aṇḍân (அம்மங்கியாண்டான்).
55. Âḷavandâr Âṇḍân (ஆளவந்தார் ஆண்டான்).
56. Dêvarâja Muni (அருளாளப்பெருமாளெம்பெருமானார்).
57. Toṇḍanoor Nambi (தொண்டனூர் நம்பி).
58. Marudoor Nambi (மருதூர் நம்பி).
59. Maḻuvoor Nambi (மழூவூர் நம்பி).
60. Tirukkrunguḍi Nambi (திருக்குறுங்குடிநம்பி).
61. Kuruva Nambi (குருவநம்பி).
62. Muḍumbai Nambi (முடும்பைநம்பி).
63. Ândhra Pûrṇa (வடுகநம்பி).
64. Vankipurattu Nambi (வங்கிபுரத்துநம்பி).
65. Parânkuṣa Nambi (பராங்குசநம்பி).
66. Ammangi Ammâḷ (அம்மங்கியம்மாள்).

67. Varadârya (பருத்தி கொல்லையம்மாள்).
68. Utkala Ammâl (உக்கலம்மாள்).
69. Chottai Ammâl (சொட்டையம்மாள்).
70. Mudumbai Ammâl (முடும்பையம்மாள்).
71. Komândoor Pillai (கொமாண்டூர் பிள்ளை).
72. Komandoor Ilayavalli (கொமாண்டூர் இளையவல்லி)
73. Kidâmbi Perumâl (கிடாம்பிப்பெருமாள்).
74. Pillân of Arcot (ஆர்க்காட்டுப்பிள்ளான்).

B.—Others.

Sannyâsins	700.
Êkângis	12,000.
Kothis (women)	300.
Non-Brahmins—Innumerable.	

(*T.G.*)

ÂNDHRA PÛRNA.

Of the numerous disciples of Râmânuja none was so wholly devoted to him as Ândhra Pûrna (வடுகநம்பி). His daily worship was offered not to any god, but to his Master's sandals, which he claimed to be the means and the end of all his aspirations.

Once, during a journey to Tiruvellarai, 10 miles north of Srirangam, he was observed by the Master to convey together his sandals (the object of Ândhra Pûrna's daily worship) and the image of Varadarâja, the household god of Râmânuja.

"What is this you are doing?" exclaimed the Master in horrified tones; "see you not that it is sacrilege extreme to place together my sandals and the image of the Lord of Kâuchi?"

"Ah! Even so?" replied the disciple, coolly enough. "I knew it not. But will you deign to let me know wherein *my* household deity falls behind *yours* in merit?"

Even when he accompanied the Master in his visits to the Temple, he would offer his worship to the Master alone, entirely ignoring the Lord Ranganâtha. The Blessed One happened to notice it, and said to him:

"Son, see you the grand beauty of the eyes of the Lord?"

Vaṭuka looked at them and at the eyes of the Master and replied in the words of Ṣrî Ṣaṭhakôpa:

"He that has gazed even once at the features of *my* Lord of Immortality can have no eyes for any other object." The Master was overcome with this instance of superhuman devotion, and ever afterwards his heart went out to Ândhra Pûrṇa as it did to no one else.

When the Master asked him to partake of the remains of his meals, Vaṭuka used to receive it with reverence, and instead of washing his hands as usual, wiped them on his head. (Ṣrî Vaishṇavas do not wash their hands with water after they have partaken of the offerings to the Lord, when they are distributed in His presence—the magnetism is so pure and beneficial that they cannot afford to throw it away, but they wipe them upon some object near. Again, they do not wash their feet when they return from a visit to the Lord's house, for the same reason.)

One day the Master chanced to notice it and rebuked him: "Absurd! Go and wash your hands." The next time they happened to be in the temple, the remains of the food that was offered to the Lord was given to the Master. He partook of it and gave the remains to Vaṭuka, who received it, but called for water to wash his hands. The Master was naturally shocked and exclaimed in amazement:

"How is this Vaṭuka? You seem to forget where you are."

"Not in the least, my Lord. I but try to follow, as strictly as I can, your directions to me yesterday."

Another day, Vaṭuka was preparing milk for the Master, when the latter called out:

"Vaṭuka, come out instantly; the Lord is coming out in procession; let us go and offer our worship to him."

"Well, if I come away to worship *your Lord*, who will prepare milk for *my Lord*? I will not come."

On another occasion, when some of his relatives (who were not in the faith) came and stayed with him, he took the earliest opportunity after their departure, to throw out every utensil that was rendered impure by their touch, and reflected over the best method of purifying the house. All at once he went to the backyard of Âṇḍân's house, and from the rubbish heap there collected all the cast-off utensils for use in *his* house. He would regard as impure nothing that had been in any way connected with any of the disciples of the Master. They were, in his eyes, holy beyond description.

He would never partake of any holy water except what had washed the feet of his Teacher. He preserved it reverently in his Holy of Holies (கோயிலொழுவார்): the sandals of the Master formed the object of his daily worship and constant meditation.

In his last moments he pointed them out to his dearest friends, (those who, he thought, were advanced enough,) and said:

"This is your stay and refuge. This is the priceless treasure I leave behind me. Guard it carefully and spare no pains to see that due worship is rendered to it."—(*T.G.*)

He is one of the eight Dig-gajas (the Elphants that support the Earth in the eight quarters) or the Guardians of the Good Law.—*G.L.R.*

ÂṈḌÂN THE YOUNGER.

(சிறியாண்டான்).

His last words:—"If the Lord were to forget for a second his own merciful nature and think of my sins, the hells now in existence-are not bad enough for me. But if he were to forget my nature and think of his alone, then the glorious Vaikuṇṭha is not good enough for me. He must furnish me some better residence."

MARUDOOR NAMBI.

(மருதூர்நம்பி.)

His last words: "Śiśupâla who offended the Lord in his three births, was taken unto his Holy Feet. I have offended you, Lord of Mine, during births innumerable; all the more reason why I should reach them sooner, as the greater sinner." Nṛisimha took him unto his Holy Feet that very day.

Nambi Tiruvaludi Vaḷanâḍu Dâsa.

(நம்பிதிருவழுதி வளநாடு தாஸர்.)

During his last moments, a Srī Vaishṇava standing by, wept aloud.

Nambi rebuked him saying: "What! are you mad? *I* have greater reason to weep in that I am going away from among the Lord's Own; but you who are more fortunate, in that you are privileged to hear Parâṣara teach, what cause have *you* for grief?"

Piḷḷai Tiruvaḻudi Vaḷanâḍu Arayar.

(பிள்ளை திருவழுதி வளநாடரையர்.)

was observed, in his last moments, to shed tears; his friends and followers looked at one another in amazement, at what they believed to be a sign of human weakness, which they never expected in one so far advanced.

The dying one happened to notice it and said: "See you not that I grieve for the worldly ones and not for my miserable self? Alas! how slight is the difference between them and the faithful! We but take refuge in the Lord and lay our heads at His Holy Feet. We throw away the bonds of material existence and secure to ourselves Everlasting Life and Light. How slight the effort and how grand the results! And yet the worldly ones know it not, but are whirled powerless upon the Wheel of Change."

EMBÂR.

When the Master was about to depart, Embâr embraced his feet and said: "I was wandering in the dark forest of Ignorance, when Srî Saila Pûrṇa took pity on me and brought me unto Life and Light. Later on he made me over unto you and said 'Râmanujâ is your father and mother, your friend, your Master, your Teacher, your God. He is everything to you here and hereafter.' And you have been unto me all this and more. I am the shadow of your feet and how can I remain away here when you go back?"

"Very true" replied the Master, "I took you from Srî Saila Pûrṇa as a free gift. He made you over to me, body and soul, so you can never remain away from me. And the Lord on High would not break such an indissoluble tie. But do thou come unto me some time hence, when you have prepared Parâşara for his future work. The Cause is dearer to every one of us than our individual interests, is it not?"

Some time after, Gôvinda presented himself before Ranganâtha and said all meekly: "Lord, I am useless here. My heart is with my Master and he is in Vaikuṇṭha. I cannot but go unto him. Have I your permission, Lord?"

Ranganâtha was overcome with grief and pity at these simple yet touching words, and said "Have thy wish. Thou art dear to us there, as here."

Gôvinda went back to his Maṭha and said to Parâşara: "My son, I go back to my Master. And you, the

Hope and Mainstay of the future millions, lay this to your heart of hearts. You are the son of Âlvân, the Eye of the Faith; you have sounded the depths of knowledge; the Lord has adopted you as His dear son. *But all this will serve you nothing* and will only tend to make you proud and conceited. Your hope of Salvation lies, not in these, but in the Feet of the Master, wherein do you take humble refuge."

And he went back to the side of his Master. (*T.G.*)

An Exception.

The Srî Vaishnavas keep holy the day of departure of the Teachers of the Doctrine, but make an exception in the cases of the Âlvârs and Râmânuja. The latter are still present among us in spirit and through their images, and lead us on the Path of Light to the Throne of Glory. And so to the End of Time. (*T. G.*)

CHAPTER XXIII.

BEHIND THE VEIL.

Need we any testimony to the greatness of the Blessed One and his divine Mission of Mercy? I think not. But if there be any who want it, the following would convince the most sceptic among them:—

1. Said the **Lord Ranganâtha**: "We give unto you and to yours the Lordship of this world and the next.

2. This was reiterated by the **Lord Vênkatêsa,** when the Master visited Tirupati.

On that occasion, a shepherdess, named Kondi, came unto the Master and his disciples to offer them milk and curds for sale. When she asked for the price of the articles, the Master directed Pranatârtihara to feed her. The holy influence of the sacred food was so potent that she came back unto the Master and, falling at his feet, said :

"Lord, my eyes are no longer sealed. I ask you not for the price of the articles I have supplied you with, but grant unto me the right of passage to the House of the Lord."

"That is for the Lord Vênkaṭêṣa to confer" replied the Holy One.

"Then" rejoined the acute woman, "give me a note of recommendation to Him."

The Teacher smiled and complied with her request. She went up the Holy Mount and was met half way by the Lord, who felt Himself honored in that the Master had made over, for once, the authority delegated to him. He read the note and forthwith took the humble one unto Himself.

3. VARADA: When the Master found himself worsted in the disputation with Dêvarâja Muni, he applied to Varada, who furnished him with the necessary arguments. Again, Varada appeared to Yâdava Prakâṣa in his dreams and declared into him that to go round Râmânuja was as efficacious as making a tour of pilgrimage all around the globe.

4. THE LORD OF TIRUNÂRÂYAṈAPURA appeared to the Master in his dreams and led him to the place where He was to be found; and Sampatkumâra was so much attached to the Master as to be called by him "My dear son, my precious one."

5. THE LORD Sundarabâhu: One day the Lord directed the disciples of the Master to come unto him. All present there (and among them there were many Teachers) came up and stood with reverently joined hands; but there were some who were related to Mahâ Pûrṇa and they kept away.

"What is the matter with you that you come not?" said the Lord.

"Oh," replied they, "you but ordered the disciples of Râmânuja to come up."

"Yes and who are *you*?"

"*We* belong to Mahâ Pûrṇa and Râmânuja stands to us as a disciple."

"What!" exclaimed the Lord in great amazement, "do I hear aright? Râmânuja your disciple! This recalls to my mind a far-off incident, a similar misconception of my mortal parents Daṣaratha and Vasudêva, when they regarded me as their son during my incarnations as Râma and Kṛishṇa."

Another day, He called out to Praṇatârtihara and asked him to recite a stanza. Âcchân began with the famous one of Yâmuna beginning with अपराधसहस्रभाजनं and when he came to the words अगतिं the Lord stopped him short and said "What! अगति did you say—friendless, none to offer you refuge? You must be either mad or ungrateful to say so when you have our Râmânuja with you."

6. THE LORD—at Kuruṅguḍi. (*Vide* Text.)

7. NAMMÂḺVÂR.—He wagered with the Lord that he would bring back unto the Path those with whom the Lord failed. But, after superhuman efforts, he had to give up in despair and confess himself defeated. And, looking far into the future, he said, "Surely Kalî and his black hosts would be foiled"—referring to the incarnation of the Master.

8. NÂTHAYÔG.—"The Waters of Wisdom, if they ran down into a small hole, will not slake the thirst of a sparrow; but if they ran into the lake of Vîranârâyaṇapura (his birth-place) they would spread plenty over a whole country."

"A great cloud which they call Srî Sathakôpa hung over the waters of a vast sea (The Lord) and drank to its fill of the Waters of Immortality. It travelled on and on and rested on the high Mahâ Mêru (Nâthayôgi). It poured its sweet waters on the tops and these ran down the mighty slopes (Pundarîkâksha and Râma Migra) in tiny rivulets which united into one broad noble river (Yâmunâchârya). A spacious lake received the voume of waters (Râmânuja) and through skilfully constructed sluices and aqueducts (the later Teachers) watered the dry wastes of Samsâra (material existence) and kept them in perennial freshness and loveliness."

9. YÂMUNÂCHÂRYA.—"If this Râmânuja were to enter the Faith, he would restore the reign of the Good Law. He is your Future Teacher."

10. VARA RANGA—caused his brother Chottai Nambi to become the disciple of Râmânuja, as he had himself no son of his own to offer him.

11. MAHÂ PÛRNA.—One day, Râmânuja and his disciples paid a visit to his Master. Mahâ Pûrna rose up in haste and reverently saluted Râmânuja. His daughter Attulâi, who was with him at that time, asked him in great surprise: "Father! know you what you are doing? Râmânuja is your disciple, is he not?".

"Nay, nay, my dear" "replied the Sage. This head of mine is a meet pillow for such feet."

Another day, Mahâ Pûrna happened to meet the Master and his disciples on their way from the Cauvery, and reverently saluted him; and stranger still, Râmânuja accepted it and blessed him in return. His disciples ventured to question him on the propriety of the act.

"I but follow his unspoken wish" said the Master. "I do not care to look beyond."

They sought out Mahâ Pûrṇa and requested to be enlightened on the point.

"I saw but my Master Âḷavandâr and his disciples and saluted them accordingly."

"Your reasons?"

"After Yâmuna, my revered Teacher, I know of no other who unites in himself all the excellences. I see no difference between a Great Teacher and a Great Disciple."

He led his son Puṇḍarîkâksha to the feet of Râmânuja.

12. GÔSHṬHÎ PÛRṆA.—(*Vide* Text).

13. ṢRÎ ṢAILA PÛRṆA.—(*Vide* Text).

14. MÂLÂDHARA.—(*Vide* Text).

15. ÂNDHRA PÛRṆA.—"There is a heaven by name '*The world of the Teacher*' and it belongs of right to Râmânuja. His sacred feet are the ONLY Means and the Goal to all of us. Let us take our refuge in them."

16. BÂLA SWÂMY OF KRISHṆAPURA (கண்ணனூர்சிறியாச்சான்) one day bathed with his clothes on, and standing in the waters cried out with lifted hands, in the fulness of his heart: "I swear by everything I hold sacred that the feet of the Holy One are the only Refuge. He is the World-Teacher; he is the regenerator of the fallen Humanity." [The same is related of Âĩvân.—*Prap.*]

17. DÊVARÂJAMUNI—(*Vide* Text).

18. PILḺAI-PILḺAI-ÂĨḺVÂN—(*Vide* Notes).

19. MARÎCHIÂRYA—(மிளகாழ்வான்) once challenged Âṇḍân to argue with him. "What is the wager?" asked Âṇḍân.

"The victor is to ride on the shoulders of the vanquished" replied the other.

They argued and Âṇḍân won. Marîchiârya carried Âṇḍân upon his shoulders some distance and said:

"Reverend Sir, deign to to set me upon the Path."

"That is easy enough," replied Âṇḍân, "do thou take refuge in the Feet of the Blessed One."

20. Embâr—(*Vide* p. 303).

21. Parâṣara—said to his disciple and successor Mâdhavâchârya (நஞ்சீயர்): "Pride not thyself that thou hast sought me out as thy Teacher; that thou hast made over to me immense wealth; that thou art a past master in Vedânta; that thou hast explained the Sacred Collect a hundred times. Do thou take refuge, as I do, in the feet of the Blessed Râmânuja."

22. Nanjîyar—said to Nampiḷḷai, his disciple and successor: "Pride not thyself upon thy title Lokâchârya (The Teacher of the World); or upon thy marvellous skill in expounding the Sacred Collect, but do thou seek refuge in the Feet of the Ṣrî Bhâshyakâra."

23. One day, Nampiḷḷai was returning to his house resting on the arm of Ṣivikkarai Piḷḷai. When they were entering the house, the latter noticed a Ṣrî Vaishṇava lying asleep in the passage, and cried out in the excess of his zeal:

"Get up, I say; at least draw in your outstretched legs."

Nampiḷḷai at once shook him off in sorrow and said:

"I see before me one of the Lord's Elect; and the great Ṣaṭhakôpa thinks that the words 'Sacred Feet' are too irreverent to designate what you so sacrilegiously call 'legs.' I would that you would forget your way to my house."

The disciple departed in grief and despair, and after some time had it represented to his Teacher that he was like a stone hurled from a sling from between the Two Rivers, and prayed that he should not be left miserable. The Teacher sent back this characteristic reply:

"Tell the ignorant one that the Great Haven of Refuge, the Sacred Feet of Râmânuja, is open to him as to all, to the end of Time."

24. When PILLÂN was at Sirupputtûr, Somayâji Âṇḍân studied the Srî Bhâshya under him thrice; and when Pillân was about to leave the place, said to him:

"Reverend Sir, I live hereabouts and it is not given me to go with you; point out to me something wherein I can take refuge."

"Be it so" replied Pillân, "be not thou elated with pride because thou hast mastered the systems of Bhaṭṭa, Prabhâkara and the other Mîmâmsas and can skilfully expound the Srî Bhâshya; but take thy refuge in the Holy Feet of Râmânuja."

24. PILLÂN OF GÔMATHA explained the Srî Bhâshya thrice to one Âcchân of Kâkkayâḍi, and finding him proud of his learning, said to him: "My son, I fear thy great learning will cause thee to commit some grave offence to the Lord's Elect. So make haste to take thy refuge in the Holy Feet of Srî Râmânuja."

25. About ten or twelve Srî Vaishṇavas were studying the Srî Bhâshya under Naḍâdoor Ammâḷ; one day, at the close of a splendid lecture on the teachings of the Master, they gave it out that the Holy One pointed out 'devotion' as the only means of salvation. Then Ammâḷ spoke to them of the beauty and of the greatness of the Doctrine of Refuge (Prâpatti).

"Verily" exclaimed they, "the Holy One must have chosen *this* as the easiest and the shortest path."

"Then" replied Ammâḷ, "do thou take refuge in His Sacred Feet and attain Life Eternal."

16. Madhyamârya (நடுவிலாழ்வான்) was expounding the Srî Bhâshya to a host of disciples at Tirunârâyaṇapura, when Vankipuraṭṭâcchi, Choṭṭai Ammâḷ and some others exclaimed that it was beyond their grasp. "Then" said the teacher "take refuge in the Sacred Feet of its author."

27. On another occasion, VÊDA VYÂSA BHAṮṮA lectured in the same place and on the same subject to a crowded audience. The Fifty Two rose up and humbly said: "Alas! this is like the roaring waters of Ganga when it fell from the toe of the Lord of the Discus and we are nothing before it. Point out to us some easier path." "Then" said Bhaṭṭa, pointing out to the image of the Master, before which they were seated, "do you take refuge, as you were instructed, in the Feet of your Household Deity."

28. The same was said by Naḏuvil Tiruvîdippiḻḻai (நடுவில் திருவீதிப்பிள்ளை) to his disciple Iḻayavaḻagiâr (இளைய வழகியார்).

29. The BRAHMARÂKHASA—(*Vide* the incident of Yâdavaprakâṣa.)

30. THE DUMB BOY OF KANCHI.—He disappeared all on a sudden, and when he came back after a year or two, talked as well as any.

"Where have you been?" asked his friends in surprise.

"To the Milky Ocean."

"Ah! how wonderful! Brought anything for us?"

"Nothing but the news that the Lord of the Divine Hosts has come down into the world as Râmânuja." And he was seen no more among men. So said SÊNÂPATI JÎYAR.

31. ÂNDHRA PÛRṈA accused Âlvân and Âṇḏân of vacillation and called them *Trimmers* for taking refuge in

the Feet of Ranganâtha and Râmânuja conjointly; "they should have preferred the latter," said he. It was not given to everyone to say with Ândhra Pûrṇa; "I take my refuge but in the Master;"

Or with Parâṣara: "I take my refuge but in the Lord Ranganâtha;"

Or with Anantâlvân: "The Lord Vênkaṭêṣa is my only stay and refuge;"

Or with Kacchi Nambi: "I know of no other refuge but the shadow of Varada's Feet;"

Or with Râmânuja: "I take my refuge now and for ever in Thee, my Precious One, my dear Son (Sampatkumâra.)"

32. "What were your thoughts" asked Vishṇuchittârya of Âcchân Piḷḷai of Kâkkayâḍi "when the Lord spoke to you in anger?"

"Oh! I but took refuge in the Feet of the Master."

33. SARASVATI.—(*Vide* the Master's visit to Ṣaradâpîṭha).

34. The superior greatness of the Master over all the previous Teachers of the Good Law lies in that he brought home to the heart of every one the Promise of Mercy and Protection held out by the Lord (Abhaya Pradâna); he threw a flood of light on the Last Word of the Lord Ṣrî Krishṇa; he explained clearly the sayings of the holy Rishis of yore; he brought within the reach of all, prince and peasant, man and woman, young and old, the truths embodied in the Sacred Collect; he explained the Brahma Sûtras of Vyâsa in the light of the teachings of Nâtha Yôgi, Yâmuna and other great Teachers; he bequeathed to all humanity such works as the Ṣrî Bhâshya and the Gadya Traya; and in that he has exposed the fallacies and the snares of other faiths

and has irrefutably established the Doctrine of the Good Law.

35. Why should all the Teachers point out to their disciples the Feet of the Master as the only Haven of Refuge?

They had been taught so by *their* Teachers. Râmânuja was the direct disciple of the Holy Ṣaṭhakôpa, the intervening Teachers being but the medium for preserving the line of teaching till his time.

Mahâ Pûrṇa and the previous teachers were glorified by being connected with the Master as his *teachers*, and the teachers that came after him by being related to him as his *disciples*.

36. Once when the Master was holding forth on the Promise of Refuge, Dhanurdâsa stood up and prepared to go away.

"Whither away, my son?" asked the Master in surprise.

"Vibhîshaṇa, the brother of Râvaṇa" replied Dhanurdâsa, "came to Râma and took refuge in his mercy. He left behind him his kingdom, his friends, and his kin; and Ṣrî Râmachandra was to him everything—his kingdom, his happiness, his life—here and hereafter. He came to him with his four attendants and, standing in mid-air, cried out for protection. But the hosts of monkeys that formed the army of Râma made ready to kill him and his followers. And shall I, the worldly one, who have not as yet freed myself from the bonds of material existence, be admitted within the group of the Faithful? I have no place here and I go away."

"Fear not" replied the Master with a smile, "if *I* get it, *you* are sure of it; if Mahâ Pûrṇa gets it, *I* am sure of it; if Yâmunâchârya gets it, Mahâ Pûrṇa is sure of it; and if the others before him get it, *he* is sure of it. Srî Sathakôpa has said in so many words 'I am past all sorrow and desire. I have attained salvation.' It is sure that *he* did get it; so *we* too are sure of it. No one need despair so long as he has the Divine Mother to intercede for him. We are so many links in a vast chain that extends from the Lord; and He will not fail to look after His own. When the Lord held out His Promise of Protection to Vibhîshana, He did not keep out the four Râkshasas that followed their master; when the monkeys prepared to kill himthey did not mean to leave out his attendants. Again I say unto you: *If I get it, you shall get it.* The Lord never forgot Satrughna that took refuge in Bharata; nor Madhurakavi whose only god was the Holy Sathakôpa; nor Nâcchiar who trusted in Periâlvâr."

37. Said NADÂDOOR AMMÂL: "This is what I hold to. Neither Karmayôga, nor Gñyânayoga, nor Bhakthi Yoga, nor even Prapatti is the means. The Holy Feet of the Master and *they alone* are the Means and the End. Take refuge in the Master, that is Prapatti; recite his glorious name, that is the most sacred of all the Mantras. Serve him with thy heart and soul, that is the goal of all human aspirations."

When RANGÂMRITA recited his Antâdi before the Master, he came to the stanza மைக்கதிர்க்கண் and said: "It is the utmost goal of my aspirations ever to meditate upon Thy glorious form and attributes; the spot sanctified by those that sing Thy praises is to me the highest Heaven. Lord, grant unto me unswerving devotion to Thy servants and let me be admitted to the group of those that serve them." The Master listened to it graciously and expressed his approval of the same.

CHAPTER XXIV.

THE ELECT.

The Master's personal attendants:—

ÂḺVÂN, ÂNDÂN, VARADA VISHṈU ÂCHÂRYA, PARÂṢARA and his brother assisted the Master in the composition of the Ṣrî Bhâshya.

DÊVARÂJA MUNI wrote Gñâna Sâra and Pramêya Sâra. These were critically examined by the Master and approved of. He was thereafter entrusted with the daily worship of the image of Varada.

PRAṈATÂRTIHARA and KIḌÂMBI PERUMÂḺ lóoked after the refectory.

ÂṈḌÂN got ready the materials necessary for the Master's Sacred Badges and daily worship; and brought to him his sandals.

ÂNDHRA PÛRṆA attended upon the Master during his bath and tended the Master's cows.

BÂLÂRYA OF GOMAṬHA bore his bowl and slippers.

EMBÂR made his bed, shampooed him when tired, offered him his arm while walking, and took charge of his garments.

DHANURDÂSA looked after the treasury. UTKALÂRYA served out the meals.

UTKALA AMMÂḺ fanned him.

AMMANGI AMMÂḺ prepared his draught of milk.

MÂRUTI THE ELDER served him with water to wash his hands.

MÂRUTI THE YOUNGER supplied the Maṭha with the daily articles of comsumption.

TOOYA MUNI VÊḺAM brought him water for his bath.

Vanḍa and Sunḍa, nephews of Dhanurdâsa, served the king for a thousand pieces of gold each and made the same over to the Maṭha.

Akaḷankârya took charge of the enemies of the Faith.

CHAPTER XXV.

THE SPIRITUAL HIERARCHY.

The Guru Parampara.

1. The Mantra Parampara.
2. The Mantrârtha Do.
3. Srî Bhâshya Do.
4. Bhagavad Vishaya Do. (Sacred Collect)

From the Lord down to the Master the order of succession is the same for all the four:—

The Lord.
The Divine Mother.
Senêsa.
Saṭhakôpa.
Nâtha Yôgi.
Punḍarîkâksha.
Râma Misra
Yâmunâchârya.
Mahâ Pûrṇa.
Râmânuja.

I. Mantra Parampara.

After him the seventy-four Âchâryas and their descendants, the Parakâlaswâmi Maṭha and the Ahobilaswâmi Maṭha continue the line to this day.

II. Mantrârtha Guruparampara.

Râmânuja.
Kiḍâmbi Âcchân (Praṇatârtihara).
Kiḍâmbi Râmânuja Appuḷḷâr.
Kiḍâmbi Srî Ranga Râja.
Kiḍâmbi Appuḷḷâr.
Vêdânta Dêsika.
Brahmatantraswâmi.

III. Srî Bhâshya Guruparampara.

Râmânuja.
Pillân.
Vishnuchitta.
Nadâdoor Ammâl.
Appullâr.
Vêdânta Dêsika.
Brahmatantra Jîyar.

IV. Bhagavad Vishaya Parampara.

Similar to the preceding up to Dêsika; then Nainârâchârya—Brahmatantra Jîyar. (*V. G.*)

GURUPARAMPARA is of two kinds—Âsrayana and Grantha.

Âsrayana Parampara.

ÂSRAYANA—Same as the above as far as Râmânuja; then

Embâr.
Parâsara.
Nanjîyar.
Nampillai.
Srî Krishnapâda (வடக்குத் திருவீதிப்பிள்ளை).
Pillai Lokâchârya.
Srî Sailêsa (திருவாய்மொழிப் பிள்ளை).
Manavâla Mahâmuni (பெரிய ஜீயர்).

Grantha Parampara.

(*a*) RAHASYA GRANTHA — inserts Koorakulottama Dâsa after Pillâi Lokâchârya.

(*b*) BHAGAVAD VISHAYA.

Râmânuja.
Pillân.
Embâr.
Âlvân.
Bhattar.
Nanjîyar.
Nampillai.
Srî Krishnapâda.
Îyunni Mâdhava.
Îyunni Padmanâbha.
Kola Varâha Nainâr.
Nâloor Dêvarâja.
Srî Sailêsa.
Peria Jîyar or Nampillai.
Krishna Samâhvaya (பெரியவாச்சான்பிள்ளை).
Nainâr Âcchân Pillai.
Âlagia Manavâla Jîyar
Vâdi Kanthîrava.

(c) Ṣri Bhâshya.

Râmânuja.
Embâr.
Bhaṭṭar.
Nanjîyar.
Nampiḷḷai.
Ṣri Kṛishṇapâda.
Piḷḷai Lokâchârya ; or, Râmânuja.
Piḷḷân.
Vishṇuchitta.
Naḍâdoor Ammâḷ.
Appuḷḷâr.
Dêṣika.
Nainârâchârya.
Prativâdi Bhayamkara (Aṇṇan.)
Poḷippâkkam Nainâr. (*Pal*

"Here endeth what I write
Who love the Master for his love of us.
A little knowing, little have I told
Touching the Teacher and the Ways of Peace.
* * * * Showed he those
In many lands and many tongues and gave
Our *India* light, that still is beautiful ;
Conquering the world with spirit of strong grace
All which is written in the Holy Books."

—*Light of Asia* (adapted.)

श्रीकृष्णार्पणमस्तु.

FINIS.